AF478538

ADVANCES IN
THE ECONOMICS OF
ENERGY AND RESOURCES

Volume 9 • 1995

SUSTAINABLE ECONOMIC GROWTH

ADVANCES IN
THE ECONOMICS OF
ENERGY AND RESOURCES

SUSTAINABLE ECONOMIC GROWTH

Editor: JOHN R. MORONEY
Department of Economics
Texas A&M University

VOLUME 9 • 1995

Greenwich, Connecticut   *London, England*

CONTENTS

LIST OF CONTRIBUTORS — vii

INTRODUCTION
John R. Moroney — ix

ECONOMIC SUSTAINABILITY
John R. Moroney — 1

FOSSIL FUEL USE AND SUSTAINABLE
DEVELOPMENT: EVIDENCE FROM U.S.
INPUT-OUTPUT DATA, 1972-1985
Richard W. England and Stephen D. Casler — 21

SUSTAINABLE GROWTH AND VALUATION
OF MINERAL RESERVES
M.A. Adelman — 45

COMMENTARY
Teofilo Ozuna — 69

ECONOMIC CONSERVATION POLICY:
IMPLICATIONS FOR ECONOMIC GROWTH
AND CONSUMER WELFARE
Donald A. Norman — 71

COMMENTARY
Jeff Talbert — 105

U.S. PETROLEUM SUPPLY:
HISTORY AND PROSPECTS
Edward D. Porter — 111

COMMENTARY
Bryan Maggard — 163

TRENDS IN U.S. NATURAL GAS PRODUCTION
Robert A. Wattenbarger and Mauricio Villegas

169

COMMENTARY
James M. Griffin

197

DISTRIBUTIONAL AND ENVIRONMENTAL
CONSEQUENCES OF TAXES ON ENERGY
*Hadi Dowlatabadi, Raymond J. Kopp, and
F. Ted Tschang*

203

COMMENTARY
M. Douglas Berg

237

LIST OF CONTRIBUTORS

M.A. Adelman

Department of Economics
Massachusetts Institute of
Technology

M. Douglas Berg

Department of Economics
Texas A&M University

Stephen D. Casler

Department of Economics
Allegheny College

Hadi Dowlatabadi

Department of Engineering and
Public Policy
Carnegie Mellon University

Richard W. England

Center for Business and Economic
Research
University of New Hampshire

Irma Gomez

Department of Agricultural
Economics
Texas A&M University

James M. Griffin

Department of Economics
Texas A&M University

Raymond J. Kopp

Resources for the Future

Bryan Maggard

Department of Petroleum
Engineering
Texas A&M University

John R. Moroney

Department of Economics
Texas A&M University

Donald A. Norman

Policy Analysis and Strategic
Planning
American Petroleum Institute

Teofilo Ozuna

Department of Agricultural
Economics
Texas A&M University

Edward D. Porter

Policy Analysis and Strategic
Planning
American Petroleum Institute

Jeff Talbert

Martin School of Public Policy
University of Kentucky

F. Ted Tschang

Department of Engineering and
Public Policy
Carnegie Mellon University

Mauricio Villegas

Department of Petroleum
Engineering
Texas A&M University

Robert A. Wattenbarger

Department of Petroleum
Engineering
Texas A&M University

INTRODUCTION

This volume stems from a highly productive conference held at Texas A&M University November 9-10, 1994. The scholars were mostly economists and petroleum engineers, but included political scientists, statisticians, environmental scientists, and participants from government and industry. The papers were available well in advance to all discussants, so their comments were carefully considered. They often led to very helpful clarification, and sometimes to searching revisions by the authors.

Morry Adelman focuses on estimating the user costs of mineral reserves, and the monetary adjustment to net domestic product (NDP) necessary to estimate sustainable NDP. Adelman believes that mineral reserves should properly be viewed as social capital assets, similar to reproducible physical capital. A "depletion charge" should be made each year for mineral reserves used up. Accordingly, to reckon the *sustainable* NDP of a country its ordinary NDP should be adjusted downward for the monetary value of mineral reserves produced during the year. Adelman reasons that the monetary value applied to physical depletion should be the user cost of the reserves depleted. He makes such calculations for U.S. oil reserves. This sort of approach is now being developed by national income accountants at the U.S. Department of Commerce and the United Nations.

Donald Norman centers on the costs and benefits of energy conservation. The benefits of conservation are chiefly in reducing atmospheric pollution—carbon dioxide, sulfur dioxide, and other particles. Several environmental groups have proposed policies to reduce energy consumption, but have *assumed* no concomitant reduction in economic growth. But Norman carefully marshals a range of evidence showing that energy is an important determinant of growth. Given this fact, lower energy consumption reduces real growth: the environmental benefits of energy conservation should properly be weighed against the cost of potentially lower living standards.

Edward Porter carefully reviews the history of U.S. oil reserves and production, then forecasts reserves and production until the year 2010. His forecasting model is one developed and refined at the American Petroleum Institute. The model incorporates several taxes that must be subtracted from the gross wellhead price to compute the net producer price. Porter shows that drilling activity is the key determinant of new reserve findings. As you would expect, drilling responds to expected net cash flows. Successful exploration and development adds to reserves. And because oil production follows reserves, production is linked, with some lag, to economic variables. Porter's is a sophisticated and very useful econometric model.

Robert Wattenbarger and Mauricio Villegas, petroleum engineers, attempt to track U.S. natural gas production by fitting a modified logistic function suggested originally by the late M. King Hubbert. The basic idea behind Hubbert's approach is that production of a mineral reserve follows a life cycle. As the mineral industry develops from infancy, annual production increases initially at an increasing rate. As the industry matures, annual production continues to grow but at a decreasing rate. Production finally peaks. Then in Hubbert's model it declines each year along a path symmetrical to the path it charted during expansion.

The Hubbert model is short on economics. Nonetheless, Wattenbarger and Villegas find that it tracks annual gas production very well during the industry's expansion phase (1918-1973). Production peaks in 1973, then follows a path of slow, erratic decline. Then from an engineering viewpoint, a strange thing happens around 1985: annual production begins to increase despite the fact that proved reserves are falling. Wattenbarger and Villegas explain this engineering anomaly by stressing that annual gas production is constrained by market demand. And market demand for natural gas increased sharply after 1985 partly because of declining real prices and partly because of tighter environmental restrictions, which increased the demand for clean-burning gas and decreased demand for dirtier fuels, especially coal. To adequately explain oil and gas production, a hybrid model incorporating both engineering and economic variables offers a great deal of promise. Work along these lines by Moroney and Wattenbarger is progressing at Texas A&M University.

Dowlatabadi, Kopp, and Tschang analyze the tax burden U.S. households would bear under two widely-discussed energy taxes: (1) a BTU tax (levied on the heat content of various fuels) and (2) a carbon tax (levied on their carbon content). Not surprisingly, they find that the burden of either tax would differ a bit among different regions, being highest in the Mountain region and lowest in the Pacific region. They analyze energy consumption and tax burdens using three different frameworks: a "naive" model with zero elasticity of demand for energy, a "conservation" model allowing consumers limited opportunity to reduce fuel consumption following higher energy prices, and a "long-run" model permitting consumers to fully adjust their energy using capital stocks in response to higher energy prices. All three models produce qualitatively similar results concerning regional tax burdens.

They then analyze the environmental consequences of the two taxes. Their long-run models yield strikingly similar results: with either a BTU or a carbon tax, annual carbon emissions from U.S. household energy consumption would decrease by about 46 or 47 million tons per year. That's an encouraging result.

The paper by Richard England and Stephen Casler was not given at the conference. But it is a natural for this volume. England and Casler write an interesting empirical study about sustainability and fossil fuel use. They develop an input-output model of the direct and indirect use of fossil fuels (coal, natural gas, and oil) in the United States. Their model has 11 major sectors. Five sectors produce and refine nonrenewable resources. A sixth sector, biological resources, produces renewable resources. Five others (electric utilities, durable manufacturing, nondurable manufacturing, transportation services, and other services) consume nonrenewable and renewable resources.

Comparing final demands in 1972 (when energy prices were very low) and in 1985 (after real energy prices increased four-fold), consumption changed pretty much as you would expect: the household sector reduced its consumption of refined petroleum, and the government sector sharply curtailed consumption of refined petroleum, electricity, and natural gas.

England and Casler then compute the changes in direct and indirect input coefficients between 1972 and 1985 (their Table 9). Most energy-consuming sectors reduced fossil fuel consumption (measured in BTU) per unit of output. The biological resource sector is a real success story: its total energy input requirements dropped from 33 to 19 thousand BTU per unit of gross output. But other major sectors remained energy addicts: the mineral production sector scarcely reduced its total energy requirements from 69 to 62 thousand BTU per unit of gross output; and the transportation sector made a tiny reduction from 51 to 48 thousand BTU per unit.

England and Casler have made a good start linking up fossil fuel consumption to sustainability. Yet some vitally important questions remain open. What is the degree of macroeconomic substitution between biological resources and fossil fuels? What sort of macroeconomic substitution can we get between physical capital stocks and fossil fuels? Can new capital stocks easily be produced with much less energy? Can their methodology, which makes a lot of sense, be extended from the United States to other energy-hungry countries—Western Europe, Russia, and China? They haven't tackled these questions yet, but I hope they will.

Ms. Jacqueline Henderson gracefully orchestrated the entire conference. She cheerfully arranged for lodging, meals, and transportation of all conference participants and skillfully kept track of the myriad administrative details so vital to a smooth conference. She had a lot of assistance from Doug Berg. Without the diligent efforts of Ms. Henderson and Doug Berg, the conference would have been chaotic. No—it would not have taken place. I am deeply indebted to them both.

The conference was generously supported by grants from the Texas A&M Program on Interdisciplinary Research Initiatives and a Texas A&M Professional Development grant. The American Petroleum Institute also provided financial assistance. Several A&M graduate students participated either as co-authors or discussants: Doug Berg from the Department of Economics, Jeff Talbert from the Department of Political Science, Bryan Maggard and Mauricio Villegas from the Department of Petroleum Engineering, and Irma

Gomez from the Department of Agricultural Economics. Several other graduate students attended the sessions, as did all undergraduates in my Natural Resource course. They are direct beneficiaries of this stimulating and highly productive conference. We are each of us indebted to Texas A&M University and The American Petroleum Institute for underwriting the conference.

John R. Moroney
Series Editor

ECONOMIC SUSTAINABILITY

John R. Moroney

ABSTRACT

An economically sustainable society is one that preserves its long-run living standards indefinitely. Sustainability is an appealing idea: surely a consensus goal of any generation is to leave its successor at least as well off as itself. Sustainability is scientifically interesting because any society must consume some exhaustible resources (like fossil fuels and metal ores). To preserve long-run living standards for the future, the current generation must leave more physical capital and better technology as a substitute for the exhaustible resources it has consumed.

Bequeathing more and better physical capital for future generations is what advanced Western economies have done for more than 200 years. Most other societies have not. They would do well to adopt the economic ways of the West, at least in this respect.

Advances in the Economics of Energy and Resources, Volume 9, pages 1-19.

ISBN: 1-55938-922-2

I. THE PRINCIPLE OF SUSTAINABILITY

Sustainability has received a lot of attention in the last twenty years. It has become a focal point of the World Resources Institute, the United Nations, and numerous scientists and social scientists. Some have focused narrowly on purely physical aspects of sustainable development (*World Resources, 1992-1993*, Chapter 1; Goeller and Weinberg, 1976). Using environmental indicators, researchers at the World Resources Institute stress the need to reduce various measures of pollution—atmospheric pollution, hazardous wastes, and water pollution.

Others include in their definition of sustainability the need to relieve worldwide poverty. They correctly emphasize that a finite Earth cannot sustain indefinite population growth. Still others take a broader view that sustainable development should globally improve health care, education, and social well-being.

Among all the scholars who have studied the question, I think Robert Solow best pinpoints the crucial issue. According to Solow, *a sustainable society is a society that preserves its productive capacity for the indefinite future.* Put a little differently, Solow views sustainability as a generalized capacity to produce constant economic well-being generation after generation (1992, p. 14). To quote Solow:

> The duty imposed by sustainability is to bequeath to posterity not any particular thing, but instead to endow them with whatever it takes to achieve a standard of living at least as good as our own and to look after their next generation similarly. Sustainability means we are not to consume humanity's capital in the broadest sense.

We can think of society as a series of overlapping generations. Each generation necessarily consumes a certain volume of nonrenewable resources like crude oil, natural gas, coal, and iron ore. Consuming exhaustible resources today means that less of them are left to the future. So to preserve stable living standards indefinitely, each generation must replace used-up resources with something else. But with what? Each generation can in principle replace the exhaustible resources it uses up by leaving a larger, more efficient stock of reproducible capital to the next generation.

Substitution is a cornerstone of sustainability. To simply live, each generation must consume some exhaustible resources. But it can (and usually does) leave a larger, more productive stock of capital for the next one. The crucial substitution question is this: How easily can physical capital be substituted for (and thus *compensate for*) the exhaustible resources used up? Sadly we don't know. As I mention in a moment, the estimates of subsitutability are too scattered to give a consensus.

As Solow puts it, "Each year there are two decisions: How much to save and invest, and how much of the remaining stock of exhaustible resources to use up. There is a sense in which we can say that this year's consumers have made a trade with posterity. They have used up some of the stock of exhaustible natural resources; in exchange they have saved and invested, so that the next generation will inherit a larger stock of reproducible capital" (1992, p. 9).

Solow's idea of sustainability boils down to this: Each generation necessarily consumes some exhaustible resources; but if it leaves a sufficiently larger and more productive stock of reproducible capital to compensate for the irreplaceable resources it has consumed, then future living standards can be preserved. This is an appealing idea that makes a lot of sense. It can in principle be accomplished. But to do so requires that each generation save and invest efficiently for the future. If it does not, the required growth in physical capital won't occur.

But invest how much? How much growth in the reproducible capital stock will compensate the next generation for the exhaustible resources we consume during our lifetimes? And compensate them in the sense that the larger capital stock enables the next generation to enjoy a standard of living as high as ours? To get at a numerical measure of sustainability, two important adjustments to the national accounts are necessary.

A.   Properly Charging Today's Generation
for Consumption of Exhaustible Resources

Let's accept Net Domestic Product (NDP) as an approximate measure of society's welfare. Recall that NDP is GDP adjusted downward for the depreciation of physical capital. To obtain a measure of *sustainable* net domestic product we need to make a further deduction: a deduction for the net depletion of exhaustible resources. The correct charge for depletion should value each unit of any specific resource extracted at its net price. The correct net price is its market price minus the marginal cost of extraction. This is exactly the user cost of the exhaustible resource, or the Hotelling rent per unit of resource (Solow, 1974).

What about aggregate resource depletion? Solow suggests that the correct measure of each year's overall exhaustible resource depletion is simply the aggregate value of Hotelling rents in the mining industry. In theory, this aggregate value is the proper way to put a valuation on what is taken from the ground in a given year. An effort in this direction is now being made by the United Nations and the U.S. Department of Commerce (*Survey of Current Business*, 1994).

Estimating the net value of exhaustible resource depletion is easier said than done. Recall that the correct unit value of resource depletion is the user cost. User cost is correctly calculated by subtracting the *marginal* cost of extraction from the market price of the resource. But marginal cost is usually hard to estimate. An assumption now becomes handy. Specifically, assume that long-run *marginal* extraction cost is the same as long-run *average* extraction cost. Then an approximation to the value of depletion can be made by subtracting all economic costs (costs of labor, costs of capital including the competitive rate of return, and costs of all other inputs used to extract the resource) from the gross value of an extractive industry's sales.

If the industry is effectively competitive, this may not be a bad approximation. But if instead the industry were a monopoly or collusive oligopoly, then this residual or gross margin wraps in monopoly profits with the value of resources depleted. In this instance the number that we call the value of depletion overstates the true value of depletion.

I should add something else. Even with competition, to get the "correct" prices of exhaustible resources the private markets need to have some foresight about their exhaustibility. This is a strong, perhaps infeasible requirement. But we certainly have no reason to expect government planners to have clearer foresight than private markets.

B.   Correcting Net Domestic
Product for Environmental Realities

Recent developments in so-called "green accounting" attempt to correct conventional national accounts for environmental changes. The principles involved are straightforward. In any year during which perceptible environmental damage occurs, a deduction should be made from NDP to record the spoils to the environment. And whenever a notable environmental improvement is achieved, a country's NDP should be increased to reflect the value of the improvement. The World Bank, the OECD, and the U.S. Department of Commerce are preparing a framework of shadow national income accounts along these lines. Put simply, an economic value should be assigned to environmental changes. An aggregate value of environmental degradation could be subtracted from each year's NDP, and an aggregate value of environmental improvement could be added to it.

The principles are clear enough. But obtaining even approximately correct estimates is very tough business. The usual method used in imputing a value to an environmental amenity for which there is no market is *contingent valuation.* But contingent valuation is itself highly controversial. Diamond and Hausman (1994) believe contingent valuation estimates to be so badly flawed, it is better to not even attempt them.

Solow (1992, pp. 12-13) suggests the possibility of treating environmental quality as a kind of capital stock whose value is depreciated by the addition of pollutants and increased by successful pollution abatement. For example, the continued (or increased) emission of sulphur dioxide or carbon dioxide would be treated as a deduction from NDP. Likewise, the value of a program of successful emission abatement would be added to the environmental capital account. Treating environmental changes like environmental capital is an appealing thought. In principle it is like treating an improving (or deteriorating) labor force as a change in human capital. The difference is that an improving labor force has a tangible (recordable) outcome: higher real earnings. To correctly place a value on environmental change is not so easy.

II. FEATURES OF THE SUSTAINABLE STEADY STATE

All models of sustainable steady state economies share some common features. They appear in the models of Daly (1973, 1974), Goeller and Weinberg (1976), and Solow (1992).

1. *Real NDP per capita will be constant.*

2. *Real consumption per capita will be constant.* Goeller and Weinberg (1976) peg real sustainable consumption per capita to the cost of primary energy. As they put it, "In the Age of Substitutability energy is the ultimate raw material. The living standard will almost surely depend on the cost of prime energy."

There is an intrinsic paradox here, mentioned to me in a letter from Robert Solow. It's tough to improve on Solow's clarity, so I take the liberty of quoting his view of the sustainability paradox. "Suppose the Founding Fathers had written sustainability into the Constitution. Then we would still be 'enjoying' the standard of living of 200 years ago. Would that have been a good thing? If doubtful, why are we so sure that sustainability should start now?" I'm not so sure.

3. *World population will be stable.* Daly and Solow do not specify a number, but both state that their long-run steady state requires a stable population. Goeller and Weinberg (1976) and Goeller and Zucker (1984) assume a steady state world population of 8.5 billion.

4. *Substitution is vital.* Solow emphasizes substitution of reproducible capital for exhaustible resources. So in Solow's steady state reproducible capital per person must be growing continuously. Daly's (1973, 1974) steady state involves a constant physical capital stock (he calls them artifacts) which are just maintained at a constant level in the steady state. In the Goeller-Weinberg model the crucial substitution occurs between specific inexhaustible resources for exhaustible resources. Of course no exhaustible resources are ever physically exhausted; instead they eventually become too expensive economically so that substitutes are found.

Substitution is a fact of life. Ethanol (made from renewable resources) can be used instead of gasoline. Propane or methanol can likewise be substituted for gasoline. Low-grade lignite can be substituted as boiler fuel for high-grade bituminous coal. And natural gas can be substituted as boiler fuel for either bituminous coal or lignite. PVC can be substituted for copper tubing. PVC is cheaper, and has pretty much replaced copper in plumbing applications. Substitutions among different materials are discussed extensively by Goeller and Zucker (1984). Estimates of elasticities of substitutions between physical capital and specific exhaustible resources are given by Moroney and Trapani (1981); between physical capital and certain exhaustible resources and between physical capital and other renewable resources by Moroney and Toevs (1977). Elasticities of substitution between physical capital and energy resources have been estimated by Berndt and Wood (1975), by Griffin and Gregory (1976), and others. The estimates are regrettably all over the map.

5. *Technological progress is important.* Technological progress is also a fact of life. At the macroeconomic level technological progress has been estimated by Solow (1957) for the period 1909-1949 at approximately 1.5% per year; more recently aggregate technological progress was estimated by Moroney (1992) for the period 1950-1984 to be about 1.3% per year. If a lot of technological progress must be embodied in new capital, it just makes reproducible capital investment all the more important in a sustainable steady state.

Goeller and Weinberg (1976) and Goeller and Zucker (1984) do not discuss specific rates of technical progress. But they emphasize the crucial importance of finding new technologies that permit the technical substitution of new types of energy (especially fission breeder reactors and solar energy) for fossil fuels that dominate today's energy budget. Technological progress in harnessing new types of commercial energy is the heart of the Goeller-Weinberg model.

6. *The environment should be preserved.* Solow is not explicit as to how, but states only that "It may be possible to treat environmental quality as a stock, a kind of capital that is "depreciated" by the addition of pollutants and "invested in" by abatement activities. Goeller and Weinberg (1976) are quite explicit. They believe that society's reduced reliance on coal for energy would carry two environmental benefits. First, it would sharply diminish mine spoils for which coal mining accounts for the lion's share. Secondly, it would reduce atmospheric emission of CO_2 (today's major greenhouse gas) and SO_2 (the main source of acid rain). Using fission breeder reactors on the scale they envision would necessarily entail much larger production of radioactive wastes. But they believe the technology is currently available to safely store the increased volumes.

How do the papers that follow shed light on economic sustainability?

In "Sustainable Growth and Valuation of Mineral Reserves" Adelman agrees with the modern principle of calculating *sustainable* net domestic product: It is necessary to subtract the value of net mineral assets used up in a year from the net domestic product. But what monetary value should be placed on the net change in mineral assets consumed? Adelman thinks it is *the current market value of a barrel in the ground.* Solow thinks it is user cost (Hotelling rent).

Adelman correctly denies the basic Hotelling notion that there is a "fixed stock" of oil or gas. He believes the idea of a fixed stock is an ethereal phantom—the stock of any exhaustible resource is not ever known and not ever knowable. Adelman argues that how much of the original stock was in the ground before extraction began and how much is left when extraction stops are both unknown and unimportant. The amount extracted is what is important; and the amount extracted depends on marginal cost of extraction and price, nothing more. As long as the net price exceeds marginal extraction cost, more will be produced. At the point when marginal cost exceeds net price, production stops. Adelman talks straight microprinciples.

Thus far, new knowledge about extraction and new discoveries of previously unknown deposits have dominated any tendency toward diminishing returns. Adelman is on target: he documents that in the past 60 years or so the real (inflation-adjusted) prices of more basic metals have fallen than have risen. This contradicts the simplest theory of depletion and scarcity, based as it is on the assumption of fixed and known mineral stocks. The hard fact is that new reserves are "created" by development investment.

A.   Creating New Reserves by Development

Once an oil field is found, new reserves are "created" by development investment over time. As an example, Adelman cites the Kern River field which was discovered in 1899. In 1942, after 43 years of depletion, its "remaining reserves" were 54 million barrels. But in the next 44 years this field produced not 54 but 736 million barrels, and had another 970 million barrels "remaining" in 1986. Adelman emphasizes that the field had not changed, but knowledge had. Science, technology, and the detailed geological knowledge of the field changed by development investment.

As another example, Adelman notes that in 1944 an expert mission estimated Persian Gulf reserves at 16 billion proved, and 5 billion more as "probable." By 1975 Adelman states that *those same fields* had already produced 42 billion barrels and had 74 billion "remaining," or more than 5 times the combined reserve estimates made 30 years before. In fact, cumulative 1945-1993 Persian Gulf output (from all fields, not just those that were developed by the year 1944) was 188 billion barrels, 9 times the 1944 reserve estimates. Adelman stresses that new reserves added in existing fields are not gifts of nature but instead *growth of knowledge* paid for by investments.

Operators strive to produce from lowest-cost reserves. This means that investment for exploration competes with investment for development, which competes with investment for new reservoirs, new fields, and even with new "plays" in unexplored territory. Adelman believes that estimated finding costs are prone to large errors.

Nonetheless, he calculates the user cost (Hotelling rent) for U.S. oil in 1984 and 1992 to be less than 12% of gross wellhead price and less than 20% of gross wellhead price net of operating expenses, royalties, and taxes (Adelman, this volume, Table 1).

For Adelman, the in-ground value of a developed barrel of oil minus its development cost is the value of an undeveloped barrel (or its user cost). This user cost is sacrificed, over and above development cost, by the decision to produce: A barrel produced today is irretrievable in the future. Adelman finds that his rough estimate of user cost, a residual, declined from $3.10 per barrel in 1984 to $1.84 per barrel in 1992. User cost in the United States was falling, contrary to the prediction of the simplest Hotelling model. Yet reserves added in 1992 (1.5 billion barrels) were much lower than reserves added in 1984 (3.8 billion barrels). Whether one uses gross wellhead price, net wellhead price, or Adelman's residual estimate of user cost as the measure of scarcity value, the evidence shows reduced, not increased, scarcity of oil!

B.   Scarcity in the World Oil Market, 1944-1994

Estimates of worldwide reserves are prone to large errors. Yet Adelman believes that changes in reserve estimates over several years have meaning, but not precision. World reserves were first calculated for 1944 at 51 billion barrels. By the end of 1993, the world had produced and consumed 690 billion barrels and had an estimated 999 billion barrels left in reserves. Most net growth in reserves has been in OPEC. Adelman validly concludes that long-term movements in estimated reserves show no worldwide oil scarcity— quite the contrary. Over the past half-century the worldwide oil supply curve shifted far to the right (as did worldwide demand). But increase in supply was sufficient to prevent a long-term increase in real price. From Adelman's Figures 5 and 6 (this volume), real user cost may have decreased slightly between 1955 and 1986.

C.   Valuation of Reserves Used Up: Sustainability

Adelman states the correct way to evaluate reserves used up is to multiply the net reserve decrease by the current market value of a barrel in the ground (line 3 in Table 1, this volume). This is not the same as multiplying the net reserve decrease by *user cost* (line 5 in Table 1), which is the theoretically correct method according to Solow (1992).

Adelman's suggestion of valuing by the current market value of a barrel in the ground amounts to ignoring development cost and operating cost. These two costs are legitimate long-run marginal costs of extraction. It seems to me that they should properly be subtracted from in-ground market value to obtain an estimate of user cost.

III.   GAINS AND COSTS OF CONSERVATION

What does a society gain and what does it give up by using less energy? The gains usually include a cleaner environment and prolonging known energy reserves. The costs are slower economic growth; and in an energy-intensive culture such as the United States, some unwanted changes in lifestyle. In his chapter on "Energy Conservation Policy," Donald Norman focuses squarely on these issues.

Let's begin with some important facts. *Fact 1*: The aggregate per capita output of a country can grow at the same time it reduces per capita energy consumption. The United States and other industrial countries did in fact grow while stabilizing or reducing per capita energy consumption between 1973 and 1986. But they grew more slowly than they otherwise would have. How did these countries manage to increase real per capita GNP at the same time they reduced per capita energy consumption? By substituting physical capital for energy and by continuing to gain technological improvements— features (4) and (5) of a sustainable steady state noted earlier.

Fact 2: It is feasible for Country A to achieve roughly comparable overall living standards with Country B but to consume much less energy per capita. France, Germany, and Switzerland have living standards about like the United States, but these European countries consume less than one half the energy per capita of the United States. Why? First, because the European countries are much more compact than the United States, so they require much less energy per capita to transport goods and services. Second, for many decades the countries of Europe have had higher energy prices than the United States, so the European capital stocks (autos, houses, factories) are designed to use energy more efficiently than U.S. capital stocks.

Fact 3: Environmental quality is not linked in a simple way to energy consumption. It matters what kind of energy is consumed and how stringently energy byproducts are controlled. Natural gas is a "clean" fossil fuel and the United States is fortunate to consume a lot of it. High sulfur coal is a much dirtier fossil fuel and China's heavy reliance on it with no environmental restrictions contributes to China's high output of SO_2, CO_2, and nitrous oxide. Electricity from hydro power causes no pollution, and Norway gains environmentally by having so much of it.

Norman's starting point is that energy is a productive input just like physical capital and labor. Over time, energy, capital, and labor are substitutable. It follows that to maintain a given growth in output per worker, if energy per worker declines then capital per worker must grow even faster. Even if energy is a small share of an economy's total input cost it can still play a key role in economic growth, as shown by Moroney (1992).

Norman reviews three scenarios concerning future U.S. energy consumption. The Department of Energy Reference Case is based on these assumptions: (1) aggregate real GDP growth of 2% per year, (2) a stable real oil price of $22.50 per barrel until the year 2000, then (3) a gradual increase to $29 per barrel in 2010. In this reference case total U.S. energy consumption grows from 85 quadrillion BTU (quads) in 1990 to 106.7 quads in 2010.

One environmental group (including the Alliance to Save Energy, the American Gas Association, and the Solar Energy Industry Association) thinks a much lower energy path to be feasible. Again assuming 2% aggregate real GDP growth, this group obtains conservation from energy efficient heating and appliance technologies and major substitution of natural gas for oil. In *America's Energy Choices* this group projects a very slight decrease of aggregate domestic energy consumption from 83.8 quads in 1990 to 82.3 quads in 2010.

Yet a different group of conservationists (the American Council for an Energy Efficient Economy, the Alliance to Save Energy, and the Union of Concerned Scientists) makes several energy consumption forecasts, each based on a different goal. All forecasts assume aggregate real growth of approximately 2.1%.

Their stiffest plan is a "Climate Stabilization Scenario," involving a 25% reduction in CO_2 emissions by 2005 and a 50% reduction by 2030. In this setup, total domestic energy falls from 85.3 quads in 1988 to 68.9 quads in 2010, a decrease of about 22%. Oil consumption falls from 33.5 quads in 1988 to 20.0 quads in 2010. The scientifically important question is this: Is it feasible to sustain real economic growth of 2.1% in the face of such a sharp reduction in energy use? To increase real GDP by 58% while reducing energy consumption by 22% requires approximately doubling aggregate energy efficiency. To achieve this, U.S. energy use in 2010 would look more like today's consumption in France or Germany than today's consumption in the United States.

Norman's evidence from six industrial countries shows that rapid GDP growth in the years 1950-1973 was linked to (not necessarily caused by) rapid energy growth. Following the 1973-1984 hike in energy prices, energy consumption stabilized or declined in all six countries, and GDP growth plummeted. Norman is rightly skeptical of models that assume reductions in energy consumption can be achieved without sacrificing any economic growth. There is a tradeoff.

A. Sustainable Growth

There are two keys to sustainable growth: substitutability among inputs and technological progress, broadly conceived. Economists know what technological progress is at the micro-level. The pentium chip is a quantifiable improvement over the 486, which was in turn a quantifiable improvement over the 386, and so on. Aggregate technological progress is a different thing. It is an imperfectly understood combination of micro-improvements. Whatever it is, aggregate technological progress will be a major source of sustainable growth.

To focus strictly on input substitution, let's ignore technological progress. Then the only way to increase output per worker is to substitute other inputs for labor. Historically, capital and energy have been jointly substituted for labor; but in an economy that simultaneously grows and conserves energy, a higher rate of capital formation is the only hope. (Indeed in Solow's model reproducible capital formation is *the key* to a stable long-run living standard.)

IV. U.S. OIL RESERVES ARE DWINDLING

By 1993, oil production in the lower 48 states was 44% below its 1970 peak. Using a petroleum supply model developed at the American Petroleum Institute, Edward Porter suggests that domestic crude oil production by the year 2010 is expected to be roughly 3 million barrels per day below the 1990 level. Opening new federal lands, particularly the Arctic National Wildlife Refuge, to exploration and development could offset perhaps 50% or more of this decline.

Virtually all forecasters in 1980 *seriously underestimated* actual domestic oil production in 1985. The slight increase that actually occurred between 1981 and 1985 took place simultaneously with a decline in real oil price. An increase in production concurrent with the decline in real price is not consistent with a simple supply model. But then oil and gas production is not a simple business.

Porter emphasizes that taxation and regulation sensitively affect exploration and development. Domestic taxes drive a big wedge between the domestic wellhead price and the after-tax price received by producers. Even after the sharp world oil price increases of the mid 1970s, producers of conventional onshore oil received after-tax real prices in 1978 equivalent to real prices in 1966. The effect of regulated prices and on long-oil supply is a very complex business.

A. Discovery and Production

The stock of known oil reserves is constantly changing: Reserves decrease because of current production, but increase because of new discoveries and development investment. Porter shows that by 1990 the United States had produced a total of 305 billion barrels equivalent (crude oil plus natural gas production expressed as equivalent barrels of oil). Of the 305 billion barrels, 263 billion (or 86%) were produced from the lower 48 onshore, 32 billion barrels, (10.5%) from the lower 48 offshore, and 10.2 billion barrels (3.5%) from Alaska.

Porter estimates an empirical model to account for cumulative reserves added. In his model, cumulative reserves added depend on cumulative footage drilled and technological progress that improves drilling productivity. Porter estimates reserves added for three separate regions: Lower 48 onshore, lower 48 offshore, and Alaska. Empirically he cannot separate the positive effect of technological progress from the negative effect of depletion; but he finds strong evidence of diminishing returns to cumulative footage drilled.

Between 1965 and 1990 large volumes of oil and gas new reserves were discovered domestically. In this 25-year period, crude oil reserves increased from 31.4 billion barrels in 1965 to 38.9 billion in 1970, chiefly because of a ten billion reserve increase in Alaska, then declined steadily to 26.2 billion in 1990.

Gas reserves show a roughly similar pattern. Aggregate gas reserves from the lower 48 onshore, the lower 48 offshore, and Alaska decreased from 57.4 billion oil equivalent barrels in 1970 to 35.7 billion barrels in 1990. Porter shows that *combined* domestic oil and gas reserves reached a peak of 96.3 billion barrels in 1970 then declined to 61.9 billion barrels in 1990. Because the largest fields tend to be the first discovered, most of the giant domestic reservoirs have been found. New reserves will assuredly be found; but domestic reserves will diminish. Porter estimates that combined oil and gas reserves will fall from 61.9 billion barrels in 1990 to only 35.5 billion in 2010. This decrease is the net result of 60 billion barrels of oil and gas reserves being added but 86 billion barrels being produced, yielding a net reserve decrease of 26 billion barrels.

Production follows reserves. Both respond positively but inelastically to price. Porter suggests as a point of reference that if the real price of oil were to remain constant at $20 per barrel and the real price of gas were likewise to remain constant, combined domestic oil and gas production would fall from about 14.5 million barrels of oil equivalent per day in 1994 to roughly 9.3 million barrels per day in 2010. Using a higher real oil price of $25 per barrel, his simulation yields a flatter decline to roughly 10 million barrels per day in 2010. But with a lower real price of $15 per barrel his simulation yields a somewhat faster decline to 8.4 million barrels per day in 2010. The implied long-run price elasticity of supply is between 0.3 and 0.4.

Government policies are important in Porter's model. He explicitly considers two. First, he believes that if the Arctic National Wildlife Refuge were opened to development and were to yield 9.2 billion barrels of new oil reserves, domestic oil production in 2010 might be 5.5 million barrels per day instead of 4.0 million barrels without prospective ANWR production. Second, Porter considers the effects on production if materials associated with exploration and production not currently classified as hazardous waste were to be reclassified and regulated under the Resources Conservation and Recovery Act. Not surprisingly, the effect of stricter environmental regulation is to decrease oil production by approximately .5 million barrels per day below the Reference Scenario Path (see Porter's Figure 23, this volume).

V.   U.S. GAS RESERVES ARE DWINDLING TOO

Wattenbarger and Villegas estimate trends in U.S. gas production using a method developed by the late physicist/geophysicist M. King Hubbert. Hubbert's essential idea is that the lifetime production of an exhaustible resource such as oil or natural gas follows a logistic curve. By taking the first derivative of cumulative production with respect to time, the annual production rate increases to a maximum, then decline along a path symmetrical to the path of expansion during the growth phase.

Wattenbarger and Villegas show that the U.S. gas industry developed from a fledgling production rate of 2.0 billion cubic feet (BCF) per day in 1918 to a peak production rate of 62 BCF in 1973. During this expansion phase, 1918-1973, the Hubbert curve closely tracks actual annual gas production.

But between 1973 and 1978 gas production dropped from 62 BCF to 55 BCF per day, sharper than the decline predicted by Hubbert's model. Between 1979 and 1983 actual production rates came back into line with the Hubbert curve prediction, falling in 1983 to a rate of 46 BCF per day.

Then an astonishing thing happens: instead of continuing to decline, after 1986 gas production steadily increases to almost 53 BCF per day in 1993. The post-1986 growth in domestic gas production is completely at odds with the Hubbert curve prediction of steady decline (see Wattenbarger and Villegas, Figure 3, this volume). Because actual production increases between 1986 and 1993, the prediction errors from the Hubbert model get progressively larger: Forecast production for 1993 on the Hubbert curve is about 26 BCF per day but actual production is nearly 53 BCF per day. After 1984 the Hubbert curve consistently underestimates production with a growing margin of error.

Why does the Hubbert model fit actual production so closely between 1918 and 1970, consistently overestimate production between 1974 and 1978, then vastly underestimate production after 1985?

Wattenbarger and Villegas suggest two answers. First, proved gas reserves are a moving target. U.S. gas reserves have moved downward from 250 trillion cubic feet in 1973 to 165 trillion cubic feet in 1992. In the years 1986-1993 gas production increased at the same time proved reserves fell, pulling the reserve/production ratio down from 12 in 1986 to about 9 in 1992 (as shown in Figure 7, this volume).

What caused gas producers to pull harder from their dwindling reserves? Hubbert's geophysical model offers no guidance because it omits the crucial economic variables: price and cost. Wattenbarger and Villegas recognize these economic variables, but do not explicitly model their influences. Priced on a BTU basis, the average price of gas was only 26% as high as the price of oil in 1974. Then the price of gas rose in a jagged pattern to 90% of the price of oil in 1986, dropped back to 50% of the price of oil in 1990, then rose back to 82% of the price of oil by 1993. On a BTU equivalent basis, gas was priced at about 70% of the price of oil in the period 1986-1993. By contrast, the average price of gas was only about 45% of the price of oil during the years 1974-1979 (see Figure 10, Wattenbarger and Villegas, this volume). Thus gas became much more profitable relative to oil in the years 1986-1993 than in the period 1974-1979. They believe this increase in relative profitability helps explain the increase in actual gas production in these later years.

A second part of the answer is that gas production is constrained by demand. The demand for gas was comparatively low during the period 1979-1984 when the average price of gas was relatively high (see Wattenbarger and Villegas, Table 2, this volume). Low demand, because of relatively high prices, constrained the amount actually produced and marketed. But the price of gas fell from $3.63 per MCF in 1984 to $1.73 MCF in 1991. Producers who could not find buyers at $3.63 could find customers at $1.73, so the quantity produced increased during the years 1985-1993. The demand curve for gas also increased during these later years because of environmental concerns: natural gas is a cleaner burning fuel than coal or oil. Declining gas prices combined with stricter environmental standards to induce some fuel switching from coal and oil in favor of gas.

VI.   ENERGY TAXES

Dowlatabadi, Kopp, and Tschang (DKT) consider the burden of two proposed energy taxes among households in the United States. Their motivation is correct: any tax scheme will be an easier political sell if members of Congress view it as "equitable"—the burden being shared about equally among households in different jurisdictions. DKT analyzed the burden of two energy taxes: first, a BTU tax and second, a carbon tax levied on the carbon content of various fossil fuels (coal, oil, and natural gas).

They begin by analyzing average household energy consumption in the nine U.S. census regions for 1990. Interestingly, the regional variation in household energy consumption is moderate: energy consumption is greatest in the Mountain region (369 million BTU per year) and smallest in the Pacific region (262 million BTU per year), a maximum regional difference of about 35%. But consumption in the Northeast, East North Central, West North Central, and West South Central regions is very nearly the same as that in the Mountain region. Average U.S. household expenditure on energy was $3,104, ranging from a minimum of $2,914 in the Pacific region to a maximum of $3,931 in New England.

Higher energy taxes will increase energy prices. The burden of higher taxes therefore depends on the extent of energy conservation with higher prices. But how much will be conserved? DKT tackle the question with three models. The "naive" short-run model assumes zero price elasticity of energy demand. The "conservation" model allows some substitution of more energy efficient capital, chiefly appliances, following higher energy prices. The long-run model allows households to completely replace physical capital stocks in response to higher energy prices.

What's really interesting is that they find very little difference in the household tax burden regardless of the energy model chosen (on the order of only $30 to $40 per year). In addition, they find very little regional difference in the burden of the two tax schemes. So if either scheme turns out to be a political hot potato, it will be about the same temperature in all regions.

What about environmental effects of the two taxes? In the naive (zero demand elasticity) model there are of course none: energy consumption is the same before and after either tax. But the long-run model gives rise to a much larger reduction in carbon emissions than the conservation (medium-run) model. This result holds equally for the BTU tax or the carbon tax. For example, DKT estimate that after full long-run adjustments U.S. carbon emissions would be reduced by about 46 or 47 million tons if a BTU or a carbon tax were imposed. The environmental benefit of either tax appears to rest in the long-run result of lower carbon emissions.

VII. CONCLUSIONS

Economic sustainability is an important matter. Most of us would like to provide later generations an opportunity for a steady or rising living standard. If approached correctly, useful numerical answers can be given to the important questions.

To be worth their salt, the answers ought to include realistic assessments of the rate of capital formation required to offset long-run depletion of specific resources. Fossil fuels will almost certainly begin to be economically depleted (more costly in real terms) in the next century. But their depletion will not be a catastrophe, and need not be even much of a burden—provided that substitutes are found.

The answers should also include substitution of non-fuel resources for one another. For most, the range of substitutes is enormous. Additional work along the lines of Goeller and Weinberg (1976) and Goeller and Zucker (1984) should be extremely useful. In any case the feasible substitutions need to be quantified. So do the costs and the benefits of specific environmental changes. The most important environmental questions still remain unanswered. We remain ignorant at our peril.

ACKNOWLEDGMENT

I am pleased to thank Robert Solow for his most helpful comments on an earlier draft.

REFERENCES

Berndt, E., and D.O. Wood. 1975. "Technology, Prices, and the Derived Demand for Energy." *Review of Economics and Statistics 57* (August): 259-268.
Daly, H.E. (ed.) 1973. *Toward a Steady-State Economy.* San Francisco: W.H. Freeman and Co.

Daly, H.E. 1974. "The Economics of the Steady State." *American Economic Review* 64 (May): 15-21.

Diamond, P., and J. Hausman. 1994. "Contingent Valuation: Is Some Number Better Than No Number?" *Journal of Economic Perspectives* 8 (Fall): 45-64.

Goeller, H.E., and A. Weinberg. 1976. "The Age of Substitutability." *Science* 191 (February): 683-689.

Goeller, H.E., and A. Zucker. 1984. "Infinite Resources: The Ultimate Strategy." *Science* 223 (February): 456-462.

Griffin, J., and P. Gregory. 1976. "An Intercountry Translog Model of Energy Substitution Responses." *American Economic Review* 66 (December): 845-857.

Humphrey, D.B., and J.R. Moroney. 1975. "Substitution Among Capital, Labor, and Natural Resource Products in American Manufacturing." *Journal of Political Economy* 83 (February): 57-82.

Moroney, J.R. 1992. "Energy, Capital, and Technological Change in the United States." *Resources and Energy* 14: 363-380.

Moroney, J.R., and J. Trapani. 1981. "Factor Demand and Substitution in Mineral-Intensive Industries." *Bell Journal of Economics* 12 (Spring): 272-284.

Moroney, J.R., and A. Toevs. 1977. "Factor Costs and Factor Use: An Analysis of Labor, Capital, and Natural Resource Inputs." *Southern Economic Journal* 44 (October): 222-239.

Solow, R. 1957. "Technical Change and The Aggregate Production Function." *Review of Economics and Statistics* 39: 312-320.

Solow, R. 1974. "The Economics of Resources or the Resources of Economics." *American Economic Review* 64 (May): 1-14.

Solow, R. 1992. "An Almost Practical Step Toward Sustainability." Fortieth Anniversary Lecture for Resources for The Future, October 8.

Survey of Current Business. 1994. Washington, DC: U.S. Government Printing Office.

World Resources, 1992-1993. 1992. New York: Oxford University Press.

FOSSIL FUEL USE AND SUSTAINABLE DEVELOPMENT:

EVIDENCE FROM U.S. INPUT-OUTPUT DATA, 1972-1985

Richard W. England and Stephen D. Casler

ABSTRACT

This chapter addresses a serious question which can be stated quite simply. Are recent trends in fossil fuel use compatible with sustainable development? Although we cannot claim to have discovered a definitive answer to that question, our research has pointed to some clues. We begin our discussion by briefly surveying a number of theoretical debates concerning the definition of sustainability and by describing some empirical trends relevant to its measurement. We then turn to an analysis of U.S. input-output tables for 1972 and 1985 which emphasizes the dynamic connections among economic growth, structural change in the macroeconomy, dependence on fossil fuels, and sustainability.

Advances in the Economics of Energy and Resources, Volume 9, pages 21-44.

I. THEORETICAL AND EMPIRICAL TRENDS

Nearly a quarter century ago, classical concerns about whether economic growth could be sustained in the long run began to resurface within economics. The position that economic growth cannot continue indefinitely because of biophysical constraints on the scale of human activity was advanced by Daly (1971) and Meadows and colleagues (1972), among others. This *limits-to-growth* hypothesis, which received a great deal of popular and scholarly attention at that time, seemed to imply an eventual and inevitable transition to a steady-state economy:

> A steady-state economy fits easily into the paradigm of physical science and biology...Why not our economy also, at least in its physical dimensions of [human] bodies and artifacts?...[T]he fact that wealth is measured in value units does not annihilate its physical dimensions...[V]alue could conceivably grow forever, but the physical mass in which value inheres must [eventually] conform to a steady state...(Daly, 1971, p. 17).

A steady state, according to Daly (1971, pp. 29-31), would be characterized by constant stocks of human beings and physical capital and by the lowest feasible flows of materials and energy to maintain and reproduce those stocks.

This point of view encountered stiff opposition within the mainstream of academic economics during the early 1970s (Cole et al., 1973; Nordhaus, 1973). For a time, the limits-to-growth debate subsided, and the expectation of exponential growth once again became an uncontested premise of modern economics.[1] During recent years, however, the debate of a quarter century ago has begun to revive, albeit in an altered form (Gever et al., 1986; Meadows et al., 1992; Nordhaus, 1992; Pimentel et al., 1994). Two characteristics of this revival deserve mention. One is the current effort to formulate *sustainability* as a scientific concept and as a guide to economic policy. The other is growing recognition that *energy production and use* are intimately connected to issues of sustainable development.

Although the sustainability concept has been construed somewhat differently by various authors, its essence is that current income must be viewed as the maximum amount that a community can consume over some time period and still be as well off at the end of the period as at the beginning. Being as well off means having the same capacity to produce the same income in the next year—that is, maintaining capital intact (Hicks, 1946, chap. 14). Hence, sustainability requires that a society live on its current income and renounce the consumption of capital.

As Turner (1993) has pointed out, this capital-preservation criterion has weaker and stronger versions. In its weaker form, sustainability requires that society transfer an *aggregate* capital stock to the next generation no smaller than that inherited from the previous generation. This version would permit a *reallocation* of aggregate capital among its various forms (e.g., computer codes, human skills, factories and skyscrapers, coal deposits and forests) so long as the overall capacity to produce useful services was not impaired. As both Daly (1994, p. 24) and Turner (1993, p. 6) have recognized, weak sustainability assumes that human capital, business capital, and natural capital easily *substitute* for one another in production. If they do not, if the various forms of capital actually *complement* one another in production, then sustainability requires preservation of ecosystems and restrained use of mineral deposits, not the unrestrained conversion of natural capital into human beings and their physical artifacts.[2] Hence, in the face of strong complementarities, sustainable development requires intensive efforts to conserve natural capital and to create technologies which ease substitution among the forms of capital.

Ironically, the empirical connection between energy use and sustainability is both straightforward and also hard to discern. On the one hand, it is quite clear that modern industrial economies have become utterly dependent upon the use of fossil fuels and that geological deposits of coal, oil, and natural gas are currently being consumed at unsustainable rates. As Smil (1991, p. 150) has noted:

> [P]reindustrial civilizations depended on practically *instantaneous solar energy flows*. In contrast, industrial civilization has been tapping *stores of fossil fuels* transformed from biomass...mostly between 10^6 and 10^8 years ago.... We are living in an energetic interlude: the stores powering our way of life are finite and even the best conversion efficiencies and conservation measures cannot extend their life [indefinitely]....[3]

Whether or not economic activity in forthcoming decades will remain heavily dependent upon dwindling physical reserves of fossil fuels is not so obvious, however. There are significant cross-sectional differences in current energy use among nations at similar levels of economic development (Smil, 1991, p. 273). Hence, it appears that there is no particular flow of energy use which is technologically required to support any given scale of macroeconomic activity. Furthermore, as individual economies grow and develop, their aggregate degrees of dependence on fossil fuels typically evolve. In the United States, for example, the ratio of fossil fuel use to real GDP fell 31% from 1960 to 1990 (U.S. Census, 1993, p. 572; U.S. Commerce Dept., 1992, p. 42). Thus, although pioneering efforts to forecast energy demand typically assumed a constant ratio of energy consumption to real aggregate output (Griffin, 1993), we now know that the macroeconomy possesses a certain degree of flexibility in its use of fossil fuels and other energy sources.

The perplexing scientific and public policy question is whether that flexibility is extensive enough to permit sustainable development. As Cleveland (1991, p. 292) has observed, neoclassical theory presupposes a very high degree of flexibility:

> According to the neoclassical model, the means of escape from increasing scarcity lies in the market mechanism.... Price increases stimulate a host of resource-augmenting mechanisms: increased exploration for new [i.e., previously unknown] deposits, recycling, substitution of alternative resources, increased efficiency of converting resources into goods and services, and, most importantly, technical innovation in resource exploration, extraction, processing, and transformation into [products]....

In its *World Development Report 1992*, the World Bank exhibited this neoclassical optimism in unqualified form: "For natural resources that are nonrenewable, increases in consumption necessarily imply a reduction in the available [physical] stock. The evidence, however, gives no support to the hypothesis that marketed nonrenewable resources such as [fossil fuels]... are becoming scarcer in an economic sense" (p. 37).[4]

It seems to us that the issue of sustainability involves both the physical depletion of natural resources and also the adjustment of the economy to growing scarcity of those resources. Therefore, more empirical research is warranted before we conclude that market incentives alone will inevitably uncouple macroeconomic activity from fossil fuel use, thereby facilitating "sustainable growth" during the decades to come.[5] In the following sections, we analyze energy-output linkages within the U.S. economy and how those relations evolved from 1972 through 1985. The two global oil price shocks which occurred during that era generated excellent data with which to test the hypothesis that higher energy prices will suffice to induce the input substitutions and technological innovations required for continued expansion of the macroeconomy.

II. INPUT-OUTPUT DATA AND ENERGY ANALYSIS

The use of input-output tables to analyze the structure of and trends in national energy use has become a well established research method within energy and ecological economics. Building upon the pioneering efforts of Leontief (1966), authors such as Bullard and Herendeen (1975) and Hannon (1982) have shown that published input-output tables can be modified to highlight the interdependencies between the energy-producing and energy-consuming sectors of the aggregate economy. As Miller and Blair (1985, pp. 200-201) have aptly summarized this energetic methodology:

> Energy input-output [analysis] typically determines the total energy required to deliver a product to final demand, both directly as the energy consumed by an industry's production process and indirectly as the energy embodied in that industry's [other] inputs.... The sum of these two is the *total energy requirement.*

Expressing this method more formally, suppose that the economy has n productive sectors, m of which produce and ship energy products and $(n-m)$ of which provide nonenergy products.[6] If x is the gross output of and Y_j the final demand for the product(s) of the jth sector, and if a_{ij} is the commodity flow from sector i to sector j directly required per unit of gross production in sector j, then one can express the sectoral interdependencies within the aggregate economy according to equation (1):

$$
\begin{bmatrix} X_i \\ \cdot \\ \cdot \\ \cdot \\ \cdot \\ X_m \\ X_{m+1} \\ \cdot \\ \cdot \\ \cdot \\ X_n \end{bmatrix}
=
\begin{bmatrix} a_{11} & \cdots & a_{1m} & \cdots & a_{1n} \\ \cdot & & \cdot & & \cdot \\ \cdot & (I) & \cdot & (II) & \cdot \\ \cdot & & \cdot & & \cdot \\ a_{m1} & \cdots & a_{mm} & \cdots & a_{mn} \\ \cdot & & \cdot & & \cdot \\ \cdot & (III) & \cdot & (IV) & \cdot \\ \cdot & & \cdot & & \cdot \\ a_{n1} & \cdots & a_{mm} & \cdots & a_{nn} \end{bmatrix}
\begin{bmatrix} X_i \\ \cdot \\ \cdot \\ \cdot \\ \cdot \\ X_m \\ X_{m+1} \\ \cdot \\ \cdot \\ \cdot \\ X_n \end{bmatrix}
+
\begin{bmatrix} Y_i \\ \cdot \\ \cdot \\ \cdot \\ \cdot \\ Y_m \\ Y_{m+1} \\ \cdot \\ \cdot \\ \cdot \\ Y_n \end{bmatrix} \quad \cdot \quad (1)
$$

Equation (1) can be expressed more compactly as

$$X = A \cdot X + Y, \tag{2}$$

which, in turn, implies that $(I - A) \cdot X = Y$, I being the identify matrix, and hence

$$X = (I - A)^{-1} \cdot Y. \tag{3}$$

This standard result in input-output economics invites the interpretation that A is the matrix of *direct* input coefficients linking productive sectors whereas $(I\text{-}A)^{-1}$ is the Leontief inverse matrix of *total* input requirements, direct and indirect alike. That is, elements of the inverse matrix measure the amount of each input directly required to produce a unit of output plus the amount of each input indirectly used elsewhere in the economy to produce the other inputs required to produce a unit of output.

In order to emphasize that energy is physically conserved from the moment of its economic production through the moment of its use and to highlight that energy use tends to physically deplete various energy sources, let us measure the elements of A and of $(I\text{-}A)^{-1}$ in a "hybrid" fashion. The elements of quadrant I in (1) are therefore measured as British thermal units (Btu's) of energy input per Btu of gross energy output. The elements of quadrant II, on the other hand, are measured by Btu's of energy input per deflated dollar of gross nonenergy output. The elements of quadrant III measure deflated dollars of nonenergy inputs required per Btu of gross energy production in various energy sectors. Quadrant IV, which focuses attention on interdependencies between nonenergy sectors, requires customary ratios of deflated dollars to measure its elements. Having implemented this measurement strategy, one can then easily extract the first m rows from the Leontief inverse matrix to reveal the total energy input requirements (measured in Btu's) per Btu or constant dollar of final demand for any sector's output.

This analytical framework has been used to study the evolution of energy use within the U.S. and other national economies. In an Office of Technology Assessment report (U.S. Congress, 1990), for example, "hybrid" input-output tables for the years 1972 and 1985 were inspected to reveal changes in energy use and associated changes in the U.S. economy. The report's authors concluded optimistically:

The future holds a unique opportunity for achieving economic growth without incurring the costs associated with increased energy use.... History illustrates that economic growth can be achieved with little or no increase in energy use (p. 48).

Although the OTA report provides valuable insights into the relationship between energy use and economic growth, we cannot accept its sanguine conclusions without attaching a few sobering provisos. In the following sections, we report on our efforts to reanalyze U.S. data for 1972 and 1985 in order to extract lessons about the *sustainability* of recent U.S. economic growth. In doing so, we hope to make a modest contribution to an already enormous literature which analyzes U.S. energy use during the seventies and eighties (e.g., Schipper, Howarth, and Geller, 1990).

III. AGGREGATE SECTORS AND SUSTAINABILITY

In an effort to highlight the issue of sustainability, we have aggregated the detailed sectors described in the OTA and similar studies into five energy sectors and another six sectors producing nonenergy commodities. These grand sectors, which are listed in Table 1 and which are based on the U.S. Bureau of Economic Analysis classification scheme, are meant to focus analytical attention on the production and use of renewable and nonrenewable natural resources (including fossil fuels) and their linkages to industrial and service activities.

Table 1. Aggregate Sectors
of the U.S. Economy

1.	coal mining
2.	crude oil and natural gas
3.	petroleum refining
4.	electric utilities
5.	gas utilities
6.	biological resources
7.	mineral resources
8.	durable manufacturing and construction
9.	nondurable manufacturing
10.	transportation services
11.	other services

Source: Appendix.

In this conceptual scheme, both the coal mining and also the crude oil and natural gas sectors are populated by primary producers which extract fossil hydrocarbons from geological deposits. The mineral resources sector also extracts materials from geological deposits to be used within the human economy. The petroleum refining, electric utility, and gas utility sectors, in turn, process fossil fuels and other energy sources and then deliver energy commodities to other producing sectors and to final customers.

The biological resources sector (which includes agriculture, ranching, fishing, and forestry) offers the promise of sustainable supplies of commodities into the distant future. If harvest rates did not exceed the reproduction rates of the animal and plant populations being exploited for human use, then gross output of the biological resources sector could remain the same indefinitely. Unfortunately, however, there is abundant evidence that fisheries, tropical forests, and even the soils of agricultural lands are presently being exploited at unsustainable rates (Meadows et al., 1992; Pimentel et al., 1995).

In sharp contrast with the biological resources sectors, the sector producing mineral resources depends heavily on tapping depletable natural deposits of metals and other materials. Since these natural deposits are typically not renewable, the sustainability of mineral supplies is problematic. Some combination of human recycling of previously extracted minerals and development of renewable substitute materials will be required to avert worsening physical scarcity of nonrenewable minerals as economic activity proceeds (and even expands in scale).[7] For both the biological and mineral resources sectors, however, dependence on energy-intensive production methods could hinder productivity long before agricultural lands and mineral deposits are depleted.

The four remaining productive sectors engage in construction, manufacture of durable and nondurable products, and provision of transportation and other services. This quartet accounts for the lion's share of employment and sales generated by the U.S. economy. The manufacturing and construction sectors are heavy users of both energy and materials. The reliance of the U.S. transportation system on motor vehicles and aircraft implies heavy dependence on fossil fuels. The service sector, on the other hand, is frequently assumed to operate almost "on thin air." As we shall see, however, service activities in the United States do require significant direct and indirect inputs of fossil fuels and other energy commodities.

IV. ENERGY USE PATTERNS: SCALE AND FINAL DEMAND

What, then, were the macrodynamic connections among economic growth, structural change, and fossil fuel use in the United States between 1972 and 1985? We begin with an examination of the overall scale of economic activity. As reported in Table 2, U.S. society experienced substantial economic and population growth during that interval of history. Population grew by 14%, and per capita real output grew by nearly 21%, for a combined increase in total real gross domestic product approaching 38%. Simultaneously, there was a relatively modest increase in total energy consumption (3.8%) and a decline in consumption of fossil fuels (-2.2%). The fact that the average deflated price of fossil fuels during 1980-1985 was roughly *triple* that of 1970 surely helps to explain this restrained growth of energy use and the shift from fossil fuels to other energy commodities (U.S. Bureau of Census, 1993, p. 580). Hence, empirical evidence which appears to confirm the optimistic assessments of the OTA (1990, p. 48) and World Bank (1992, p. 37) is not difficult to find.

In order to discover whether these optimistic assessments are fully warranted, however, it is necessary to look beneath the surface appearance of macroeconomic *aggregates* and to analyze the *evolving structure* of the macroeconomy, that is, secular changes in the sectoral composition of final demand and in the technologies commonly used to produce various commodities. In the absence of this more detailed look, one can conclude very little about the sustainability of the U.S. economy.

Table 2. Aggregate Data for U.S. Economy

Variable	1972 Level	1985 Level	Percent Change
population (millions)	209.3	238.5	+14.0%
real per capita GDP (1987 $)	14,845	17,945	+20.9%
real GDP (billions 1987 $)	3107	4280	+37.8%
energy consumption (quadrillion Btu)	71.3	74.0	+3.8%
fossil-fuel consumption (quadrillion Btu)	67.7	66.2	-2.2%

Sources: Survey of Current Business, September 1992, p. 42
Statistical Abstract of the United States: 1993, pp. 8, 572.

Looking first at the composition of final demand, several intersectoral differences and historical trends stand out (see Tables 3 and 4). First, the markets for depletable natural resources (coal, crude oil and natural gas, and minerals) made a minor contribution to final demand in both 1972 and 1985, especially for domestic uses.[8] Second, biological resources constituted a modest, but rapidly expanding, share of final demand. Third, non-transportation services (the provision of which requires relatively little energy) comprised a huge and rapidly expanding share of final demand in the United States. Finally, durable manufacturing and construction continued to provide a large and expanding volume of final demand, an expansion tending to increase fossil-fuel use by the U.S. economy. Thus, although the composition of final demand did shift in the direction of a "service economy" between 1972 and 1985, agriculture and industry continued to play major roles in the United States.

Perhaps more surprising than these shifts in the sectoral composition of final demand were the differential responses of government and households in the United States to higher energy prices and uncertain energy availability. As shown in Table 4, U.S.

Table 3. Final Demand, All Sectors
(billions 1977 $)

Sector	1972 Level	1985 Level	Percent Change
coal	2.0	3.3	+63%
crude oil & natural gas	-7.6	-10.7	+40%
refined petroleum	34.2	36.9	+8%
electric utilities	25.9	37.9	+46%
gas utilities	17.8	12.4	-30%
biological resources	17.3	35.5	+105%
mineral resources	-1.3	-0.6	-56%
durable manufacturing & construction	463.1	676.5	+46%
nondurable manufacturing	213.6	252.6	+18%
transportation services	44.2	58.9	+33%
other services	723.8	1156.9	+60%
total	1532.9	2259.6	+47%

Sources: Calculations based on Hannon et al. (1983) and Casler (1989).

Table 4. Final Demand for Energy
(trillions Btu)

Sector		Final Domestic Use			International		
		Consumption (C)	Investment (I)	Government (G)	Exports	Imports	Total
Coal	1972	179	487	62	1335	-1	2062
	1985	99	-626	125	2466	-64	2000
Crude Oil &	1972	0	52	0	1	-4848	-4795
Natural Gas	1985	0	109	0	435	-6896	-6352
Refined	1972	12,584	-399	1608	464	-5345	8912
Petroleum	1985	11,279	-253	1087	1223	-3713	9623
Electric	1972	1745	0	424	9	-36	2143
Utilities	1985	2775	0	359	17	-157	2994
Gas	1972	5148	11	757	80	-1051	4946
Utilities	1985	5161	-243	201	58	-951	4227

Sources: Calculations based on Hannon et al. (1983) and Casler (1989).

households cut their use of refined petroleum by more than 10% from 1972 to 1985 while simultaneously increasing electricity use by 59% and holding utility gas consumption steady. Government departments and agencies, on the other hand, cut their final use of energy sharply and across the board: refined petroleum by 32%, electricity by 15%, and utility gas by almost three-quarters. Hence, there is evidence that U.S. households *substituted* among forms of energy to some degree whereas the public sector pursued a more comprehensive program of energy *conservation.*[9]

V. ENERGY USE PATTERNS: GROSS PRODUCTION AND INTERMEDIATE INPUT USE

Our story up to this point is seriously incomplete, however, since it has concentrated on the sectoral composition of final demand and neglected *gross production* and *intermediate input use* of the five energy and six nonenergy commodity groups. Tables 5 and 6 help to remedy that analytical imbalance. Note, for example, that the gross output of biological resources in 1985 was roughly equal in market value to the gross output of transportation services. Turning to depletable natural resources, we find that U.S. gross output of coal,

Table 5.   Gross Output, All Sectors
(billions 1977 $)

Sector	1972 Level	1985 Level	Percent Change
coal	14.1	22.2	+57.7%
crude oil and natural gas	48.5	48.9	+0.8%
refined petroleum	76.8	92.4	+20.4%
electric utilities	56.4	80.7	+43.0%
gas utilities	52.9	46.1	-12.8%
biological resources	120.2	147.2	+22.5%
mineral resources	10.5	9.9	-5.0%
durable manufacturing and construction	871.5	1166.6	+33.9%
nondurable manufacturing	484.9	594.1	+22.5%
transportation services	108.7	144.2	+32.6%
other services	1119.6	1826.9	+63.2%

Sources: Calculations based on Hannon et al. (1983) and Casler (1989).

Table 6.   Energy Sectors
(trillions Btu)

Sector		final domestic use (C+I+G)	gross domestic output	net exports
coal	1972	728	14,172	1334
	1985	-402	19,325	2402
crude oil and	1972	52	42,336	-4847
natural gas	1985	109	34,549	-6461
refined petroleum	1972	13,793	27,562	-4881
	1985	12,113	27,849	-2490
electric utilities	1972	2,169	5,992	-27
	1985	3,134	8,654	-140
gas utilities	1972	5,916	20,851	-971
	1985	5,120	16,017	-894

Sources: Calculations based on Hannon et al. (1983) and Casler (1989).

crude oil, and natural gas in 1985 ($71 billion) was seven times the gross output of mineral resources. Hence, the scale of fossil fuel extraction within the United States remained quite substantial during the eighties despite the nation's growing dependence on imports of crude oil. Most important of all, we find that gross production of energy commodities was greatly in excess of domestic final use for all five energy categories, with net imports actually supplementing domestic production in four of the five energy sectors. These large differences signify the extensive use of energy commodities as intermediate inputs in the production of nonenergy commodities.

VI.   ENERGY USE PATTERNS: CHANGING TECHNOLOGICAL REQUIREMENTS

The heavy dependence of the U.S. economy on depletable fossil fuels is documented quite clearly in Tables 7 and 8.[10] We find that coal, refined petroleum, and utility gas were essential direct inputs to the electrical power sector throughout the period studied, providing 1.68, 0.13, and 0.36 Btu's of physical inputs per Btu of electricity generated in 1985. Although the direct input coefficients for oil and gas declined from 1972 to 1985, those reductions were partially offset by an increase in the direct input coefficient from coal mining into the electric utility sector. On balance, then, the total direct input of fossil fuels into the electricity-generating sector declined fairly modestly in the wake of escalating fossil fuel prices, from 2.55 to 2.17 Btu's of inputs per Btu of electricity produced.[11]

The pervasive and direct dependence of nonenergy sectors on fossil fuel inputs can be seen in Table 8. Not surprisingly, construction activity and the production of minerals and manufactures were heavily dependent upon direct inputs of coal, refined petroleum, and utility gas. Transportation services also required a hefty direct input of fossil fuels, mainly in the form of refined petroleum. The direct energy requirements of the biological resources sector were modest compared to mining, nondurable manufacturing, and transportation, requiring 7420 Btu's of refined petroleum, electricity, and utility gas per dollar of output in 1985. However, the unavoidable fact that those Btu's came overwhelmingly from depletable fossil fuels implies that current practices in the biological resources sector are not sustainable.

Table 7. Direct Input Coefficients: Energy-to-Energy
(Btu per Btu)

From \ To		Coal	Crude oil and natural gas	Refined petroleum	Electric utilities	Gas utilities
coal	1972	.01	0	0	1.38	0
	1985	0	0	0	1.68	0
crude oil &	1972	0	.04	.90	0	.92
natural gas	1985	0	.03	.91	0	.85
refined	1972	0	0	.06	.49	0
petroleum	1985	.01	0	.06	.13	0
electric	1972	0	0	0	.11	0
utilities	1985	0	0	0	.09	0
gas utilities	1972	0	0	.04	.68	.09
	1985	0	.01	.02	.36	.06

Sources: Calculations based on Hannon et al. (1983) and Casler (1989).

Table 8. Direct Input Coefficients: Energy-to-Nonenergy
(10^3 Btu per 1977 $)

From \ To		Biological resources	Mineral resources	Durable manuf. & construction	Nondurable manufacturing	Transportation services	Other services
coal	1972	.01	2.75	3.18	1.79	.11	.07
	1985	.02	9.75	1.39	1.64	.03	.04
crude oil &	1972	0	0	.02	2.69	.50	.01
natural gas	1985	0	0	.02	1.67	.06	0
refined	1972	8.74	13.94	3.61	5.44	34.65	2.78
petroleum	1985	6.28	9.24	1.92	3.63	34.92	2.55
electric	1972	.81	5.89	1.13	1.54	.40	.99
utilities	1985	.75	9.11	1.03	1.70	.50	1.12
gas utilities	1972	1.36	19.93	3.59	7.56	.83	1.37
	1985	.39	11.59	1.83	4.89	.25	1.01

Sources: Calculations based on Hannon et al. (1983) and Casler (1989).

The reputation of the "service sector" as a modest direct user of energy inputs is also confirmed in Table 8. However, even in this sector, significant physical inputs of refined petroleum and utility gas as well as coal transformed into electricity were required for each dollar of services produced. Hence the technologies employed to produce financial and other services consumed fossil fuels directly just like farming, mining, and manufacturing, albeit at a lesser rate per real dollar of gross output.

These differences among nonenergy sectors in their degree of addiction to fossil fuels seem less dramatic once one accounts for both direct *and also* indirect energy inputs, as shown in Table 9. In 1972, for example, construction and durable manufacturing required roughly 32,000 Btu's of coal, crude oil, and natural gas inputs, directly and indirectly, per real dollar of gross output. In that same year, however, the biological resources sector of the U.S. economy utilized 33,000 Btu's of fossil fuel inputs, directly and indirectly, per deflated dollar of product. Agriculture in the United States, for instance, relied upon fossil hydrocarbons to manufacture tractors and irrigation pumps and to supply the gasoline and electricity used to operate those forms of farming equipment.

Table 9. Direct and Indirect Input Coefficients: Energy-to-Nonenergy
$(10^3$ Btu per 1977 \$)

From	*To*	*Biological resources*	*Mineral resources*	*Durable manuf. & construction*	*Nondurable manufacturing*	*Transporta- tion services*	*Other services*
coal	1972	4.54	15.11	9.43	8.39	2.70	3.16
	1985	4.11	30.47	6.68	9.11	3.05	3.76
crude oil &	1972	28.52	54.43	22.49	37.85	48.80	11.60
natural gas	1985	14.77	31.22	10.90	21.88	45.09	8.09
refined	1972	20.37	24.05	12.02	17.22	45.18	6.92
petroleum	1985	12.24	15.31	6.53	11.04	45.31	5.61
electric	1972	2.56	8.03	2.85	3.62	1.36	1.82
utilities	1985	2.12	11.73	2.54	3.80	1.62	2.03
gas utilities	1972	8.82	32.79	11.17	18.03	5.82	4.99
	1985	3.34	19.12	5.18	10.28	2.88	3.05

Sources: Calculations based on Hannon et al. (1983) and Casler (1989).

Although the mineral resources, nondurable manufacturing, and transportation sectors required roughly 69,000, 46,000, and 51,000 Btu's of direct and indirect fossil fuel inputs per dollar produced, even the service sector required nearly 15,000 Btu's of coal, crude oil, and natural gas as a consequence of its technological links to the rest of the economy. The manufacture and delivery of computers and office furniture to banks and brokerage houses, for example, could not avoid the utilization of fossil fuels. By implication, even if 1972 final demand in the United States had consisted totally of financial and other services, sectoral interdependencies within the macroeconomy would have dictated continuing consumption of fossil fuels, albeit at a slower pace.

In reaction to the enormous increases in real energy prices that occurred between 1972 and 1985, did the U.S. economy become less addicted to inputs of fossil fuels and other energy sources? Tables 8 and 9 do not support an unambiguous answer to that question. On the one hand, direct inputs of utility gas fell sharply to all six nonenergy sectors during that era of escalating energy prices. In addition, the direct input coefficients from petroleum refining to biological and mineral resources, to manufacturing and construction, and to nontransport services also fell significantly. These changes are consistent with the neoclassical belief that changes in relative input prices will induce profit-seeking producers to implement input substitutions and technological innovations, thereby helping to conserve increasingly scarce inputs.

In certain other respects, however, trends in the U.S. economy from 1972 to 1985 were less favorable to the physical conservation of remaining fossil fuel reserves. The direct input of refined petroleum to the transportation sector remained essentially the same (over 34,000 Btu's per 1977 dollar of transport service) even as real final demand for transport services grew by a third (see Tables 3 and 8). In addition, the direct inputs of coal and electricity to minerals production grew sharply between 1972 and 1985, even as the coefficients for utility gas and refined petroleum declined. Hence, the reaction of the minerals sector to higher energy prices was primarily one of substitution among forms of fossil fuels, not a program to reduce the overall energy intensity of the sector.

What can we say about changes in the direct as well as indirect dependence of nonenergy sectors on fossil fuels between 1972 and 1985? Three sectors stand out as major success stories. Biological resource producers lowered their average input of coal, crude oil, and natural gas from 33 to 19 thousand Btu's, directly and indirectly, for each dollar of gross output. The construction and durable manufacturing sector lowered its direct and indirect coefficient for fossil fuels from 32 to 17 1/2 thousand Btu's. Nondurable manufacturing lowered its total input requirement from 46 to 31 thousand Btu's. Major sectoral changes such as these help to explain the modest growth of total energy use in the United States which occurred during a period of substantial macroeconomic and demographic expansion (recall Table 2).

The other trio of productive sectors, however, adjusted to higher energy prices in a far less impressive manner. Direct and indirect use of coal, crude oil, and natural gas by the minerals sector declined modestly from 69 to almost 62 thousand Btu's per dollar of gross output. The corresponding input-output ratio for the transportation sector fell from 51 to 48 thousand. Financial, retail, and other services also experienced a modest decline, from nearly 15 to almost 12 thousand Btu's used per dollar of service provided. Hence, these three sectors (which comprised 50% of final demand in 1972) barely reacted to the tripling of real fossil fuel prices which rocked global energy markets during the seventies.

VII. CONCLUSIONS

Are there grounds for optimism regarding the sustainability of fossil fuel use? Based on our analysis of trends in energy requirements from 1972 to 1985, the answer depends on how one defines the term. On the one hand, our data show that U.S. energy consumption virtually stabilized at its 1972 level, while real output growth continued at a reasonable pace. In addition, the fraction of gross output or final demand composed of energy commodities declined. These trends indicate that a large industrial economy can adapt to suddenly higher prices for nonrenewable inputs. For the foreseeable future, there will be sufficient physical supplies to support current energy use patterns and rates of output growth.[12]

On the other hand, the transition period from low to high energy prices was not smooth—there were costly recessions and a painful redistribution of real income and wealth.[13] Despite the more restrained use of fossil fuels after 1972, the overall level of economic activity continues to place a large strain on depletable resources. As indicated by the rise in imports of crude petroleum products and the insignificant rise in domestic oil and gas output, the limits of exploitation for crude oil and natural gas have probably been reached in the United States. Given widespread concern over the environmental impact of coal use and nuclear power, the continued importance of liquid-fuel-based transportation as a major source of energy demand, and the limited progress made in developing renewable energy sources, it is unlikely that we will see large-scale substitution from oil in the coming decades. Continued economic growth will therefore rely more and more on imported sources of petroleum. With about two-thirds of known oil reserves located in the Persian Gulf region and limited success in discovering major new sources of supply, we expect growing dependency on Mideast oil and the potential for future energy price shocks.

This likely increase in dependency on Mideast oil suggests we should be wary of the current structure of cheap energy prices since those prices will not evolve smoothly.[14] Serious risk of future supply shocks implies a much higher real cost of fossil fuel use than one might expect. By inducing the use of a highly energy-intensive capital stock, the low-energy-price regime of the 1950s and 1960s contributed to retarded productivity growth and major recessions in the 1970s and early 1980s. It would be foolhardy to ignore or forget that lesson of recent economic history. By accounting for the future costs of current energy use, we can reduce the rate of exhaustion of a finite resource, buy time to develop new energy technologies, and help to ensure the achievement of Hicks' notion of sustainability—the preservation of our capital stock so that economic development can continue in the future.

APPENDIX

Classification of Industries into Aggregate Sectors

Energy Sectors	*BEA Codes*
1. Coal Mining	7.00
2. Crude Petroleum + Natural Gas	8.00
3. Petroleum Refining	31.01
4. Electric Utilities	68.01
5. Gas Utilities	68.02

(continued)

Appendix (Continued)

Nonenergy Sectors		BEA Codes
6. Biological Resources	Livestock + Livestock Products	1.00
	Other Agricultural Products	2.00
	Forestry + Fishery Products	3.00
	Agricultural, Forestry, and Fishery Services	4.00
7. Mineral Resources	Iron + Feroalloy Ores Mining	5.00
	Nonferrous Metal Ores Mining	6.00
	Stone + Clay Mining and Quarrying	9.00
	Chemicals and Fertilizer	10.00
8. Durable Manufacturing and Construction	New Construction	11.00
	Maintenance + Repair Construction	12.00
	Ordinance and Accessories	13.00
	Lumber and Wood Products	20.00
	Wooden Containers	21.00
	Household Furniture	22.00
	Other Furniture + Fixtures	23.00
	Glass + Glass Products	35.00
	Stone + Clay Products	36.00
	Primary Iron + Steel Manufacturing	37.00
	Primary Nonferrous Metals Manufacturing	38.00
	Metal Containers	39.00
	Heating, Plumbing, and Fabricated Structural Metal Products	40.00
	Screw Machine Products	41.00
	Other Fabricated Metal Products	42.00
	Engines and Turbines	43.00
	Farm Machinery	44.00
	Construction, Mining, Oil Field Machinery and Equipment	45.00
	Materials Handling Machinery and Equipment	46.00
	Metal Work Machinery and Equipment	47.00
	Special Industry Machinery and Equipment	48.00
	General Industrial Machinery and Equipment	49.00
	Machine Shop Products	50.00
	Office, Computing and Accounting Machines	51.00
	Service Industry Machines	52.00
	Electric Transmission and Distribution Equipment	53.00
	Household Appliances	54.00

(continued)

Appendix (Continued)

Nonenergy Sectors		*BEA Codes*
	Electric Light and Wiring Equipment	55.00
	Radio, Television and Communication Equipment	56.00
	Electric Components and Accessories	57.00
	Misc. Electrical Machinery and Equipment	58.00
	Motor Vehicles + Equipment	59.00
	Aircraft and Parts	60.00
	Other Transportation Equipment	61.00
	Professional, Scientific and Controlling Instruments	62.00
	Optical, Opthmalic and Photographic Equipment	63.00
	Misc. Manufacturing	64.00
9. Nondurable Manufacturing	Food + Kindred Products	14.00
	Tobacco Manufactures	15.00
	Fabrics, Yarn and Thread	16.00
	Misc. Textile Goods and Floor Coverings	17.00
	Apparel 18.00 Paper + Allied Products	24.00
	Paperboard Containers + Boxes	25.00
	Printing and Publishing	26.00
	Chemicals and Selected Chemical Products	27.00
	Plastics + Synthetic Materials	28.00
	Drugs, Cleaning + Toilet Preparations	29.00
	Paints + Allied Products	30.00
	Paving Mixture + Blocks	31.02
	Asphalt Coatings	31.03
	Rubber + Misc. Plastic Products	32.00
	Leather Tanning and Industrial Leather Products	33.00
	Footwear and Other Leather Products	34.00
10. Transportation Services	Railroads	65.01
	Local, Suburban and Interurban Highway Passenger Transport	65.02
	Motor Freight	65.03
	Water Transportation	65.04
	Air Transportation	65.05
	Pipeline Transportation	65.06
	Transportation Services	65.07
11. Other Services	Communications Except Broadcasting	66.00
	Radio and TV Broadcasting	67.00

(continued)

Appendix (Continued)

Nonenergy Sectors	*BEA Codes*
Water and Sanitary Services	68.03
Wholesale and Retail Trade and Eating and Drinking Places	69.00
Finance and Insurance	70.00
Real Estate and Rental	71.00
Hotels and Lodging, Personal Services	72.00
Business Services	73.00
Auto Repair and Services	75.00
Amusements	76.00
Medical, Educational and Nonprofit Organizations	77.00
Federal Government Enterprises	78.00
State and Local Government Enterprises	79.00

ACKNOWLEDGMENTS

The authors would like to thank the U.N.H. Vice President for Research and Whittemore School of Business and Economics for their financial support. We would also like to thank Sinthy Kounlasa for her secretarial support and William Strauss for his research assistance. Finally, our thanks go to Richard Norgaard, David Pimentel and members of the U.N.H. Graduate Economics Seminar for their valuable comments on an earlier draft.

NOTES

1. The commitment of most academic economists to exponential growth probably reflects some combination of scientific and ideological beliefs. See England (1994a) for one attempt to analyze the roots of that widespread commitment.

2. For a detailed discussion of "natural capital," see Jansson et al. (1994). Daly (1994, pp. 25-26) uses the Aristotelian distinction between efficient and material causes to argue that human artifacts and natural capital are complements, not substitutes, in production.

3. For similar points of view, see Gever et al. (1986, pp. 12-14), Meadows et al. (1992, pp. 66-78), and Norgaard (1994, pp. 220-221). See Smil (1991, pp. 303) for global energy consumption trends from 1700 to the present.

4. This unbridled optimism is also displayed in a stylized graph which projects the *complete delinking* of pollution from the level of real GDP (World Bank 1992, p. 40).

5. Daly (1993) has argued that continued economic growth and sustainability are contradictory and that "sustainable growth" is therefore an oxymoron.

6. This exposition follows that of Miller and Blair (1985, ch. 6).

7.   This is clearly an important and controversial issue but one beyond the scope of this paper. For various perspectives on scarcity of minerals, see Goeller and Weinberg (1978), Georgescu-Roegen (1977), and England (1994a).

8.   Note, however, that the physical volume of U.S. coal exports grew by nearly 85% during that period whereas U.S. imports of crude oil and natural gas expanded by more than 42%. For a discussion of the dependence of industrial nations on oil imports from the Mideast, see England (1994b).

9.   To what extent reduced government use of refined petroleum resulted from the 1975 withdrawal of U.S. military forces from Vietnam is unclear and warrants additional research.

10.   Note that Table 7 reports the 1972 and 1985 elements of quadrant (I) in the matrix of equation (1), whereas Table 8 reports the corresponding elements in quadrant (II). The elements for quadrants (III) and (IV) are available from the authors in unpublished form.

11.   Perhaps U.S. electric utilities would have been willing to substitute nuclear energy for fossil fuels to a greater extent than actually occurred, but that technological path was strewn with environmental, political, regulatory and financial hurdles. See England and Mitchell (1990) and Cohn (1990).

12.   See, for example, the energy use projections in Energy Information Administration, "Annually Energy Outlook, with Projections to 2010." Washington, DC: U.S. Government Printing Office, 1991.

13.   On the painful effects of the energy price shocks, see Bina (1992) and Nicolini (1985).

14.   The Hotelling model of exhaustible natural resources envisions the smooth exponential growth of an exhaustible resource's price until the moment of stock depletion. For a critique of the Hotelling model, see England (1994b).

REFERENCES

Bina, C. 1992. "The Laws of Economic Rent and Property: Application to the Oil Industry." *American Journal of Economics and Sociology* 51(2): 187-203.

Bullard, C., and R. Herendeen. 1975. "The Energy Costs of Goods and Services." *Energy Policy* 1(4): 268-77.

Casler, S. 1989. "Energy Flows through the U.S. Economy: 1980, 1982, and 1985." Report prepared for U.S. Office of Technology Assessment.

Cleveland, C.J. 1991. "Natural Resource Scarcity and Economic Growth Revisited: Economic and Biophysical Perspectives." In *Ecological Economics*, edited by R. Costanza. New York: Columbia University Press.

Cohn, S. 1990. "The Political Economy of Nuclear Power (1945-1990): The Rise and Fall of an Official Technology." *Journal of Economic Issues* 24(3): 781-811.

Cole, H.S.D. et al. (eds.). 1973. *Models of Doom*. New York: Universe Books.

Daly, H.E. 1971. "Introduction to Essays toward a Steady-State Economy." Pp. 11-47, reprinted in *Valuing the Earth*, edited by H.E. Daly and K.N. Townsend, 1993. Cambridge: M.I.T. Press.

Daly, H.E. 1993. "Sustainable Growth: An Impossibility Theorem." Pp. 267-273 in *Valuing the Earth*, edited by H. Daly and K. Townsend. Cambridge: M.I.T. Press.

Daly, H.E. 1994. "Operationalizing Sustainable Development by Investing in Natural Capital." Pp. 22-37 in *Investing in Natural Capital*, edited by A. Jansson et al. Washington: Island Press.

England, R. 1994a. "On Economic Growth and Resource Scarcity: Lessons from Nonequilibrium Thermodynamics." Pp. 193-211 in *Evolutionary Concepts in Contemporary Economics*, edited by R. England. Ann Arbor: University of Michigan Press.

England, R. 1994b. "Three Reasons for Investing Now in Fossil Fuel Conservation: Technological Lock-In, Institutional Inertia, and Oil Wars." *Journal of Economic Issues* 28(3): 755-776.

England, R., and E. Mitchell. 1990. "Federal Regulation and Environmental Impact of the U.S. Nuclear Power Industry." *Natural Resources Journal* 30: 537-559.

Georgescu-Roegen, N. 1977. "The Steady State and Ecological Salvation: A Thermodynamic Analysis." *BioScience* 27(4): 266-70.

Gever, J. et al. 1986. *Beyond Oil*. Cambridge: Ballinger.

Goeller, H.E., and A. Weinberg. 1978. "The Age of Substitutability." *American Economic Review* 68(6): 1-11.

Griffin, J.M. 1993. "Methodological Advances in Energy Modelling: 1970-1990." *Energy Journal* 14 (1): 111-124.

Hannon, B. 1982. "Analysis of the Energy Cost of Economic Activities: 1963 to 2000." *Energy Systems and Policy Journal* 6(3).

Hannon, B. et al. 1983. "A Comparison of Energy Intensities: 1963, 1967, 1972." *Resources and Energy* 5: 83-102.

Hicks, J.R. 1946. *Value and Capital*. Oxford: Oxford University Press.

Jansson, A. et al. (eds.). 1994. *Investing in Natural Capital*. Washington, DC: Island Press.

Leontief, W. 1966. *Input-Output Economics*. New York: Oxford University Press.

Meadows, D.H. et al. 1972. *The Limits to Growth*. New York: Universe Books.

Meadows, D.H. et al. 1992. *Beyond the Limits*. Post Mills, VT: Chelsea Green.

Miller, R., and P. Blair. 1985. *Input-Output Analysis: Foundations and Extensions*. Englewood Cliffs, NJ: Prentice-Hall.

Nicolini, J.L. 1985. "The Degree of Monopoly, the Macroeconomic Balance and the International Current Account: The Adjustment to the Oil Shocks." *Cambridge Journal of Economics* 9: 127-140.

Nordhaus, W. 1973. "World Dynamics: Measurement without Data." *Economic Journal* 83: 1156-83.

Nordhaus, W. 1992. "Lethal Model 2: The Limits to Growth Revisited." *Brookings Papers on Economic Activity* 2: 1-59.

Norgaard, R. 1994. "The Coevolution of Economic and Environmental Systems and the Emergence of Unsustainability." Pp. 213-225 in *Evolutionary Concepts in Contemporary Economics*, edited by R. England. Ann Arbor: University of Michigan Press.

Pimentel, D. et al. 1994. "Achieving a Secure Energy Future: Environmental and Economic Issues." *Ecological Economics* 9(3): 201-220.

Pimentel, D. et al. 1995. "Environmental and Economic Costs of Soil Erosion and Conservation Benefits." *Science* 267 (February 24): 1117-1123.

Schipper, L., R. Howarth, and H. Geller 1990. "United States Energy Use From 1973-1987: The Impacts of improved Efficiency." In *Annual Review of Energy* (volume 15), edited by J. Hollander, R. Socolow, and D. Sternlight. Palo Alto, CA: Annual Reviews Inc.

Smil, V. 1991. *General Energetics*. New York: John Wiley & Sons.

Turner, R.K. 1993. *Sustainable Environmental Economics and Management*. London and New York: Belhaven.

U.S. Bureau of Census. 1993. *Statistical Abstract of the United States: 1993*. Washington, DC: U.S. Government Printing Office.

U.S. Congress, Office of Technology Assessment. 1990. *Energy Use and the U.S. Economy*. Washington, DC: U.S. Government Printing Office.

U.S. Department of Commerce. 1992. *Survey of Current Business* (September).

World Bank. 1992. *World Development Report 1992*. Oxford: Oxford University Press.

SUSTAINABLE GROWTH AND VALUATION OF MINERAL RESERVES

M.A. Adelman

ABSTRACT

The annual change in the value of an in-ground mineral is equal to the increase or decrease of inventories ("reserves"), multiplied by the market value of a reserve unit. The limited shrinking resource does not exist as an economic fact. Its intergenerational optimizing is a phantom problem. If there is any "Hotelling rent" it is captured by the reserve market value, which is created by investment in knowledge (exploration) and in productive capacity (development). There are problems of concepts and data. But examples for recent years suggest that mineral value changes are small.

To reckon the sustainable national product for any year, we must subtract the value of assets used up, including minerals in the ground.

Advances in the Economics of Energy and Resources, Volume 9, pages 45-68.

ISBN: 1-55938-922-2

We focus on oil and natural gas, which account for nearly three-fourths of value added in the mineral industries. For this task, we need a theory of mineral values and depletion.

I. INTRODUCTION

A paper published ten years ago (Boskin, Robinson, O'Reilly, and Kumar, 1985) calculated the value of the U.S. Government's mineral assets, mostly oil, by taking 1981 prices and assuming they would increase by 3% real, that is, by 43% by 1993. In fact, the real oil price fell about 70%. The overstatement is by a factor of 4.8. Then the authors discounted future income at a riskless 2%. If one uses a conventional 10%, that shows overstatement by a factor of 5, or a total overstatement of 24 times. This was no aberration. It followed what is still the received theory of mineral depletion.[1]

A. The Received Theory

In its current professional form the doctrine now comprises a large body of theory and econometrics, and a systematic treatise by DasGupta and Heal (1979). There are many variations on a simple and apparently self-evident proposition.

There is only so much of the mineral resource. Every unit used today means one less for the future. As the finite stock shrinks, its value rises. The owner must find the optimal way to ration it out, the correct rate of exchange between present and future use. If conduct is rational, the present value of any barrel in the ground must equal that of every other barrel, regardless of when the barrel is to be produced. Otherwise it would pay to shift the barrel from a lower-value year to a higher-value year. As compensation for keeping the asset in the ground for later use, the price must rise at the "appropriate" discount rate. It follows, and is basic to the theory, that the value of a unit in the ground is equal to the current price, net of extraction cost.[2]

What is the correct discount rate for discounting a flow of output from a deposit in-ground? Market discount rates will not do, because they relate to the supply and demand for investible funds. But the distinguishing mark of a mineral resource is that it precedes investment. The value is born not made.

Some economists think the time to exhaustion is so long that market prices do not express real scarcities. The market cannot work. Even those who do not go that far still seek a rate unrelated to investment and investment risk, as did Boskin and his colleagues (1985). Perhaps it is the riskless rate, or a "social discount rate" generated by some political process. Higher discount rates mean faster depletion, threatening social catastrophe.

Applying the theory runs into problems, and I think they are insuperable. First, mineral prices should rise over time; in fact, the trend is, if anything, down. Second, if the value of the in-ground barrel equalled its current net price, that would have been remarked and acted upon by the oil industry. In fact, a rule of thumb for many years has been: a barrel in-ground is worth one-third the gross wellhead price, or *half* the net price.   Moreover, since it should not matter whether the barrel is sold early or late, a barrel which is to be produced quickly should be worth no more than one which is to be produced slowly. Yet papers written forty years ago—I regret that there is nothing more recent—show clearly that a reserve with a high production:reserve ratio sells for more than a reserve with a low ratio. Coal reserves are sold, invariably with many more years' production than oil or gas reserves; and at a much lower ratio of value to net price. (For the theory, see Appendix, paragraph 3; Adelman, 1993, p. 228; Gordon, 1966.)

B.   The Nonexistent "Fixed Nonrenewable Irreplaceable" Mineral Resource

The physicist Max Planck once described "phantom problems." One of them "used to keep many a great physicist busy for many years: the study of the mechanical properties of the luminiferous ether" (Planck, 1949, p. 56). In time, physicists decided they could not find the luminiferous ether, they did not need it, and had best forget it. (As chemists had forgotten phlogiston.)

Particularly after 1970, the study of "an exhaustible natural resource...a fixed stock of oil to divide between two or more periods" (Stiglitz, 1976) and the "basic upward tilt" to the price, kept some fine economists "busy for many years." But the fixed stock is like the luminiferous ether—it isn't there. Its optimal allocation over time to do justice as between us and our posterity is a phantom problem.

No mineral, including oil, will ever be exhausted. Only a portion of what is underground will ever be extracted. If and when the cost

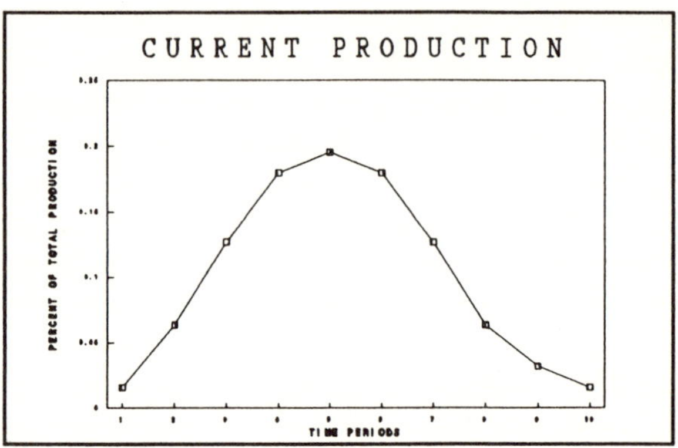

Figure 1.

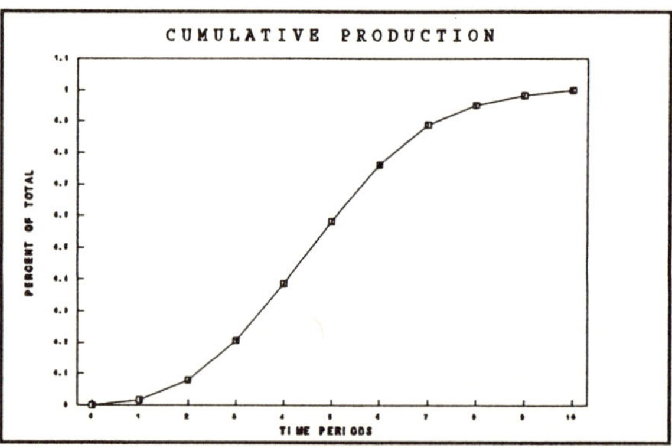

Figure 2.

goes above the price which consumers are willing to pay, the industry will begin to disappear. How much was in the ground before extraction began, and how much is left when it stops, are both unknown and unimportant. The amount extracted depends from first to last on cost and price, nothing more.

Curves like Figures 1 and 2 please the eye and sum up the history of many industries. On the horizontal is time, on the vertical is production. The upper curve shows it for each period, and the lower cumulates it up to the end of each period. The cumulative curve first grows at an increasing rate, then flattens to approach the limit.

For 1948-1990, the graphs are a fairly good picture of the production of 33 1/3 RPM phonograph records; for 1953-2000, of production of mainframe computers, which IBM expects will cease by the end of the decade (*Wall Street Journal*, 1994, p. B4). As was pointed out 60 years ago, most manufacturing industries have followed similar curves, whereby the rate of growth at first increases, then declines (Burns, 1934). Nobody suggests that the total cumulative output of a manufactured product over time is somehow fixed in advance, and must stop when there is "nothing left to produce."

The cumulative amount cannot be estimated in advance, unless future costs and prices are known. A forecaster might extrapolate the growth of phonograph records or mainframes (or vacuum tubes, typewriters, horseshoes, whale oil, etc.) into a logistic curve, based on his gut feeling for prices, costs, and how long it would take until the product was displaced by something better. He could be right; people know much more than they can prove. But there would be no way to tell. A logistic curve for a mineral industry is no different.

C.   A Simpler Theory: Reserves = Inventories

Mineral production is a flow from an unknown physical resource, first via exploration investment into identified "fields" and "reservoirs," then via development investment into current inventories or "proved reserves," to be extracted and sold. Reserves are renewable and constantly renewed, if—and only if—there is enough inducement to invest in creating them. The illusion of a fixed resource, forever running down, hides the real problem.

D.   The Real Cost-price Problem

There is a good reason why the costs of renewing mineral reserves should keep rising, and prices with them. All else being equal, the larger more accessible fields would be found first, even by chance. Once found, the better deposits (lower cost or higher quality) would be developed first. As mankind went forever from good to bad and from bad to worse, minerals should become ever more scarce, and prices rise.

What really happens is shown in Figure 3: six important metals over 50 years. A simple time trend shows three statistically significant decreases (aluminum, lead, iron ore); one significant increase (tin); one borderline decrease (zinc); and increase (copper). There is an endless tug-of-war, diminishing returns versus increasing knowledge, which includes formal science and technology in a two-way interaction with a vast amorphous body of know-how.[3] Mankind has won big—so far. I think our successors will wonder why it took economists so long to see that the ghost of mineral scarcity should be laid to rest along with the ghost of land scarcity.

One should not think of Figure 3 as "three downs, one up, two undecided, the downs have it." It shows that each mineral price has fluctuated as one or another force has dominated. Therefore a unit in the ground is a risky asset. The discount rates which govern holding it, or creating another unit, are risky rates.

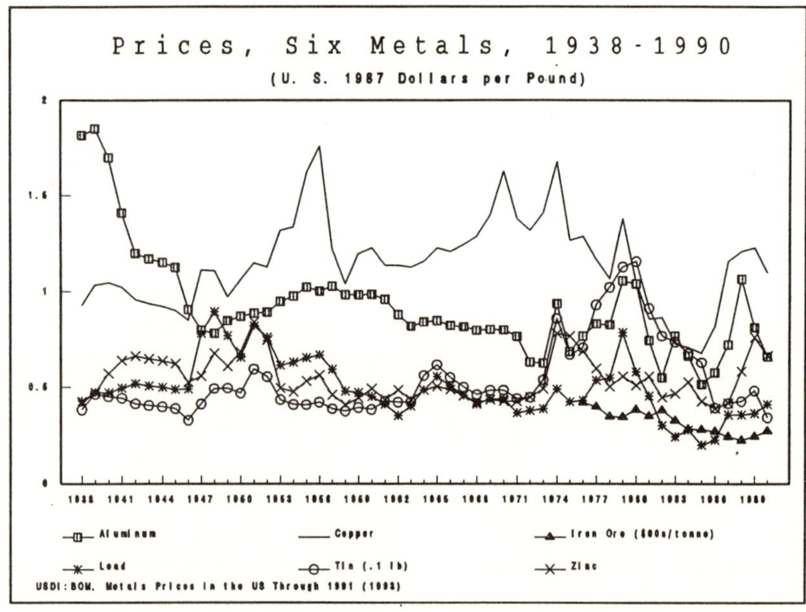

Figure 3.

E.   Mineral Depletion Theory Restated

The received theory of mineral depletion excludes investment, ours has room for little else. Once we trace the investment process, we will see how accounting for mineral depletion is more simple and accurate (if less precise) than accounting for other types of capital consumption.

II.   CREATING OIL RESERVES

A new well can produce an initial daily amount, which will decline over time because of pressure loss, water encroachment, and so on. (Additional investment in improved recovery may bounce the output back up.) Operating expenses per well are fairly constant, hence cost per barrel must rise as output declines. When it just equals the market value of the output, production stops at the "economic limit." The estimated aggregate output of the new wells over time is the "proved reserves added" or "reserves booked."[4] This is the marginal cost of providing inventory. The unit value and the marginal cost of renewal constantly gravitate toward each other throughout the market network.

In the United States, annual reserve estimates are accurate enough to permit estimating the annual net and gross additions to reserves. There are also reliable data on the expense of drilling and connecting new wells. Until 1992, we also had a record of non-drilling investment outlays. Investment data lags do not always closely match those in the reserve data, but one can estimate cost per barrel added, year by year, over a long period, within tolerable error limits.

A.   Reserve Growth in a Field

Once a field is found, reserves are created over time. In California, the Kern River field was discovered in 1899. In 1942, after 43 years of depletion, its "remaining reserves" were 54 million barrels. In the next 44 years it produced not 54 but 736 million barrels, and had another 970 million barrels "remaining" in 1986. The field had not changed, but knowledge had—science, technology, and not least, the detailed local geology learned by development.

In England, as the onshore Wytch field was developed, it was perceived to extend under the sea. A 1991 development plan for drilling the undersea section from an artificial island was rejected because it was in a scenic area. Two years later the undersea reservoir was reached by drilling horizontally from the onshore, to a record length. The investment was actually 56% less than with the island (*Oil & Gas Journal*, 1994, p. 30). Wytch reserves will be increased accordingly. These examples are unusual but help us understand how most reserve creation is in old fields, how reserves eventually booked are many times the initial estimate, and why production may stubbornly keep growing in areas where it "must" decrease.

B.   Persian Gulf

A special expert mission estimated Persian Gulf reserves in 1944 at 16 billion barrels proved, 5 billion probable. By 1975, those same fields, excluding later discoveries, had already produced 42 billion barrels and had 74 billion "remaining." Both numbers are much larger today, but not published. Indeed, since 1981, we no longer have Persian Gulf production by fields. We cannot tell when fields grow together into one, as several grew into the Saudi giant Ghawar. But Gulf discovery effort has been small. Probably most output is still from those pre-1944 fields. Cumulative 1945-1993 Gulf output was 188 billion barrels, nine times the 1944 estimate. At end-1993, Gulf "remaining reserves" were 663 billion—estimated, to be sure, more generously than they would be in the United States.

C.   "Ultimate Reserves"

Along the way, predictions of "undiscovered" or "ultimate" reserves have repeatedly been made, then surpassed, sometimes with embarrassing speed. At end-1984, it was estimated that there was a 5% probability of another 199 billion barrels remaining to be added at the Gulf, ever. Within five years, it had already happened.

These "ultimate reserves" are implicit forecasts: how much it will be profitable to find, develop, and produce, given current costs and current knowledge. The estimator of "ultimates" is doing economics without knowing it. We pointed out earlier that a forecast may be right,[5] but we cannot tell. As knowledge grows, so do the "ultimates."

D.   United States

In the United States, crude oil discovery peaked in 1930, when proved reserves were 13 billion barrels. In the next 60 years, the U.S. ex-Alaska produced 130 billion. The inventory turned over ten times and is today about 17 billion (with another 6 in Alaska). Many small fields were found. More important was the continuing expansion of old fields. In 1966-1977, the only years when comparison is possible, 19 billion reserve barrels were added, of which 17 billion were in fields discovered before 1966.

These huge new reserves in old fields were no gift of nature. They were a growth of knowledge, paid for by investment, mostly in development. This history explains why today, in various parts of the world, there is interest in letting foreign companies develop so-called "marginal" fields. Much oil can be added in these fields, an additional return on the knowledge gained by operators elsewhere, especially in the United States.

E.   The Sensing-selection Instrument

At any given moment, reserves are being added everywhere. The industry is a great sensing-selection instrument, scanning all deposits, old and new, to develop the cheapest increment or tranche into a reserve. The reserve increments of any given period are overwhelmingly in existing fields. Nobody "finds" a reserve, just as nobody finds a factory. Oilmen find new basins, within which they keep finding fields. They find new reservoirs in old fields, and new strata or pools in old reservoirs. Discovery may lead nowhere, or to development, which usually leads to discovery. The constant search for least-cost prospects takes the industry to the fringes of known reservoirs, and beyond it. The process is driven by cost comparison.

III.   PETROLEUM DEVELOPMENT COST

In a brief treatment, we can safely neglect operating costs, and treat them largely as a subtraction from price. Development investment expenditures are made to drill and complete wells, install equipment, and connect to a pipeline or tanker terminal. Marginal development investment is the amount spent per barrel newly booked into reserve inventory, or per barrel of newly installed capacity. (Note 3 shows the conversion between reserve-additions and capacity-additions.)

The harder we squeeze a sponge, the less the additional liquid from squeezing still harder. The more intensive the development of a reservoir, measured by the ratio of production to reserves, the higher the marginal cost per unit. Development expands reserves and capacity so long as the cost is below the value.

But the value, allowing for location and quality, is the same for all pools because it is derived from the market price. Therefore, over any area where capital can flow freely, marginal cost in every single project is in competition with marginal cost in every other project. Under competition, operators keep expanding the better projects most, driving marginal costs up toward equality everywhere.[6] But the average cost, the total of all expenditures made from the start, divided by the total of all reserve barrels added from the start, varies enormously among pools. The rent per barrel produced, which is the difference between marginal and average cost, will vary even more, and there is no reason to expect equality, ever.

If the process continued indefinitely, lower-cost wells would expand most. Their marginal cost would rise until it became equal everywhere. This result is postponed as new choices appear.

A.   The Discount Rate (Return on Investment)

Return on investment drives the whole process of reserve-addition. Since there is no preexisting stock, there is no preexisting value. The discount rate in any given kind of oil development is governed by risk, as in any other investment.

More intensive development means a higher ratio Q/R, production to reserves. This raises the required investment per barrel. But—it speeds up the inflow of revenues, and raises present value. A higher discount rate penalizes slower depletion. It also raises the operator's cost of investing more to deplete faster. Thus it makes quicker depletion more desirable, but less accessible.

Macbeth's porter said of strong drink: "Lechery, sir, it provokes and it unprovokes. It provokes the desire, but it takes away the performance." So too, a change in the interest rate affects development both ways, to speed it up *and* to slow it down. The net effect is probably small.

IV.   DEVELOPMENT COST, IN-GROUND VALUE, FINDING COST, "SCARCITY RENT"

A.   Substitution Among Development, Purchase, Discovery

Operators invest in a wide gamut of projects: improved recovery; more wells into the same pool; wells into adjacent strata or adjacent pools; prospects which are completely known; less completely known...and so on to the deliberate search for new reservoirs and new fields or even new "plays" in new areas expected to contain an array of fields. "Development" shades into "exploration," or in French *recherche*, that is, research.

All these methods of reserve-addition are imperfect substitutes for each other, and all are in competition. If development is becoming more expensive, it pays more to explore for new pools and fields to freshen the mix and moderate the increase in development cost. Conversely, if the newly-found fields are getting smaller, deeper, more heterogeneous and faulted, and so forth, then development cost per unit of reserves booked into those new fields will be higher. This pushes operators into drilling more wells into and around the older pools, and to drain the older pools faster. Thus, higher finding cost is registered in higher development cost.

But there is no way to calculate past finding cost per unit. (A popular expedient, "finding cost (or replacement cost) per barrel of oil equivalent" is well worth avoiding. See Appendix, note 2.) Annual exploration expenditures in the United States were tabulated in 1955-1991, but we have hardly an idea how much was discovered in a given year. A discovery engenders a stream of reserve-additions over decades, perhaps over more than a century. At any moment, operators calculate the odds on finding a new pool of a given size and development cost in a given place. There is no way to aggregate those estimates, even if we knew them.

So finding cost is a blank, but there is often a proxy. An alternative to adding reserves by any combination of developing-finding is simply to buy them. Reserves of oil and gas are frequently bought and sold, as are companies which own them. Hence the market value of developed reserves is comparable to the cost of all other methods of reserve-addition. Because all are substitutes, changes in the cost of any are an indicator of changes in the cost of all the others.

Increasing oil scarcity means increasing values and costs across the board. A higher cost of finding and developing raises the value of a barrel already developed. Conversely, a higher value of a barrel in the ground is a greater incentive to invest more to create more. This drives up the cost. Thus in-ground value and finding-plus-developing cost always gravitate toward each other.[7]

V. MEASURING CRUDE OIL DEPLETION

I think mineral depletion can be measured far more precisely than most capital consumption. Most assets are measured by the value of original investment, perhaps adjusted for later price changes which may or may not fit the assets. The loss of productive power in a given year is usually measured by some depreciation formula whose purpose was to enable the accountant to recapture original cost over some forecast or standard lifetime. It is rare to have any objective or market-determined measure of lost value of fixed capital.

But mineral assets ("reserves") are inventories. Estimated changes in physical quantities are often available. Those for oil and gas in the United States and a few other places are of good quality. The value per unit has long been a market fact, the need is to record and measure it.

A. The Structure of Prices, Costs, and Values

Table 1 shows the layers in the United States in two recent years. Let the reader beware: Comparison of any two years is chancy. Some of the statistics are subject to wide error. The "value" estimates are a fragment from a current research project by G.C. Watkins and myself. But by looking at actual numbers we can put some flesh on the bones of economic theory. Then we can look at long-term changes to gain perspective. I conclude with a suggested procedure for calculating the value of oil assets used up in a given year.

The traditional industry rule of thumb, that the market value of an in-ground reserve fluctuates around one-third of the gross price, or one-half the net, has held fairly well in the past, but seems to understate today. In the United States, a reserve barrel is held in the ground for production on average in 6 to 7 years. The increase in value from line 3 to line 2 is compensation for the investment in

Table 1.   Price, Cost, In-ground Value Two Recent Years USA
(Dollars per barrel)

		1984	1992
1	Gross wellhead price	25.88	15.99
2	Net price (ex operating costs, royalties, taxes)	16.67	10.68
3	Developed reserve market value	6.94	4.71
4	Development cost	3.84	2.87
5	Undeveloped reserve value	3.10	1.84
	("User cost," "discovery value")		

Note: The operating margin (line 1 less line 2) includes 15% of the price as royalty. This is no cost, but rather a share of the profit. Another 5% corresponds to excise taxes, which are in part a charge for services (police and fire protection, etc.), in part a taking of profit. The true social current cost is not a third, but less than 20% of the price. However, the in-ground value of the reserve depends on the net to the owner, not the net to society. The development cost has been reduced by 11% to reflect the tax allowance. Thus lines 2 and 4 are private values, comparable with line 3, and permit the subtraction of line 4 from line 3 to arrive at line 5.

Factors affecting the cost of holding the asset oil in-the- ground, to get from line 3 to line 2:

	1984	1992
Production/reserves	0.108	0.101
Decline rate	0.096	0.091
Holding time (half life) of asset, years	6.131	6.574
Annual appreciation in value	0.154	0.133
Riskless rate	0.096	0.034

Production and reserves data from DOE/EIA, decline rate computed by formula in the Appendix. Holding time computed from formula $T'=\ln(1-(.5aR/Q))/-a$. Riskless rate, 3-month Treasury bills.

Sources: Line 1, Department Of Energy, *Monthly Energy Review*
Lines 2,4, factors from [Adelman 1993,p.248-250]
Line 3, average of "pure oil" market transactions, with no gas reserves. (From a current research project with G.C. Watkins)
Line 5 = line 3 less line 4

holding the barrel. The measure is inexact, but it is within the range of industry discount rates. It decreased with interest rates generally as inflation eased.

The difference between in-ground value of a developed barrel and its development cost is the discovery value of an undeveloped barrel, "user cost." It is sacrificed, over and above development cost, by the decision to develop. Under stable conditions, it is a proxy for finding cost. When this discovery value equals or exceeds expected finding cost, it is the signal for an investment inflow into exploration. Where cost exceeds value, there is no investment.[8]

Aside from errors, especially for a residual like line 5, domestic oil is getting more scarce. True, development cost per reserve unit declined from 1984 to 1992. But reserves-added in 1984 were 3.8 billion barrels; in 1992, only 1.5 billion. The lower marginal costs resulted from discarding the poorer prospects.[9] The supply curve swung to the left. The industry moved down the curve. Discovery value fell more than development cost, and, I think, was below finding cost.

Figure 4 shows diverging development cost trends for oil and gas since factor supply prices approximately stabilized in 1984. Of course the supply coefficients are very crude, but I doubt that better ones would make much difference. I have no explanation for the divergence. But oil and gas values are set in very different markets. Gas is a self-contained market, where prices and costs are mutually determining. But the wellhead price of oil is set exogenously. It is equal to the world price, hence the cost is no longer a floor.

B. Price, Cost, and Reserve Values in the United States—A Test of Depletion Theory

Table 1 presented four measures of oil scarcity, short and long run. Figures 5 and 6 show them over a long period, but much of it based

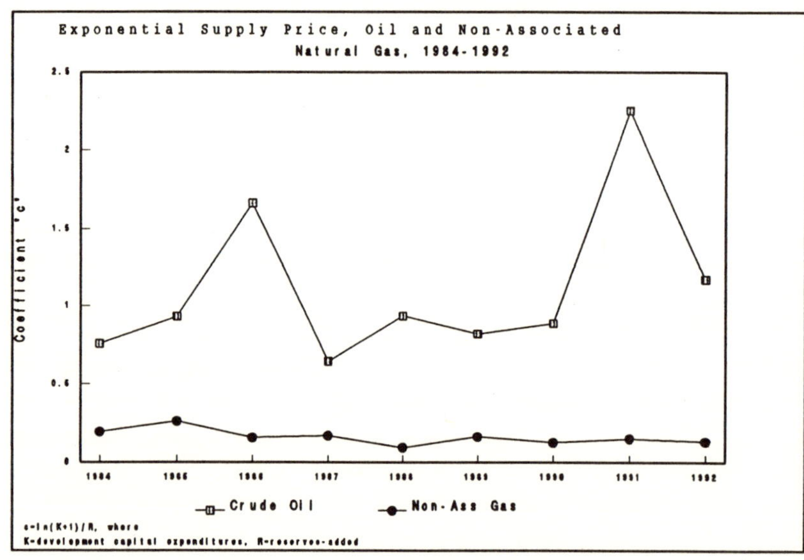

Figure 4.

on inferior data. The year 1948 marked the end of the repressed wartime inflation and industry distortion.

A long-run increase in prices and reserve values because of the fixed stock of "nonrenewable resources," and so forth, would cumulate over 24 years, even at 2% per year, to a 61% rise. Since the price level doubled from 1948 to 1972, the nominal increase—in oil prices, reserve values, and development costs—should have been by a factor of 3.2. There was no such thing. Real prices and values actually declined.

Additions to reserves were fairly stable before 1972, between 2.5 and 4 billion barrels per year. Incremental development cost fell after 1960, but this was a one-time gain from gradual easing of wasteful regulation. The stable price, over and above remaining regulatory waste, was enough to pay for an inflow of reserves which was slightly greater than the current outflow. U.S. oil reserves were in a steady state; production even grew slowly.

C.   Conclusion on Oil Scarcity and "Scarcity Rents"

Development cost is a measure of long-run scarcity. So is reserve value, which is driven by future revenues. They move in the same direction, up or down. In the United States, they were steady to declining for many years, then fluctuated sharply with the price shocks after 1970.

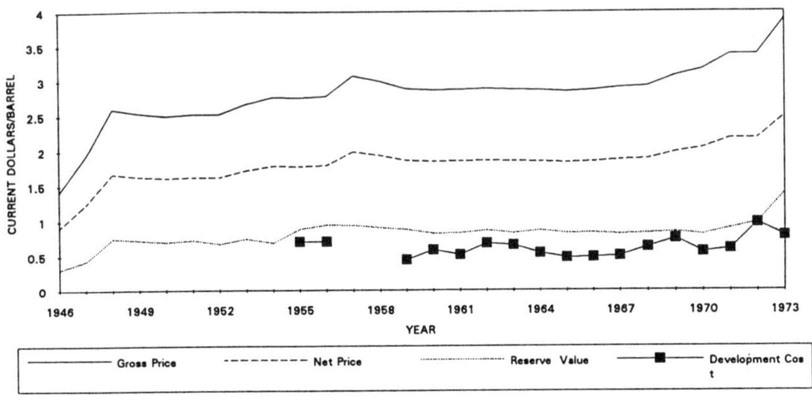

Figure 5. Crude Oil: Price, In-ground
Value, Development Cost USA 1946-1973

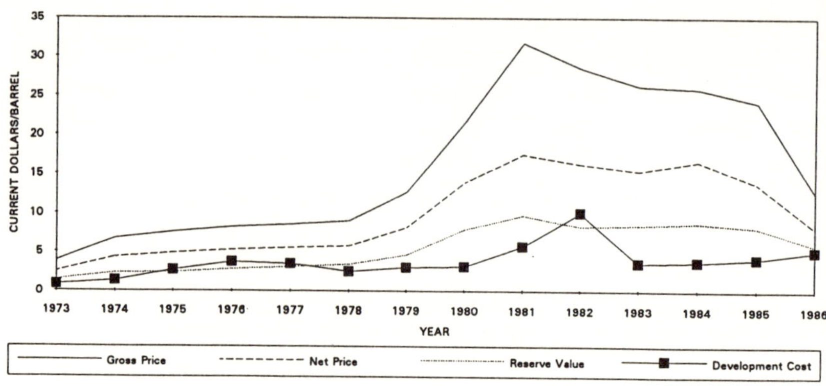

Figure 6.   Crude Oil: Price, In-ground
Value, Development Cost USA 1973-1986

VI.   SCARCITY IN THE WORLD MARKET 1944-1993

Except for the United States and a very few other countries, published
reserves are not well defined, and estimation methods are not
revealed. Year-to-year changes usually do not mean much. But over
several years, changes have meaning, although not precision.

World reserves (Table 2) were first calculated for 1944, at 51 billion
barrels. By the end of 1993, the world had produced and consumed
690 billion barrels, and had 999 billion barrels left. The worldwide
production/reserves ratio is half of what it was in 1944. Strong
conclusion should not be drawn from weak numbers, but they do
not suggest increased scarcity or shortage at any time.

Most of the net growth has of course been in OPEC. We are often
told that non-OPEC producers will "empty out their reserves." Very
true. Each decade, they use up most of what they have, and replace
it with more. This need not continue forever, but cost trends show
it is a good bet to continue for years. Thus the value of reserves in
the United States is now governed by the difference between the
worldwide price and the level of domestic operating costs.

In principle, changes in development cost are an indication of
change in value, in finding cost, and in oil scarcity in general. If we
array, from lowest to highest, development (and much exploration)
investment per unit of new capacity, for each country outside North

Table 2. World Production and Reserve-Additions 1960-1990
(in Billions of Barrels)

	1944	1945-60	1961-70	1971-80	1981-93	1944-93
			O P E C			
Cumulative Production	—	26	55	103	100	284
Gross Reserve-Additions	—	219	251	128	434	1032
Reserves at End	22	215	412	436	770	770
			NON-O P E C			
Cumulative Production	—	51	64	102	190	407
Gross Reserve-Additions	—	98	187	114	207	607
Reserves at End	29	76	200	212	229	226
			TOTAL WORLD			
Cumulative Production	—	77	119	205	289	690
Gross Reserve-Additions	—	318	439	242	640	1639
Reserves At End	51	291	611	648	999	999

Source: Reserves:1944, from *History of the Petroleum Administration for War* (Washington, 1947), Appendix 12, Table 1. Later years from *Oil and Gas Journal*, annual "World Wide Oil" survey. Production from DeGolyer and MacNaughton, *Twentieth Century Petroleum Statistics.*

America and Western Europe in 1955, 1965, 1975, and 1985, for 1955-1985, there was clearly no strain on resources. The supply curve moved far to the right (Adelman, 1993, p. 225). The "long lead times" of which we hear so much are only for exploration in new areas, much like research and development in manufacturing. There were no wild investment swings between 1933 and 1973. There was continuous addition to capacity, which expanded sevenfold while the price fell.

As for the value of oil in the ground, we have only one Persian Gulf observation: the value of a new-found barrel in Saudi Arabia (corresponding to line 5 of Table 2) in 1976: 1 to 2 cents per barrel. This is of course a value under monopoly, related not to price but to marginal revenue, which approaches zero (Adelman, 1995, ch. 4).

VII.   CONCLUSION: CALCULATION
OF OIL ASSET CONSUMPTION

Table 3 sums up two methods, following two theories. The upper panel treats the resource oil as initially fixed. Hence all production is a subtraction from it. The estimator follows (but does not explicitly cite) the "Hotelling rule" (Das Gupta and Heal, 1979), whereby the value of the asset in-ground must equal the current net price. Thus

Table 3. Alternative Calculations of
Oil Asset Consumption in Recent Years

	1984	1992
A. Assumption: an initial fixed stock		
1 Liquids produced, million barrels	-3813	-3219
2 Net value at well head, dollars per barrel	16.67	10.68
3 Asset consumed, billions of dollars	-65.6	-34.4
B. Assumption: reserve as inventory		
4 Liquids reserves, net change, million barrels	+453	-950
5 In-ground value, dollars per barrel	6.94	4.71
6 Net change in inventory, billions of dollars	+3.1	-4.5

Sources: lines 1,4 from DOE, Reserves Annual Report
              lines 2,5 from Table 1.
Method: panel A, method from Repetto, Magrath, Wells, Beer, and Fossini (1989)
              panel B, this paper

value losses are respectively $66 billion and $35 billion. A milder version of the method of Panel A is to subtract total production, but credit output only with a charge for "resource rent" per barrel, the present value of the inevitable increase of the limited stock. But, first, there is no inevitable increase. But if there were any increase expected, its value is included in the current market value, cited in Panel B.

The method used in Panel B treats the resource as unknown and irrelevant. The net inventory (reserve) increased in 1984 by $3 billion and decreased in 1992 by $4.5 billion, about 13% of the estimate in Panel A.

Obviously I regard the method of Panel A as massive error, because what came out of the stock was nearly all replaced. The milder variant, assigning an allowance for resource rent, is a smaller error. What pervades all variants is the lack of any reference to investment in oil, of all industries. It is *Hamlet* without the Prince or the rest of the cast.[10]

VIII.   DEPLETION OF DATA

The asset valuations used are from a current research project by G.C. Watkins and myself. We hope to have some better numbers soon, despite serious data and econometric problems.

But we should be clear on the theory. The way to measure the value of oil assets used up is to multiply the net reserve decrease by the current market value of a barrel in the ground. A partial measure is the development cost of such a barrel. The value of a barrel in-ground sums up the expected trajectory of prices, up or down. Because expectations are uncertain, reserves are risky assets, their returns discounted at normal risky rates. Reserve values are forecasts made by qualified observers with an interest in guessing right. The sale of a producing lease or of a security concentrates the minds of scientists, engineers, bankers, and oilmen. They may be, and often are, beautifully wrong. But the only basis for disregarding them is to assume that private markets cannot—somehow—value mineral assets properly.

But much basic data is disappearing. The annual reserves reports are still of high quality, but not as useful as they were before 1980, on the basis of API-AGA groups estimating for small areas, year in, year out. Mindless hostility to the oil industry dictated that they be compiled by government, and the sampling frame is now companies not areas. Investment and operating costs for oil and natural gas were last tabulated in 1991; I have extrapolated one year; it becomes less defensible as we move away from the benchmark. The oil development issues of the *AAPG Bulletin* ceased after 1991, both for North America and outside, and the worldwide investment expenditures tabulated by the Chase Manhattan Bank ceased after 1987. We are now afflicted with useless estimates of corporate "finding cost," and of worldwide capital "needs," invincible against any analysis because sources and methods are not known, and replication impossible. These pseudo-statistics will infect and burden all discussion, whether of sustainable growth or anything else.

APPENDIX

1. *Investment, capacity* R is the new reserve to be developed, in barrels, by investing K dollars. Q is the initial output in barrels per year, and the investment per annual barrel is K/Q. (It is the investment per daily barrel, divided by 365.) With a decline rate of $a\%$ per year, $R = Q \int_{o}^{T} e^{-at} dt = Q(1-e^{-aT})/a$

Decline rate In general, $a = (Q/R)-(Q^{-aT}/R)$. With slow decline over a long lifetime, we can safely neglect the second right-hand-side term, and $a = Q/R$. Otherwise, we approximate: $e^{-aT} = Q_{f/Q} \approx Q/R$, where Q_f = final output. The theory is that the more intensive the development, the higher the fixed annual outlays, hence the sooner the cutoff. Then the formula becomes $a = Q/R - (Q/R)^2$. A check: Prudhoe Bay field 1993 output was 10.29% of reserves (*Oil & Gas Journal*, 1994, 1982). By formula $a = 9.23\%$. The *Reserves* report (1992, p. 29) gives Prudhoe Bay "underlying decline rate" as 9%.

2.   *Expected price increase related to ratio of wellhead price and in-ground value* As shown elsewhere (Adelman, 1993, ch. 13), the expected rate of price increase is: $g = i + a(1-P/V)$, where i is the interest rate, a the annual exponential decline rate of production, P the net price, and V the in-ground value. If in fact $P = V$, a drops out and $g = i$. But if in fact $P = 2V$, then $g = i - a$. Recalling Figures 5 and 6: if i is the market discount rate on oil investment, it stayed for many years near the decline rate a. The predicted rate of price increase was therefore zero, and the prediction was borne out.

3.   *"Finding cost per barrel of oil equivalent"* Often cited in the financial press, this consists of (a) exploration *plus* development expenditures, divided by (b) oil reserves-added *plus* the "oil equivalent" of gas reserves-added. The number is useless.

The addition in the numerator (a) is illogical. Exploration adds knowledge and development adds reserves. These are different activities, for returns over very different time periods. Moreover, exploration outlays on oil are mingled with those on gas.

The addition of oil to gas in both the numerator (a) and the denominator (b) is wrong because there is no oil or gas equivalence. Oil and natural gas are not in a stable relation to each other with respect to costs, prices, or reserve values. They can and do move in opposite directions.

Moreover, even if "finding cost per barrel of oil equivalent" meant something for any one year, it would not be comparable with that for any other year. Changes in the exploration-development mix, or in the oil-gas mix, or both together, make comparison invalid. We are told not to add apples to oranges; this is fruit salad.

4.   *The Solow contribution* Solow (1992, pp. 8-12) states:

> Even apart from the possibility of exploration and discovery, the stock of nonrenewable resources is not a pre-existing lump of given size, but a vast quantity of raw materials of varying grade, location, and ease of extraction.

This sounds like but is not a modification of the received theory. There is said to be substitution between "greater inputs of labor, reproducible capital, and renewable resources for smaller direct inputs of *the fixed resource.*" Each year we decide "how much to save and invest and how much of *the remaining stock of nonrenewable resources* to use up.... [We] have used up some of *the stock of irreplaceable natural resources*" (emphasis added).

The discount rate is said to be "a technical assumption of convenience" and in any case is "very small." This is consistent with the lack of any attention to investment in the creation of mineral stocks. Investment is again ignored in suggesting that:

> The correct charge for depletion should value each unit of resource extracted at its net price...minus the *marginal* cost of extraction.... [T]he correct measure of depletion for social accounting prices is just the aggregate of Hotelling rents in the mining industry.

This looks like the method of Repetto (Table 2), whom Solow cites as a source. Solow does not include development investment in extraction cost. He seems, logically, to exclude consumption of the asset created by development investment. But I think that for national income accounting it cannot be ignored, any more than any other type of capital consumption.

Line 5 in Table 1, "user cost," is the value of the unit (line 3) less its *current* development investment. Line 5 is also an indirect measure of discovery investment per unit. Both these investment requirements may change in the future, and make the price change. But line 3, the present value of an asset to be sold off in the future, embodies future prices. Thus it catches the elements of price unrelated to current cost, that is, rents to the mineral owner.

Solow does not explain "Hotelling rents," whose usual meaning is the allowance for higher future value of the shrinking stock. We have argued that the shrinking stock and its increasing value are phantoms. As an empirical matter, Hotelling rent is negative in the usual case of decreasing prices, market values, and user costs. But this does not matter. What does matter is that any rent, whatever the size or sign, is captured in lines 3 and 5 of Table 1.

ACKNOWLEDGMENTS

This paper is a shortened and rewritten chapter from a forthcoming book, *The Genie Out Of The Bottle: World Oil Since 1970* (Cambridge: MIT Press,

1995). It draws on *The Economics of Petroleum Supply* (Cambridge: MIT Press 1993), particularly chapters 11-13, and on a paper, "Finding and Developing Costs in the United States 1945-1986," in John R. Moroney, ed., *Energy, Growth and the Environment: Advancement in the Economics of Energy and Resources* (volume 7) (Greenwich, CT: JAI Press, 1992). For other works referred to, see references. I am grateful for the comments of John Moroney and Campbell Watkins.

NOTES

1.   Despite the protests of some economists and engineers. See Lohrenz 1992 on the "X minus x fallacy."

2.   Hartwick (1991) mentions extraction cost and discovery cost, but does not explain them. He does not mention development. He thinks that "current quantity discovered" is an observable magnitude (p. 138). Accordingly, "the r percent rule, price minus marginal extraction cost on the marginal ton extracted at any instant rises over time at a rate equal to r, the interest rate" holds also for exploration of the "exhaustible resource" (p. 129).

3.   Zvi Griliches (1984) wrote: "Knowledge is not like a stock of ore, sitting there waiting to be mined. It is an extremely heterogeneous assortment of information in continuous flux. Only a small part of it is of any use to someone at a particular point of time, and it takes effort and resources to access, retrieve, and adapt it to one's own use." A mineral body in the real world is no exception. It is not "sitting there waiting," but is rather a heterogenous mass of information needing investment for access, retrieval, and use.

4.   *Example*: Suppose the estimate for a well is an initial 1,000 barrels daily, 365 thousand barrels per year. If the decline rate is 10% per year, production after 25 years is only 82 barrels daily, 30 thousand barrels per year. If at current prices lower output will not pay operating expenses, this is the cutoff. The reserve will be booked as 335 thousand barrels, its cumulative expected output. A higher price, or lower cost, will extend the "economic life."

In algebra, $R = Q \int_0^T e^{-at} dt = Q(1-e^{-aT})/a$, where R = proved reserves, Q = initial output, a = decline rate in percent per year, and T = time. If T is indefinitely large, this simplifies to $R = Q/a$, or $a = Q/R$, which is usually but not always a good enough approximation. For our example, $R = 365 (1-e^{-(25 \times 0.1)})/.1 = 3350$.

5.   "In the calculable future we shall live in an *embarrass de richesse* of both foodstuffs and raw materials....This applies to mineral resources as well" (Schumpeter, 1943, p. 116).

6.   Assume the price of oil is $10 per barrel. One oil well produces 10 barrels daily, the other 10,000. The average cost in the big well is only a small fraction of cost in the small well. But under competitive conditions, the *marginal* cost in both wells is $10. In each well, production is pushed to the limit, where producing one more barrel daily would raise costs on the whole operation by more than $10. Profit is maximized (or loss minimized) in both wells.

7. In theory, the contribution of discovery to in-ground value in any given place ought to stay between an extreme of zero where available reserves are unlimited, and a maximum of equality with development cost (Adelman, 1993, pp.243-244). In the United States, discovery value has long fluctuated around 60% of development cost. Moreover, exploration outlays (omitting bids for leases, which are not a cost but a sharing of profits) have been around that proportion of development outlays.

8. I estimated in 1986 (Adelman, 1993, pp. 155-156) that the U.S. industry would keep shrinking because expected finding cost exceeded value. This has in fact happened, but there has been such turbulence that one cannot be sure that the conclusion was borne out.

9. At any given time, capital expenditures have a nonlinear relation to reserve additions. One plausible relation is exponential. Then $K = e^{bR}-1$, where $K =$ expenditures in billions of dollars, $R =$ reserve additions in billions of barrels, and "b" a coefficient of greater or lesser cost. Disregarding tax benefits, $K(1984) = 16.2$, $R(1984) = 3.8$, and $b(1984) = .72$. But $K(1992) = 4.9$ billion, $R(1992) = 1.5$ billion, and $b(1992) = .91$, an increase of 26%. The precision of these numbers is deceptive. Other mathematical forms would give other results. But they would all show a strong increase for oil. Over this period, the coefficient decreased for nonassociated gas reserve-additions.

10. One might ask: why not apply user cost rather than in-ground market value to place a value on net reserves added or subtracted? This would underestimate the loss of assets, which are created by investment in both finding and development. But the neglect of development investment in the literature is striking.

REFERENCES

Adelman, M.A. 1993. *The Economics of Petroleum Supply*. Cambridge, MA: MIT Press.

Adelman, M.A. 1995. *The Genie Out Of The Bottle: World Oil Since 1970*. Cambridge, MA: MIT Press.

Adelman, M.A., and G.C. Watkins. 1995. "Reserve Asset Values and the Hotelling Valuation Principle: Further Evidence." *Southern Economic Journal* 61: 664-673.

Boskin, M.J., M.S. Robinson, T. O'Reilly, and P. Kumar. 1985. "New Estimates of the Value of Federal Mineral Rights and Land." *American Economic Review* 75: 923-936

Burns, A.F. 1934. *Production Trends in the United States Since 1870*. New York: National Bureau of Economic Research.

Das Gupta, P., and G.M. Heal. 1979. *Economic Theory and Exhaustible Resources*. Cambridge: Cambridge University Press.

Gordon, R.L. 1966. "Conservation and the Theory of Exhaustible Resources." *Canadian Journal of Economics and Political Science*, 75 (3): 19-26.

Griliches, Z. 1984. "Productivity, R&D, and the Data Constraint." Presidential address to the American Economic Association, *American Economic Review* 84 (1).

Hartwick, J.M. 1991. "The Non-renewable Resource Exploring-extracting Firm and the r% Rule." *Resources and Energy* 13: 129-143.

Heal, G., and G. Chichilnisky. 1991. *Oil and the International Economy*. New York: Oxford University Press.

Lohrenz, J. 1992. "Exploration: a Misunderstood Business." In *The Business of Petroleum Exploration*, edited by R. Steinmetz. Tulsa: American Association of Petroleum Geologists.

Oil & Gas Journal. 1994a. January 3, p. 30.

Oil & Gas Journal. 1994b. January 3, p. 82.

Planck, M. 1949. *Scientific Autobiography and Other Papers*. New York: Philosophical Library.

Repetto, R., W. Magrath, M. Wells, C. Beer, and F. Rossini. 1989. *Wasting Assets: Natural Resources in the National Income Accounts*. Washington, DC: World Resources Institute.

Reserves. 1992. Energy Information Administration, *U.S. Crude Oil, Natural Gas, and Natural Gas Liquids Reserves: 1992 Annual Report*. Washington, DC: Energy Information Administration.

Schumpeter, J. 1943. *Capitalism, Socialism, and Democracy*. New York: Oxford University Press.

Solow, R.M. 1992. "An Almost Practical Step Toward Sustainability." Published by Resources for the Future, October 8.

Stiglitz, J.E. 1976. "Monopoly and the Rate of Extraction of Exhaustible Resources." *American Economic Review* 66: 655-666.

Wall Street Journal. 1994. September 12, p. B4.

COMMENTARY

Teofilo Ozuna, Jr.

M.A. Adelman begins his paper by observing that the Hotelling Principle grossly over-predicts actual in-ground unit values of oil reserves. He suggests that this over-prediction is due to an assumption of the Hotelling model which states that a known fixed stock of a mineral, including oil, is to be allocated over time. He states that knowing how much of the resource was in the ground before extraction and how much is left in the ground after extraction is "unknown and unimportant." Adelman shifts the focus from a fixed resource to development which expands reserves and capacity (so long as its cost is less than the value of the resource).

Using the idea of development cost, Adelman presents some numbers relating to the value of crude oil reserves in the United States. The essence of the valuation principle Adelman uses is: $V = D + U$ where V is the market in-ground value of a reserve, D is development cost, and U is discovery value or "user cost" (see Adelman, 1990, 1991). In his paper, Adelman also makes reference to finding cost. Thus, Adelman suggests that if the discovery value is greater than finding cost then investment would occur, but if

Advances in the Economics of Energy and Resources, Volume 9, pages 69-70.

discovery value were less than finding cost then investment would not occur. Using his numbers, Adelman concludes that "development cost or reserve value are measures of long-run scarcity." His numbers for the United States, or the world, indicate no problem with scarcity or shortage of oil.

Adelman ends his paper by calling attention not to the scarcity or depletion of oil, but to the scarcity and depletion of basic petroleum data. The data are not only becoming scarce but are being substituted by other "useless" data. He concludes the paper by saying that this data problem "will infect and burden all discussion, whether of sustainable growth or anything else."

Overall I found Adelman's paper interesting but at the same time lacking. I was expecting to see more with respect to the relationship between sustainable growth and the valuation of crude oil reserves. Instead, all I got was a rehash of material or ideas presented in two or three of his earlier papers. Sustainable growth was cited only in the first and last sentences of the paper. Thus, no discussion is provided with respect to the relationship between sustainable growth and the value of a reserve.

I would have also liked to have seen some discussion with respect to the importance of correctly valuing oil reserves and the modification of national accounts used in macroeconomics modeling. As pointed out by Adelman, whichever valuation technique one uses will lead to different reserve values and this would be important to know when modifying national accounts. Using an "incorrect" resource value would lead to erroneous resource or development policies.

REFERENCES

Adelman, M.A. 1990. "Mineral Depletion, with Special Reference to Petroleum." *Review of Economics and Statistics* 72: 1-10.
Adelman, M.A. 1991. "User Cost in Oil Production." *Resource and Energy* 13: 217-240.

ENERGY CONSERVATION POLICY:
IMPLICATIONS FOR ECONOMIC GROWTH AND CONSUMER WELFARE

Donald A. Norman

ABSTRACT

Proposals to force energy conservation raise unresolved issues, thereby suggesting areas for further research. The research topics identified in this paper include: (1) the historic relationship between economic growth and energy growth; (2) whether constraining energy consumption necessarily would have an adverse impact on economic growth; (3) the potential for reducing energy consumption by changing lifestyles; and (4) the welfare cost implications of policies which target lifestyles. A theoretical framework for analyzing the economic growth implications of conservation policies is presented and some empirical evidence is reviewed. Arguments against the proposition that economic growth and energy growth are inextricably linked also are presented. Finally, the paper discusses the energy conservation potential from lifestyle changes and the welfare cost implications of policy-constrained lifestyles. These welfare costs can be significant and raise questions about the cost-effectiveness of some conservation proposals.

Advances in the Economics of Energy and Resources, Volume 9, pages 71-104.

I. INTRODUCTION

This paper reviews a number of issues that arise from energy conservation policy proposals whose objectives include raising energy efficiency and reducing the growth rate of energy consumption in the U.S. economy. Its purpose is to identify research topics suggested by these issues. In broad terms these topics include: (1) the historic relationship between economic growth and energy growth; (2) whether constraining energy consumption necessarily would have an adverse impact on economic growth; (3) the potential impact on trends in aggregate energy consumption assuming various changes in lifestyles which affect household energy use (including energy for personal transportation); and (4) the welfare cost implications of altered lifestyles when the choice set faced by individuals is constrained by energy conservation policies.

After reviewing some of the issues associated with energy conservation policy, policy instruments for forcing a reduction in energy consumption are identified. Next, some projections of energy and oil consumption assuming the adoption of a range of conservation policies are presented. According to these projections, a radical change in energy consumption patterns can be attained without any adverse impact on economic growth. A theoretical framework for thinking about the economic growth implications of forced conservation policies is presented and some empirical evidence based on this approach is reviewed. Various arguments which take issue with the proposition that economic growth and energy growth are inextricably linked are then discussed. The empirical work as well as the critical arguments on the energy growth-economic growth nexus lay the groundwork for further research. Finally, research topics relating to the energy conservation potential from changes in the way households use energy and the consumer welfare cost implications of constrained lifestyles are identified. The potential welfare costs, which largely have been neglected in the debate on conservation policy, may be significant and raise questions about the cost-effectiveness of some conservation proposals.

II. THE ISSUES

From 1973 to 1986, the intensity of energy consumption in the U.S. declined by 26%, or by an annual average rate of 2.2%. Although real GDP grew by 35% during this period, the level of aggregate energy consumption in 1986 was almost identical to its 1973 level. The fall in energy intensity was triggered by the two oil price shocks of the 1970s. In 1986, another oil price shock—this time an oil price collapse—occurred. As a consequence, the rate of decline in the intensity of aggregate energy consumption has slowed since 1986, averaging just 0.45% annually between 1986 and 1993. Aggregate energy consumption grew at an average annual rate of 1.76% over the same period.

A number of conservation and environmental organizations have viewed energy consumption trends since 1986 with dismay. They argue that the federal government shares some of the blame for this turn of events in that energy policy during the 1980s generally was limited to one of reliance on market forces. Indeed, some have argued that government policy has actually encouraged energy consumption through hidden subsidies.[1] As a result, potential gains in energy conservation were forsaken as government initiatives to encourage increased energy efficiency were slowed or eliminated.

These groups support policies whose goal is to significantly reduce U.S. energy consumption. For some, decisions regarding the use of energy are "too important to be left to the whims of the market." Others profess fealty to market forces, but assert that energy markets represent a special case where markets do not function efficiently. Thus, it is argued that the government should adopt conservation policies so that energy consumption is reduced below the market-determined level.

According to conservation proponents, market imperfections account for the inefficiency of energy markets. These imperfections are said to include the existence of energy subsidies which distort decisions regarding energy use; a lack of information on the full benefits of conservation technologies; an absence of economically rational behavior on the part of many consumers; and the fact that individuals and the government use too high a discount rate to evaluate the future benefits which are generated by investment in conservation technologies.

Some also claim that compared to other industrialized countries, the United States uses energy inefficiently. The intensity of energy use in most Western Europe countries and in Japan is lower than in the United States and yet many of these countries have performed quite well in terms of economic growth. For some, this indicates that energy consumption can be reduced without reducing economic growth. Reducing the intensity of energy consumption in the industrial sector also will increase the international competitiveness of U.S. firms. Further, reallocating spending away from energy industries to more labor-intensive sectors of the economy will result in a net increase in employment.

Finally, energy consumption damages the environment. Because energy prices do not fully reflect costs imposed on society, the level of energy consumption and hence harmful emissions exceed socially optimal levels. Emissions like carbon monoxide and volatile organic compounds contribute to increased rates of mortality and morbidity, while greenhouse gases like carbon dioxide are predicted to eventually raise average global temperatures, an event which, it is claimed, will impose a high cost on people throughout the world. Reducing energy consumption would help to alleviate these environmental problems.

These are the main arguments for reducing energy and oil consumption, but there are others. It has been argued that reducing oil consumption would enhance national security by reducing our dependence on oil imports. Some believe the United States (and other countries) should reduce energy use to achieve "sustainable growth," alleging that continued growth in oil and energy consumption at historical rates cannot continue indefinitely. Renewable energy sources (wind, solar, biomass) are promoted as substitutes for traditional energy sources like coal and petroleum because they are less harmful to the environment. The higher cost of these alternative energy sources is said to be offset by the fact that the social cost of traditional energy supplies exceeds their private cost.

Conceptually separate from the debate about the extent of problems associated with energy use and whether the United States uses too much is the whole topic of what the implications would be of forcing the nation to use less energy (or to substitute much higher cost energy for relatively inexpensive energy from fossil fuels like coal and oil).

Energy, like capital and labor, is a productive input that contributes to the output of goods and services. In the context of a neoclassical growth model, the maintenance of a normal economic growth rate would require increased investment in capital goods, a larger input of labor services, and/or technological improvements which raise productivity to offset the foregone contribution of energy inputs that occurs if conservation policy forces a reduction of the level of energy consumption. Thus, one possible implication of forced conservation is reduced economic growth—an implication which is in stark contrast to the claim that reducing energy use would not reduce growth and in fact would create jobs. While some analysts argue that normal economic growth can be maintained in the face of reduced energy consumption, others accept that reduced economic growth is a trade-off the United States, as well as other developed countries, will have to accept if all the problems associated with ever-increasing levels of energy consumption are to be addressed.[2]

Although most of the debate concerning policy-induced conservation has centered on its cost-effectiveness and its impact on economic growth, many conservation proposals also would affect individual lifestyles by constraining choices regarding energy use. What costs are imposed on individuals if they are constrained (say by regulation or by higher taxes) to purchase smaller cars or to live in more densely populated communities? Some believe we can "get by just fine" and that these costs are minimal or even irrelevant because society's concerns take precedence over the right of individual choice. But if the legitimacy of individual choice is accepted, these costs should be included in an assessment of the costs and benefits of conservation policy.

III. ENERGY CONSERVATION POLICY OPTIONS

A number of policy options are available for reducing the nation's consumption of energy below what is its market-determined level. First, energy taxes can be raised. Higher energy taxes are looked on with favor by conservation groups because they would raise energy prices so that they more closely approximated their full social cost. Higher prices would of course discourage energy consumption and potentially raise large amounts of revenue for the government. The additional revenues could be used to support more spending, cut other taxes, or reduce the budget deficit.

Second, regulation can force a reduction in energy consumption.[3] The government can mandate higher energy efficiency standards for major appliances, houses, and automobiles. The CAFE standards for automobiles are perhaps the most obvious example of an efficiency mandate adopted to date. Zoning regulation can increase the cost of low-density housing, thereby inducing individuals to live in more densely populated urban areas. Access to highways can be controlled to encourage carpooling or the use of public transportation. Building code regulations can require the installation of energy efficient windows. Regulation can also require that those selling products which use energy provide information on the energy efficiency of these products.

Finally, the government can subsidize conservation technologies. In the past, for example, the federal government provided tax credits for solar powered water heaters and building insulation. Many public utility commissions are encouraging or require that electric utilities under their jurisdiction subsidize conservation investments by their customers so that future electric load projections can be reduced.[4]

There is little doubt that energy conservation can be forced by government policy. But each of the policy alternatives has potential problems. For example, higher energy taxes may have an adverse impact on economic growth, especially if other taxes are not simultaneously reduced. Further, energy taxes, for example, those on gasoline, may be regressive and disproportionately impact different parts of the country. Any net increase in government revenues could be used to finance new spending programs rather than to cut other taxes or reduce the deficit. It also should be recognized that some forms of energy already are taxed and that the extent to which higher taxes can be justified by externality considerations is subject to debate. Some have argued that existing taxes on certain forms of energy, for example, gasoline, already internalize environmental externalities.[5] In addition, some environmental regulations (including some pertaining to automobiles) effectively raise the cost of driving, and thereby contribute to the internalization of using gasoline.[6]

For conservation purposes, the extent to which energy taxes would have to be raised depends on the desired reduction in consumption, the elasticity of demand for various energy products, and the strength of any negative feedback effect of higher energy prices on economic growth. For a given targeted reduction in energy consumption, the required increase in an energy tax is inversely related to the elasticity of demand, assuming no change in the rate of economic growth.

Estimates of the long-run price elasticity of aggregate energy demand are fairly low. By one estimate, this long-run elasticity is -0.35.[7] Assuming that economic growth is associated with (approximately) an equivalent rate of energy growth when energy prices are stable, this relatively low price elasticity implies that a very large energy tax would be required to hold energy consumption to its current level. It has been estimated that if economic growth averages 3%, the composite price of energy would have to rise by 103 to 135%, depending on one's assumptions about "built-in" energy efficiency improvements likely to occur over the next decade, in order to hold aggregate energy consumption constant.[8]

The long-run price elasticity for crude oil is, as expected, slightly higher. A study by the Energy Modeling Forum (1992) estimates the long-run price elasticity for crude oil as being equal to -0.44. Brown and Phillips (1991) estimate this elasticity to be -0.56. Thus, the requisite tax increase to hold oil consumption constant would not be as large.

Increased regulation can impose burdens on consumers and producers which exceed the benefits of incremental improvements in energy efficiency. As discussed here, assessments of the cost-effectiveness of proposed conservation regulations often are based on engineering cost studies in which it is assumed that costs for some prototypical conservation investment are relevant nationally when in fact their relevance is limited to specific regions of the country or to producers and consumers who are "average."[9] For those who are not average, however, the cost-effectiveness of engineering prototypes is less clear. Further, low "social" discount rates often are used to evaluate future costs and benefits, thereby increasing the likelihood that a regulation with future benefits will pass the net present value test for cost-effectiveness.[10]

Subsidies for conservation can be costly and ineffective. For one thing, they may encourage excessive investment in conservation technologies and renewable energy sources. Recent studies of several existing demand side management (DSM) programs, which typically include subsidies for customers who invest in conservation, have concluded that these programs are generally not cost-effective.[11] Sutherland (1994) argues that these programs subsidize the wrong individuals, namely, those who are likely to invest in conservation with or without subsidies, while doing little to induce such investment by others.

IV.   PROJECTIONS OF ENERGY USE, 1990–2010

Forecasts of energy and petroleum consumption levels based on the assumption that strong conservation policies are adopted provide an indication of what proponents of forced conservation believe is possible. Table 1 presents two forecasts for the year 2010, as well as the Department of Energy's (DOE) reference case forecast that appeared in its *Annual Energy Outlook 1993*. In DOE's reference case, economic growth is assumed to average 2% annually. The price of oil is expected to remain close to its 1990 level of $22.54 per barrel through the year 2000, but then rise to $29 per barrel (1991$) by 2010. Total energy consumption is expected to increase from 84.6 quads in 1990 to 106.7 quads in 2010 while oil consumption is forecast to increase from 33.5 quads to 41.2 quads over the same period.

Table 1.   Selected Forecasts of Future Energy and Oil Consumption (Quads)

	1990	*2010*	*%Δ/yr.*
I. DOE Reference Case			
Petroleum	33.5	41.2	1.04%
Total Energy	84.6	106.7	1.17
II. Alternative Energy Future			
Petroleum	33.5	25.3	-1.39%
Total Energy	83.8	82.3	-0.09%
III. America's Energy Choices			
A. Market Scenario			
Petroleum	33.5	27.6	-0.88
Total Energy	85.3	83.4	-0.10
B. Environmental Scenario			
Petroleum	33.5	22.7	-1.75
Total Energy	85.3	72.7	-0.72
C. Climate Stabilization			
Petroleum	33.5	20.0	-2.32
Total Energy	85.3	68.9	-0.97

Sources: Department of Energy/Energy Information Administration (1993); The Alliance to Save Energy, American Gas Association, and Solar Energy Industries Association (1992); Alliance to Save Energy, American Council for An Energy-Efficient Economy, Natural Resources Council, and the Union of Concerned Scientists (1991).

Recent forecasts from conservation organizations present quite a different outlook for energy consumption. In *An Alternative Energy Future*, economic growth is assumed to average 2% annually. The forecast also assumes the extensive adoption of energy-efficient heating technologies, significantly increased reliance on natural gas rather than electric space heating and water heating, substantial growth in solar water heating, more energy efficient appliances, and limited conversion from incandescent to fluorescent lighting. As a result, total energy consumption is expected to decline slightly from a base level of 83.8 quads to 82.3 quads. Oil consumption is projected to decline from 33.5 quads in 1990 to just 25.3 quads in 2010. Much of this decline is attributed to increased natural gas consumption and increased solar power.

Four long-term forecasts are presented in *America's Energy Choices*. The forecasts assume an average annual rate of economic growth of approximately 2.1%. The base or reference case, not shown in Table 1, is similar to DOE's. The remaining three scenarios assume progressively stiffer policies to reduce energy consumption growth. In the Market Scenario, energy technologies that minimize the cost of energy services are selected. This scenario examines the impact of policy-driven accelerated use of conservation and renewable energy technologies that are estimated to be cost-effective based on market prices and a 3% real discount rate. Energy consumption declines from 85.3 quads in 1988 to 83.4 quads in 2010 while oil consumption falls from 33.5 quads to 27.6 quads.

In the Environmental Scenario, estimates of the cost of energy externalities are added to market energy prices. These higher prices are used to justify the adoption of additional energy efficiency and renewable energy technologies. In this scenario, total energy consumption falls to 72.7 quads by 2010 while oil consumption declines by 32% to just 22.7 quads.

Finally, the Climate Stabilization scenario is based on the goal of achieving a 25% reduction in carbon dioxide (CO_2) emissions by 2005 and at least a 50% reduction by 2030. This scenario incorporates additional technologies which reduce CO_2 emissions and assumes a more rapid penetration rate for new energy technologies included in the other scenarios. As a consequence, energy consumption falls to just 68.9 quads in 2010 and oil consumption falls by 40% to 20.0 quads. The decline in total energy consumption from the base 1988 level in this scenario is equivalent to 7.75 MMBPD.

A 1988 report by the DOE also concluded that the potential for continued improvement in aggregate energy efficiency is quite high.[12] The 1988 report reviewed six "conservation potential" studies that estimated potential energy savings for the year 2000 as ranging from 9 to 26 quads below the reference case forecasts. However, the assessment of potential efficiency gains was not limited to conservation investments judged to be cost-effective. This probably explains why the assumed reduction in energy consumption between now and 2000 in recent DOE annual long-term forecasts is less than what the 1988 report identified as a "potential" reduction.

V.   ECONOMIC GROWTH: DOES ENERGY MATTER?

A.   Theory

Historically, there are strong indications that energy has contributed to economic growth and development. It is clear, for example, that energy played a crucial role in the industrial revolution.[13] The increasing scarcity of wood in Great Britain was an important factor in slowing economic growth during the latter part of the eighteenth century. The use of coal in steam engines replaced increasingly expensive energy from wood (thereby increasing the diffusion of steam engines in manufacturing) and supplied far more energy (in a more convenient form) than could have been provided by human and animal power. The results were striking. According to Thomas (1980), real output per head in Britain in 1790 was only 3% above its level in 1760 as a consequence of the rising price of wood.[14] During the period 1790-1800 the adoption of steam power fueled by much less expensive coal resulted in real output per head rising by 20%.

The first empirical studies of economic growth investigated the roles played by the rate of population growth (a proxy for labor), and capital accumulation as determinants of a country's economic growth rate.[15] The oil price shocks of the 1970s motivated some researchers to add energy as a third factor of production and determinant of economic growth.[16] Its earlier omission may have been based on the fact that energy's average cost share as a factor of production in the U.S. economy was relatively small—perhaps on the order of 5%—and hence thought unlikely to impact growth.[17]

The growth accounting model developed by Solow (1956) and extended by Moroney (1992a) provides a framework for measuring energy's contribution to economic growth. The model is based on an aggregate Cobb-Douglas production function:

$$Y(t) = A_0 e^{\lambda t} K(t)^a L(t)^\beta E(t)^\gamma \tag{1}$$

$$\alpha + \beta + \gamma = 1$$

where Y(t) is the level of output (say as measured by GDP) at time t, K(t) is a measure of capital inputs at t, L(t) is the amount of labor services at t, E(t) is the amount of energy inputs at t, $A_0 e^{\lambda t}$ is a residual which measures the contribution to growth from factors other than capital, labor, and energy, and α, β, and γ represent elasticities of output with respect to a change in the level of each input. $A_0 e^{\lambda t}$ usually is interpreted as a measure of the total factor productivity gains attributable to technological progress, where λ is the annual rate at which (disembodied) technology grows.

Actually, one of two types of technological change, embodied or disembodied, can be incorporated in a growth accounting model. Disembodied technological change refers to improvements that, for a given level of labor, capital, and energy, raise the level of output. In contrast, embodied technological change refers to technologies that are a part of an input like a capital good. When a technology is embodied in a specific capital good, technological improvements will increase output only as existing capital goods with older technologies are replaced by newer capital goods which embody the technological improvements. Although the notion of embodied technological change has appealed to the intuition of economists, the empirical evidence to date suggests that embodied technological change is not an important determinant of economic growth[18]

In dynamic terms, the rate of growth of output is equal to the combined growth rates of capital, labor, and energy, multiplied by their respective elasticities of output, and the growth of technological progress:

$$\frac{\Delta Y}{Y} = \lambda + \alpha \frac{\Delta K}{K} + \beta \frac{\Delta L}{L} + \gamma \frac{\Delta E}{E} \tag{2}$$

The respective elasticities of output indicate the relative importance of each factor as a determinant of economic growth. The growth accounting equation also can be expressed in its labor-intensive form, derived by dividing equation (1) through by $L(t)$:

$$\frac{\Delta y}{y} = \lambda_L + \alpha\frac{\Delta k}{k} + \gamma\frac{\Delta e}{e} \tag{3}$$

In this formulation, y is a measure of labor productivity based on output per worker, λ_L is the rate of technological change per worker, k is capital per worker, and e is energy per worker. Given the elasticities of output for capital and energy, the sources of labor productivity can be decomposed into three factors: the growth of capital per worker; the growth of energy per worker; and the rate of technological change per worker.

In the context of the growth model, a reduction in the growth of energy inputs will result in a lower rate of economic growth unless the lost contribution of growth from reduced energy use is offset by increases in capital, labor, and/or technological change. Thus, viewing the determination of growth through the perspective of the neoclassical growth model forces attention on certain factors while excluding others, including macroeconomic policy and the nature of government regulation. Furthermore, the nature of technological change and how it impacts the production of goods and services is more complicated than is suggested by the growth model. Nonetheless, the model is empirically tractable and one test of its usefulness is its ability to "explain" historical trends in economic or labor productivity growth

B.   Some Empirical Evidence

A comparison of energy growth and economic growth patterns in the United States and five other industrialized countries (Table 2) provides some evidence consistent with the view that energy use contributes to economic growth. Following the oil price shocks of the 1970s, economic growth slowed more in those countries where the reduction in energy growth was greater. The correlation between the slowdown in economic growth and energy growth indicates that, on average, a one percentage point decrease in energy growth was associated with a 0.6 percentage point reduction in economic growth. The U.S. experience is roughly consistent with this estimate: energy growth slowed by 2.9 percentage points while economic growth fell by 1.4 percentage points.

Table 2.   Economic and Energy Growth Rates
for Selected Industrialized Countries, 1973-1984

	1950-1973		*1973-1984*		*Slowdown in:*	
	GDP Growth	*Energy Growth*	*GDP Growth*	*Energy Growth*	*GDP Growth*	*Energy Growth*
France	5.1	4.6	2.2	0.1	-2.9	-4.5
Germany	5.9	4.7	1.7	-0.5	-4.2	-5.2
Japan	9.4	9.2	3.8	0.5	-5.6	-8.7
Netherlands	4.7	6.6	1.6	-0.7	-3.1	-7.3
United Kingdom	3.0	1.7	1.1	-2.1	-1.9	-3.8
United States	3.7	3.0	2.3	0.1	-1.4	-2.9

Source: Derived from data in Maddison (1987).

Although there is positive correlation between energy and economic growth rates in Table 2, it is based on a limited number of observations and ignores other factors affecting economic growth. Bohi (1989) observed similar trends, for example, but argued that monetary policies, not energy price shocks, better explain why economic performance in the United States and other industrialized countries deteriorated after 1973.

A number of explanations have been offered as to why economic performance in the United States and elsewhere deteriorated after 1973, but few are supported by empirical testing. There are exceptions, however. One of the first efforts to determine the relationship between energy and economic growth also is one of the most sophisticated in terms of model complexity and detail. Hudson and Jorgenson (1974, 1978) constructed a large-scale model of the U.S. economy that included an input-out table as one component in order to assess alternative energy policies. They concluded that increases in energy prices (brought about by energy taxes) and other energy conservation measures would have a significant impact on the structure and growth of the economy. In particular, policies to restrict energy consumption "involve possible large economic cost in terms of slowed economic growth and output foregone."[19]

The complexity (and perhaps cost) of the Hudson-Jorgenson model may explain why economists have resorted to simpler models to address the impact of energy policies. Tatom (1982) estimated a modified aggregate production function using data covering 1949-1980. He found that, for a given number of labor hours and capital services, the short-run effect of a 10% rise in the relative price of energy is a 0.89% decline in private business sector output. The long-run effect of a 10% rise in energy prices is to reduce output by 1.22%.

Additional evidence pointing to a significant relationship between energy growth and economic growth has been provided by John Moroney (1992a). He estimated several variations of an aggregate production function using data for the period 1950-1984. The first variation was similar to that in equation (3), where technological progress is assumed to be disembodied while four other variations (the vintage models) were based on alternative assumptions regarding depreciation rates of equipment and structures in which technological change is embodied.

Moroney's results in the vintage models show that the elasticities of output with respect to capital and energy are very similar. In the model where technological change was assumed to be disembodied, energy actually plays a more important role. These findings led him to conclude that energy's role in economic growth is "primary" and "coequal with capital formation."

With the exception of one of the vintage models, the estimated growth rates of output per worker hour for the period 1950-1973 (calculated using the estimated elasticities of output and actual growth rates of capital and labor) are very close to the actual average annual growth rate of 2.51%. For the 1974-1984 period, the vintage models overstated the decline in productivity growth.[20] In contrast, the estimate of labor productivity derived from the model with disembodied technological progress was almost identical to the actual growth rate of 1.20% for the 1974-1984 period. For Moroney, the fact that his models generally are able to explain postwar economic growth patterns attest to their usefulness.

In a second paper, Moroney (1992b) examined energy use and economic growth across five countries (the United States, France, Canada, West Germany, and Sweden) using a simultaneous two-equation time series model. In the first equation, the demand for energy was expressed as a function of the price of energy, the level of output, and the lagged level of energy consumption in each country. The second equation was a growth accounting model for each country. This approach thus takes into account the fact that the level of output affects the demand for energy while at the same time the consumption of energy affects the level of output.

Moroney found that predicted economic growth rates across countries were fairly close to actual growth rates. His results indicated that "higher energy consumption contributed approximately one-third and capital accumulation contributed two-thirds to the actual growth in real per capita incomes" across these five countries. Again, these findings show that the growth of energy consumption has a measurable impact on economic growth.

The growth accounting approach for determining the importance of energy as a determinant of economic growth has been criticized on several grounds. It is relatively simple and attempts to explain growth of the aggregate economy by focusing on a limited number of variables. These variables themselves represent aggregate measures which necessarily fail to take account of many differences. Measures of aggregate energy consumption do not discriminate between its various users, or its composition. For example, not all energy is used as a direct input into the production of goods and services. By one estimate, 24% of aggregate energy consumption in the United States in 1990 represented direct energy purchases by households (including energy purchased for household transportation).[21]

Another criticism is that the number of explanatory variables is limited by the number of observations. Most aggregate growth models are comprised of just three or four explanatory variables. Finally, researchers using different growth accounting models have obtained strong results even though they rely on different sets of independent variables. For example, in Moroney's model (1992a), the set of independent variables includes a measure of investment (adjusted for utilization), labor services, and energy inputs. On the other hand, Mankiw, Romer, and Weil (1992) also obtain strong results with a growth accounting model based on human capital, physical capital, and labor.

Jorgenson (1988) has pointed out that the aggregate production approach involves restrictive assumptions regarding underlying sectors of the economy. As he puts it:

> All sectoral value added functions must be identical to the aggregate production function. In addition, the functions giving capital and labor inputs for each sector in terms of their components must be identical to the corresponding functions at the aggregate level.[22]

Furthermore, aggregate production function models often provide misleading results for relatively short time periods such as business cycles, since dynamic adjustments are not incorporated. This would seem to include periods following oil price shocks in which energy consumption adjusts only gradually to an increase in the price of energy.

Jorgenson attempted to identify the causes behind the slowdown in economic growth after 1973. He found that 80% of the decline in the growth of output can be attributed to a decline in rate of aggregate productivity growth. But why did aggregate productivity growth decline? To uncover the causes behind the decline in productivity growth, Jorgenson estimated production functions for 35 individual sectors of the U.S. economy. His results show that the slowdown in aggregate productivity can be traced to a decline of productivity in specific industries.[23] In 29 of the 35 industries, the use of energy as an input was found to contribute to productivity growth.[24] From this, Jorgenson concluded that the dramatic rise in energy prices and subsequent decline in energy consumption growth is more than sufficient to explain most of the decline in U.S. economic growth.[25].

Despite the problems with estimating an aggregate growth accounting model, it remains a venerable approach for analyzing the sources of economic growth. This is borne out by its use in recent papers by Moroney and by Mankiw, Romer, and Weil, as well as its continued use in research on growth accounting. The model provides a simple, but theoretically-based method for determining whether underlying data are consistent with the proposition that energy matters when it comes to long-term economic growth.

Much of the initial research on the relationship between energy and the economy was prompted by concerns about the long-term economic growth and cyclical implications of higher energy prices. Conservation policies which force a reduction in energy growth raise similar concerns, namely can normal long-term economic growth be maintained if energy growth is reduced? Studies like *America's Energy Choices* that advocate strong energy conservation policies *assume* that economic growth can be maintained while the level of energy consumption is reduced. This assumption is based on the claim that cost-effective conservation technologies already exist; if so, investment in these technologies need not reduce the rate of economic growth.

Geller, DeCicco, and Laitner (1992) used an input-output model to demonstrate that a policy-induced increase in conservation investment could create approximately 1.1 million additional jobs by the year 2010. Moreover, economic growth could be maintained at an average annual rate of 2.4%. They accept the analysis in *America's Energy Choices* regarding the cost effectiveness of increased conservation investment. This underlies their argument for policy-induced investment in energy conservation and allows them to maintain the assumption that overall productivity would increase sufficiently so that the economy could continue to grow at the same rate as in a reference scenario where conservation investment decisions are left to the market. Because the intensity of energy use is assumed to fall at the same rate as the economy grows, total energy consumption in 2010 is forecast to remain approximately equal to its 1990 level. The 1.1 million jobs created by increased conservation investment would come about as spending shifts from industries with low labor intensities and high energy intensities to those with higher labor intensities and lower energy intensities.

The effect of this shift of jobs on labor productivity and wages is not analyzed, but it would seem that raising employment in relatively labor intensive industries would tend to reduce labor productivity and wages.[26] Historically, countries have become more developed and affluent when people shifted from labor intensive activities into less labor intensive activities, not the other way around. The shift away from labor intensive activities reflects the process by which labor productivity and wages are raised.

Another issue concerns the source of the additional 1.1 million jobs. Macroeconomic conditions largely determine the overall level of employment. If the economy were at full employment, there would be no reserve labor supply to draw upon. One might argue that inefficiencies in the economy have created a pool of unemployed workers in excess of those who are frictionally unemployed. A conservation policy that created jobs in some sectors of the economy might temporarily raise the level of employment. In the long-run, however, once adjustment to regulation-induced demand shifts is complete, the total number of jobs in the economy will continue to be determined by macroeconomic policy.[27] There is no reason to expect that conservation policy would eliminate inefficiencies responsible for levels of unemployment in excess of the frictional level of unemployment.

It also would appear difficult if not impossible to engineer a sustained average annual decline of 2.4% in the aggregate intensity of energy consumption, which is assumed in this study, especially if energy prices are not rising dramatically.[28] And if energy prices were rising dramatically, it probably would be difficult to maintain a normal economic growth rate. Finally, the notion that lowering the intensity of energy use might lead to a higher level of employment is called into doubt by the persistently higher levels of unemployment and slower rates of job growth in the industrialized countries of Western Europe where the intensity of energy use generally is lower than in the United States.

C. Additional Research Topics: Why Should Energy Matter?

Despite the logic of the growth accounting model, not everyone is persuaded that continued growth of energy consumption is a necessary condition for continued economic growth. There are at least five arguments as to why energy need not matter. As a side issue, it could be argued that even if energy does matter, oil itself does not. Although some criticisms of the arguments that energy does not matter are presented here, the arguments merit further consideration in an expanded research effort which examines the relationship between economic growth and energy inputs.

The Cost Share of Energy is Too Small

Some economists have argued that because the cost of energy accounts for a relatively small proportion of total production costs— say in the range of 7-10% in the aggregate—significantly higher energy prices (and a consequent reduction in energy consumption) would have, at most, a very small impact on labor productivity and the economy.[29] Thus, even if energy prices were to rise significantly, the impact in most industries would be negligible since energy's importance, relative to other inputs, is so small.

Moroney has demonstrated that energy's small cost share does not necessarily imply that energy is unimportant as a determinant of economic growth.[30] Following Moroney, assume that in equation (3), α is equal to 0.15 or 15% and γ is equal to 0.10 or 10%. This implies that labor's cost share is equal to 75%. Further assume that the rate of disembodied technological progress, λ, is equal to 0.013, or 1.3% per year. Suppose that capital and energy per worker are growing at an initial rate of 0.025 or 2.5% per year. Substituting these values into equation (3), the growth of output per worker is found to be

0.01925 or 1.9% per year. Now suppose that the amount of energy per worker were to decline by 2% annually—as it did between 1973 and 1981. Assuming that the values for α and λ remain unchanged, the growth of output per worker falls to 0.01475, or 1.5% per year. That is, the growth of output per worker falls by almost one-half percent per year solely as a consequence of a decline in energy use and lower energy intensity.

Opportunities for Substitution

A second argument is that it is always possible to substitute labor and capital for energy. The easier it is to substitute labor and capital for energy, the smaller will be the impact of reduced energy consumption on the rate of economic growth. For example, in the Hogan-Manne aggregate model of the economy (1977), as long as the elasticity of substitution between energy and capital is equal to 0.5 or more, a significant reduction in energy use would not have a major impact on economic growth over the long run.[31]

In the Hogan-Manne model, the elasticity of substitution and the absolute value of the long-run price elasticity of demand for energy are roughly equal. As noted earlier, the long-run price elasticity of demand for energy has been estimated to be -0.35. According to the Hogan-Manne model, an elasticity of substitution of this magnitude implies that it is possible to substitute capital for energy, but that the impact on economic growth, while not disastrous, is nontrivial. However, recalling that the long-run price elasticity of demand for oil is larger, it could be argued that the potential for substituting other inputs (including other forms of energy) for oil is greater.

A separate issue is whether large-scale substitutions can be sustained given constraints on the supplies of labor and capital. That is, even supposing it is technically feasible to substitute capital or labor for energy, what is the source of additional capital and labor? Over the long run, the rate at which the labor supply grows is largely determined by demographic factors. Thus, the supply of labor cannot easily be augmented. This means that the potential for a large-scale and sustained substitution of labor for energy is limited.

The supply of capital can be augmented by increasing the level of aggregate investment. Moroney's empirical results, however, indicate that the extent to which investment would have to increase in order to offset the lost contribution of energy implied by the goal of holding energy consumption to even a zero growth rate probably could not be sustained, assuming that a normal rate of economic growth is desired.[32] For example, he found that a zero energy growth rate and a 3% rate of economic growth would be feasible only if the percentage of GNP which is invested (by the private sector and by government) increases from a normal level of about 21.5% to 32.5%. This implies an approximately equal reduction in the share of GNP accounted for by private consumption expenditures.

Because consumption spending would have to be reduced by such a large proportion, Moroney believes that the requisite increase in investment could not be sustained and hence that a zero energy growth rate and a 3% economic growth rate could not be maintained. If it is assumed that investment's share of GNP is limited to about 21.5%, the *maximum* rate of economic growth that is sustainable given a zero energy growth rate is 2.5%. But the goal of maintaining even a 2.5% rate of economic growth while attempting to *reduce* energy consumption (say to the levels projected in the various conservation scenarios in Table 1) would be virtually impossible.

Existence of Cost-Effective Conservation Technologies

Many proponents of policy-induced energy conservation claim that cost-effective conservation technologies already exist. As long as conservation technologies meet the test of cost-effectiveness, investing in them will not reduce the total output of goods and services. The cost-effectiveness of many of these technologies, however, is at issue. Indeed, if they truly were cost-effective, we would expect that firms and individuals would invest in them without government intervention. The presence of market imperfections and failures reportedly accounts for the lack of investment in these technologies.

The belief that these technologies are cost-effective typically is based on the use of a relatively low "social" rate of discount, say 3%. If private discount rates were used to evaluate future flows of costs and benefits, many of these investments would fail a net present value test.[33] Further, the estimated costs of these investments often are based on engineering prototypes. Extrapolations based on protoypical models are not very accurate due to climate differences across the country, differences in consumption habits by energy users as well as family size, and differences in the size of actual versus protypical units.[34] The experience of electric utilities with demand side management programs also indicates a bias toward overstating the cost-effectiveness of conservation programs. DSM programs are designed to reduce energy demand by subsidizing conservation investments of customers. The cost of these programs, which is included in a utility's rate base, is compared to expected benefits. Electric utilities have argued that these programs are cost-effective. Joskow and Marron (1992), and Nichols (1993) evaluated a number of DSM programs and concluded that most have not been cost-effective. The actual cost of these programs typically exceeded reported costs because relevant costs were excluded and because low discount rates were used to discount future benefits.

Technological Progress

One possibility is that technological progress will raise the efficiency with which traditional energy sources are used, thereby making it possible to reduce aggregate energy consumption and yet maintain a normal rate of economic growth. While such a possibility cannot be dismissed out of hand, it is wrong to cast technological progress as the *deus ex machina*. It is of course possible to adopt policies that raise the rate of technological progress in energy conservation by investing more on research and development. Given limits on the proportion of GDP likely to be devoted to investment over the long run, any significant increase in investment in energy efficiency will come at the expense of reduced investment in the size and overall efficiency of the capital stock. The gains from increased energy efficiency should be weighed against the costs of a smaller capital stock which is less efficient that it otherwise would have been.

Further, there are limits as to the rate at which one can reasonably expect energy efficiency gains to be realized. One could conjecture that the long-run rate of improvement in aggregate energy efficiency is bounded by the rate attained during the 1973-1986 period—a period in which energy prices increased rapidly to historically unprecedented levels. Even then, had economic growth managed to average 3% over this period, aggregate energy consumption would have increased notwithstanding the reduction in energy intensity achieved during this period. The difficulty in duplicating the rate of improvement in energy efficiency achieved in the 1973-1986 period if real energy prices remain relatively stable—or even rise moderately—should be apparent.

This difficulty is compounded by the fact that part of the decline in aggregate energy intensity during this period cannot be attributed to increased energy efficiency. According to Schipper, Howarth, and Geller (1990), about three-quarters of the decline in the energy/GNP ratio was the result of improved energy efficiency while structural change and interfuel substitution accounted for the remainder. Based on detailed disaggregated data, Preston, Adler, and Schipper (1992) demonstrate that almost half of the energy intensity reduction in the manufacturing sector from 1980 through 1988 was due to structural shifts rather than improved energy efficiency.

Although current DOE long-term forecasts are premised on a continuing reduction in energy intensity, the rate of decline is much more modest than is required to significantly slow the growth of aggregate energy consumption. In the DOE's *Annual Energy Outlook 1994*, the reference case projects that aggregate energy intensity will decline by an average rate of 0.86% per year from 1990 to 2000, and by 1.07% per year from 2000 to 2010. As noted earlier, aggregate energy intensity declined at an average annual rate of 0.45% between 1986 and 1993. The increase in the rate at which energy intensity declines over the period 1990-2000 is expected even though the real price of oil is assumed to decline from $22.22 per barrel in 1990 to $20.72 in 2000 (all prices are in 1992 dollars). The increase in the rate at which energy intensity declines after 2000 is attributable to the assumption that the real price of oil will rise to $28.16 by 2010, an increase of 36% over its assumed level in 2000.

With respect to oil, the 1988 DOE report on potential improvements in energy efficiency (discussed earlier in section IV) concluded that while the long-term potential for aggregate energy conservation is large, the potential for oil conservation is more limited. Many oil-saving activities, for example, switching from oil furnaces or boilers to natural gas or electricity, already have taken place. Also, following the oil price shocks of the 1970s, more than half of oil-heated houses had taken two or more conservation measures by 1984. In the transportation sector the technological potential for conserving oil is great, but consumer preferences for larger cars and light trucks, and higher performance vehicles is said to limit potential oil efficiency gains. These preferences, of course, are effective only if individual choice is not subject to additional constraints. If consumer preferences for larger cars and trucks are constrained in the future, the potential for conserving oil is greater.

Finally, improvements in energy efficiency might actually increase energy consumption. Saunders (1992) has demonstrated that within the context of the neoclassical growth model technological change which increases energy efficiency could, under plausible assumptions regarding substitution elasticities, the elasticity of demand for energy and the rate of technological change, raise the level of energy consumption. Improved energy efficiency has the effect of reducing the relative cost of using energy, thereby inducing the substitution of energy for capital and labor. Further, energy consumption could rise because the overall rate of economic growth is increased by technological progress.

Household Energy Consumption

Energy's role in the growth accounting model is limited to that of an input in the production process. However, as noted earlier, 24% of the energy consumed in the United States in 1990 was purchased by households. Energy used for heating and cooling a house, for running a CD player, and in household vehicles are examples of energy used in conjunction with end products used by the household.

Because a significant share of energy consumption is not devoted directly to production, it could be argued that a historical link between energy growth and economic growth is not immutable. There is no reason, for example, to expect that energy for heating and cooling houses or for entertainment will grow at the same rate as the growth of output. On the other hand, as the economy and incomes grow, so too does consumer spending. Although purchases of some energy-using final goods and services may not grow at the same rate as incomes, total consumption expenditures will, as an approximation, grow at the same rate as the economy. To the extent other final goods and services require energy, the link between energy growth and economic growth will be preserved.

Can Oil Consumption be Reduced by New Energy Technologies?

Even if growth in energy consumption is necessary for continued economic growth, it may be possible to replace oil by other forms of energy which are less harmful to the environment and whose supplies are more secure. The development of fusion power, a breakthrough in solar cell technology which reduces the cost of solar energy, or the development of improved batteries for electric vehicles could speed the process by which the importance of oil in our economy is reduced. The potential for technological breakthroughs which could reduce oil consumption constitutes yet another research project.[35]

VI. POLICY CONSTRAINTS ON LIFESTYLES

Thus far, this paper has focused on the economic growth implications of forced energy conservation. A separate issue concerns the potential costs imposed on individuals when their choices regarding energy use are constrained by policy and they are forced or induced to alter their lifestyles.

Lifestyles and economic structure affect energy demand. Much of the difference between the aggregate energy intensities of the United States and Japan is attributable to lifestyle and industrial structure differences rather than inefficiency on the part of Americans.[36] For example, in the residential sector, floor space per capita in the United States is more than three times greater than in Japan, thereby increasing the space that is heated (and cooled). In Japan, the threshold temperature for heating is just 50 degrees Fahrenheit whereas in the United States it is 65 degrees. In transportation, the Japanese typically drive smaller cars and make greater use of public transportation for commuting. Americans would have to adopt many of these lifestyle changes to achieve the relatively low aggregate intensity of energy consumption found in Japan.

Lifestyle changes can refer to changes in habits—as when a thermostat is adjusted—or to the acceptance of a substitute good or service with higher energy efficiency (like a smaller automobile) but which is inferior (in terms of the satisfaction and performance attributes) because technological progress has been insufficient to make the more energy efficient version a perfect substitute.

As an example, if one is induced by policy to replace a high performance automobile which gets 20 mpg with a more energy efficient automobile which gets 45 mpg, one can still get from point A to point B, but the satisfaction from driving, as well as safety, may decline. Similarly, if the cost of commuting to work alone in an automobile is raised by policy, an individual may choose to take public transportation or to join a car pool. One can still get to work, but the utility associated with the convenience, privacy, and comforts of private commuting is foregone and a cost has been imposed.

Some conservation proposals would have a profound effect on individuals in terms of where they live, the type of residential unit in which they live, the appliances they purchase, the type of automobile they drive, and how they get to work. A study by MacKenzie, Dower, and Chen (1992) argues that a policy goal should be to increase the population density of urban areas because public transportation will never be viable in the United States "if the ideal remains three or four dwellings per acre. Densities above seven housing units per acre are needed for cost-effective bus service while densities of over nine housing units per acre are need for cost-effective light-rail service."[37] To this end, the study recommends changes in federal funding formulas to favor public transportation, more toll roads, higher gasoline taxes, and "the adoption of land-use and zoning reforms to encourage the denser urban development that is more compatible with walking, bicycling, and public transportation."[38]

With the exception of New York City, the population density required for a viable public transportation system, as defined in the study, does not exist in the United States. Assuming there are an average of three individuals per dwelling, even large cities such as Boston, Chicago, and Philadelphia lack the population density that is required to make extensive rail systems cost-effective. Moreover, rail transit systems have their own set of external impacts which could further raise their costs if a large expansion were undertaken.

Because land is relatively inexpensive in the United States, compared to Europe or Japan, a large portion of the population has chosen to live in suburbs. Individuals already have the option of living in densely-populated central cities with mass transit systems. Judging by the fact that people choose to live with congestion and the other costs of driving, it probably would take very high taxes and zoning changes to force a significant increase in housing unit and population density. Any study attempting to estimate the value individuals place on the "suburban lifestyle" likely would come up with very large numbers in the aggregate.

With the notable exception of estimates of the costs of reduced consumer satisfaction that would result from increased automobile fuel efficiency standards, cost-benefit analyses of conservation policies generally do not recognize the costs associated with policy-constrained choices or altered lifestyles. If these costs were accounted for, some conservation proposals, especially those which affect lifestyles, would be more difficult to justify on cost-benefit grounds.

The legitimacy of individual choice and the appropriateness of recognizing the cost imposed on individuals from policy-constrained lifestyles have been questioned by some.[39] The utilitarian notion that individuals *should* have the right to make decisions solely on the basis of how it affects one's own welfare has been challenged.[40] The challenge rests on the proposition that energy consumption imposes costs on others and the belief that continued growth in energy consumption cannot, on a worldwide basis, be sustained. Accordingly, some argue that consumption should be reduced by raising energy taxes, enacting energy efficiency mandates, changing zoning laws to encourage more densely-populated communities, subsidizing mass transit, penalizing drivers who drive to work alone, and by mandating the production of fuel efficient automobiles.[41]

Some policies will impact individual choice and lifestyles more than others. A requirement that housing units meet an insulation standard imposes a cost on home buyers, but presumably has less impact on lifestyles than a policy designed to increase population density so that ridership on public transportation increases. The potential benefits of conservation policies should be weighed against the costs imposed by these policies. Several research topics are suggested by lifestyle considerations.

The Energy Conservation Potential from Lifestyle Changes

The benefits of conservation policies often are couched in terms of the potential energy savings they would achieve. For example, raising CAFE standards for passenger automobiles and extending fuel efficiency standards to light trucks and vans would further constrain the set of choices currently available to consumers. One can ask how much energy would be saved if drivers were forced to purchase vehicles that are more fuel efficient than the average vehicle currently purchased in today's market. Similarly, one can estimate the energy that would be saved if individuals were induced by zoning and tax policy to live in more densely populated communities closer to the core of a city.

Wollstadt (1990) investigated the potential for increased conservation by taking DOE's *Annual Energy Outlook, 1989*, and making stronger, but plausible conservation assumptions than those embodied in DOE's forecast. For example, his conservation scenario assumes a further increase in new-car fuel mileage from 34 miles per gallon (as assumed in DOE's forecast) to 39 miles per gallon. Despite these and other assumed efficiency gains, he finds that population growth and incomes probably will cause energy consumption to rise in the foreseeable future.[42] While the DOE long-term forecasts show energy consumption rising from 12 to 17% between 1988 and 2000, Wollstadt's conservation scenario—which embodies stronger conservation assumptions than DOE's—still shows an increase of 8%.

More recently, Norman and Tierney (1995) examined the potential energy savings as current energy technologies affecting household energy consumption are fully diffused. This effort included the assumption that older vehicles in the fleet of household vehicles are replaced by newer models so that the fleet achieved, on average, the current CAFE standard for fuel efficiency. They estimated that complete diffusion of current energy technologies would reduce the intensity of household energy consumption by approximately 16%. They also found, however, that expected population and economic growth still would result in a higher level of *total* household energy consumption.

Efficiency improvements are one brake on energy consumption growth. Altering lifestyles also could reduce household energy use. Norman and Tierney estimated the impact of hypothetical lifestyle-targeted policies aimed at reducing the size of housing units, increasing the use of car pools and ridership on public transportation, and significantly raising automobile fuel efficiency standards above the current CAFE standard. The latter policy was characterized as targeting lifestyles since, given current technology, a significant increase in fuel efficiency would necessitate the purchase of automobiles with inferior performance and safety characteristics, especially at current automobile prices. The latter policy was the only one which, by itself, appeared to have a major effect on total energy consumption. The other policies targeted at lifestyles would reduce household energy consumption, but their impact was found to be relatively small. Of course, if a sufficient number of policies impacting lifestyles were enacted, the impact on total energy consumption could be large even though the impact of any single policy was small.

The Welfare Cost of Lifestyle Changes

Reduced energy consumption is one measure of the benefits provided by increased conservation. But what about the costs? Most exercises evaluating conservation proposals assume that continued normal economic growth is feasible and hence find no cost in terms of reduced growth. Attention generally is restricted to the direct costs of increased conservation while indirect costs are ignored. But the indirect costs of constrained lifestyles may turn out to be quite large. One approach for estimating indirect costs involves estimating the consumer surplus foregone by constraints on choice, for example, on the size of vehicle that one can purchase. Reduced consumer surplus represents a pure welfare cost. An alternative is the hedonic approach whereby the demand for some good is expressed as a function of its attributes. For example, the demand for an automobile can be expressed as a function of attributes like power, size, safety, and comfort. By estimating how much one would be willing to pay for additional units of these attributes, the cost to consumers from reducing these attributes can be calculated.

Shin (1990) reviewed a number of studies that estimated the welfare cost of raising automobile fuel efficiency standards from 27 mpg to some higher level. The methodologies and assumptions in the studies differed and hence the range of estimates was large. Based on information in a study by Green and Liu (1988), Shin estimates that if CAFE standards had been raised from 27 mpg to just 32 mpg, the present value cost of reduced consumer satisfaction would have ranged between $3.2 to $8.8 billion (1988$) over the period 1992-1995. Higher CAFE standards would impose correspondingly higher costs from reduced consumer satisfaction.

Thus, consumer satisfaction associated with lifestyles potentially is important.[43] Some in the conservation community view the desire for "the American lifestyle" as a barrier to continued improvements in energy conservation, or at least to the goal of reducing energy consumption growth. Ultimately, the case for policy-induced conservation will be stronger or weaker depending on whether the lifestyle costs imposed on individuals by conservation policies are recognized as legitimate.

VII. CONCLUDING REMARKS AND SUMMARY OF RESEARCH TOPICS

This paper has identified a number of research topics relating to the potential economic growth and welfare cost consequences of policy-induced energy conservation. Few are opposed to energy conservation or doubt that the intensity with which energy is used can gradually and efficiently be reduced. What is at issue is whether market forces should be relied on to govern decisions regarding energy use or whether government should force reductions in the energy intensity of the economy. Those disposed to the former view believe that the market can best insure that energy is used efficiently. When markets guide decisions, energy efficiency is a means toward overall economic efficiency which is pursued by self-interested individuals and firms—not an end in itself. And when economic efficiency is pursued, economic growth will be enhanced.

In contrast, those arguing for policy-induced energy conservation believe that energy markets are imperfect and that government can more effectively insure that energy is used efficiently. Many argue that the growth of energy consumption can be slowed, if not reversed, without any consequences for economic growth. And some argue that the social consequences of ever-rising levels of energy consumption override the costs imposed on individuals from policy-constrained lifestyles.

Although there is a growing body of empirical evidence which shows that energy growth has measurably contributed to economic growth in the past, the question as to whether future energy growth is a necessary condition for continued economic growth remains unanswered, at least definitively. While there is a theoretical basis for the hypothesis that energy contributes to economic growth, there also are arguments as to why continued energy growth is not a necessary condition for continued growth. These arguments, some of which are variants of each other, include: (1) the cost share of energy is too small to matter, at least in the aggregate; (2) labor and capital can always be substituted for energy; (3) there exist cost-effective conservation technologies which, if adopted, would reduce energy use without reducing economic growth; (4) technological progress and projected gains in aggregate energy efficiency can eliminate the need for growth in energy consumption; and (5) not all energy consumption is directly devoted to the production of goods and services. In addition, it could be argued that although energy growth is vital to economic growth, oil itself is not.

Growth in aggregate energy consumption can be constrained by reducing energy use by households (which account for almost one-fourth of aggregate energy consumption) as well as by the industrial sector of the economy. Household energy use can be reduced by improving the energy efficiency of household appliances, equipment, and vehicles which use energy, and by constraining lifestyles. Three areas of research include: (1) the extent to which the continued diffusion of existing energy technologies for the household ultimately will reduce household energy use; (2) the potential for changes in lifestyles (e.g., living in smaller housing units, driving smaller automobiles, and using public transportation or car pools) to reduce household energy consumption; and (3) the potential welfare cost of policy-constrained lifestyles.

NOTES

1.   See Mackenzie, Dower, and Chen (1992) where it is argued that drivers receive $300 billion annually in hidden subsidies associated with externalities and other costs not directly reflected in user charges to drivers.

2.   These same analysts argue that the desire for a higher standard of living in developing countries can be fulfilled, at least in part, by redistributing incomes and wealth from the developed countries. See, for example, Durning (1992).

3.   An extensive list of regulations designed to promote energy conservation can be found in *America's Energy Choices* (1991, pp. 115-122).

4.   As an example, Virginia Power has a program whereby those purchasing a replacement heat pump, installing additional insulation, or replacing existing windows with energy efficient windows can receive a low interest loan for up to $10,000 to be repaid over a 5-year period. In the case of heat pumps, the more energy efficient the unit that is purchased, the lower is the interest rate. These programs constitute what is known as Demand Side Management, or DSM. The cost of the subsidies typically is built into the rate base.

5.   See Viscusi, Magat, Carlin, and Dreyfus (1994).

6.   Norman (1993b).

7.   See Norman (1989, pp. 11-15).

8.   Norman (1993a). The estimates represent an update of estimates found in Norman (1989). "Built-in" energy efficiency improvements refer to the rate at which the Department of Energy expects the aggregate energy intensity in the United States to fall. While the DOE assumes a continued decline in energy intensity in its long-term forecasts, the behavior of aggregate energy intensity since 1986 raises question as to whether future declines in intensity can be expected if energy prices remain stable. The estimate of 135% is based on the assumption that the energy-GDP ratio would remain constant if energy prices are approximately stable.

9. See Montgomery, Johnson, and Fauth (1993) and Jaffe and Stavins (1994).

10. See Norman (1992, pp. 6-7) and Montgomery et al. (1993).

11. See Joskow and Marron (1992), and Nichols (1993).

12. United States Department of Energy, *Oil Conservation Potential in the United States Economy*, August 1988.

13. See Landes (1972, pp. 95-104).

14. Thomas (1980).

15. See, for example, Mankiw, Romer, and Weil (1992).

16. Hudson and Jorgenson (1974) and Rasche and Tatom (1981) were among the first to incorporate energy as a determinant of economic growth.

17. This view is represented by Denison (1985).

18. See Berndt, Kolstad, and Lee (1993).

19. Hudson and Jorgenson (1978, p. 122).

20. Moroney suggests that this is because they "link technological change to gross capital formation and forbid any technological advances due to organizational improvements or learning by doing." As a result, "the lower past-1973 growth in utilized vintage capital per hour severely limits opportunities for technological change to enhance productivity." See Moroney (1992a, pp. 374-375).

21. Norman and Tierney (1995).

22. Jorgenson (1988, p. 29).

23. Jorgenson (1988, p. 34).

24. That is, productivity growth was found to be energy using. The impact of labor, capital, and materials on productivity growth varied by industry.

25. See also Jorgenson (1986).

26. Historically, countries have become more developed and affluent by moving people out of labor intensive activities and by figuring out how to make activities less labor intensive. This is the process by which labor productivity and ultimately wages rise.

27. This argument is attributable to Schmalensee (1994) who develops it in the context of the job-creating potential of environmental regulation.

28. See the discussion below on pages 91-92.

29. See example Denison (1985) and Maddison (1987).

30. Moroney (1992a, p. 366).

31. See Hogan and Manne (1977) for the derivation of this result based on an aggregate production function which is not Cobb-Douglas.

32. Moroney (1992a, pp. 375-377).

33. The use of the net present value criterion itself could overstate the level of investment justified by a given discount rate. Dixit and Pindyck (1994) propose an alternative approach to analyzing investment when there is uncertainty and when investment is irreversible. Their analysis also explains why homeowners contemplating household conservation investments appear to have very high discount rates (see pp. 411-412).

34. See Montgomery et al., (1993, pp. 5-6).

35. Henderson and Rusin (1994) recently examined efforts to develop batteries for electric vehicles.

36. See Shin (1991).

37. MacKenzie, Dower, and Chen (1992, p. 26).

38. MacKenzie, Dower, and Chen (1992, p. 26).

39. See, for example, Durning (1992).

40. See, for example, Brown, Flavin, and Postel (1991), and Durning (1992).

41. Of course, if individual choice is deemed not to be legitimate, an argument could be made that an even more efficient solution, from a central planning perspective, would be to produce just one type of automobile for personal transportation. Such a solution would dispense with the need to incur costs of product variation and would allow automobile producers to achieve maximum economies of scale at both the plant and firm level.

42. The effect of population growth on the level of energy consumption has received little attention, although some have advocated measures to reduce population growth as a means of reducing energy consumption growth.

43. One indication of the increasing relevance of lifestyles for energy conservation policy is the World Energy Council's long-term research project entitled "Energy Demand, Life Style Changes, and Technology Development" which is just getting underway. Perrels (1993) discusses the importance of lifestyle considerations for conservation policy and goals.

REFERENCES

Alliance to Save Energy, American Council for An Energy-Efficient Economy, Natural Resources Council, and the Union of Concerned Scientists. 1991. *America's Energy Choices: Investing in a Strong Economy and a Clean Environment*. Cambridge, MA.

Alliance to Save Energy, American Gas Association, and Solar Energy Industries Association. 1992. *An Alternative Energy Future*.

Berndt, E., C. Kolstad, and J. Lee. 1993. "Measuring the Energy Efficiency and Productivity Impacts of Embodied Technical Change." *Energy Journal* 14(3): 33-55.

Brown, L.R., C. Flavin, and S. Postel. 1991. *Saving the Planet*. New York: W.W. Norton & Co.

Brown, S.P.A., and K.R. Phillips. 1991. "U.S. Oil Demand and Conservation." *Contemporary Policy Issues* IX (1): 67-72.

Bohi, D.R. 1989. *Energy Price Shocks and Macroeconomic Performance*. Washington, DC: Resources for the Future.

Denison, E.F. 1985. *Trends in American Economic Growth*. Washington, DC: The Brookings Institution.

Dixit, A.K., and R.S. Pindyck. 1994. *Investment Under Uncertainty*. New Jersey: Princeton University Press.

Durning, A. 1992. *How Much is Enough?*. New York: W.W. Norton & Company.

Energy Modeling Forum. 1992. *International Oil Supplies and Demands*, EMF Report 11, Volume II, April.

Geller, H., J. DeCicco, and S. Laitner. 1992. *Energy Efficiency and Job Creation: The Employment and Income Benefits from Investing in Energy Conserving Technologies*. Washington, DC: American Council for an Energy-Efficient Economy.

Greene, D.L., and J.T. Liu. 1988. "Automotive Fuel Economy Improvements and Consumer Surplus." *Transportation Research* 22A: 203-218.

Henderson, T.P., and M. Rusin. 1994. "Electric Vehicles: Their Technical and Economic Status." Policy Analysis and Strategic Planning Department Research Study *ν*073, January.

Hogan, W., and A.S. Manne. 1977. "Energy-Economy Interactions: The Fable of the Elephant and the Rabbit?" In *Modeling Energy-Economy Interactions: Five Approaches*, edited by C.J. Hitch. Washington DC: Resources for the Future.

Hudson, E.A., and D.W. Jorgenson. 1974. "U.S. Energy Policy and Economic Growth, 1975-2000." *Bell Journal of Economics and Management Science* 5(2): 461-514.

Hudson, E.A., and D.W. Jorgenson. 1978. "Energy Policy and U.S. Economic Growth." *American Economic Review* 68(2): 118-123.

Jaffe, A., and R.N. Stavins. 1994. "Energy-Efficiency Investments and Public Policy." *Energy Journal* 15(2): 43-65.

Jorgenson, D.W. 1986. "The Great Transition: Energy and Economic Change." *Energy Journal* 7(3): 1-13.

Jorgenson, D.W. 1988. "Productivity and Postwar U.S. Economic Growth." *Journal of Economic Perspectives* 2(4): 23-41.

Joskow, P.L., and D.B. Marron. 1992. "What Does a Negawatt Really Cost? Evidence from Utility Conservation Programs." *Energy Journal* 13(4): 41-74.

Landes, D.S. 1972. *The Unbound Prometheus: Technological Change and Industrial Development in Western Europe from 1750 to the Present*. New York: Cambridge University Press.

Maddison, A. 1987. "Growth and Slowdown in Advanced Capitalist Economies." *Journal of Economic Literature* XXV(2): 649-698.

Mankiw, N.G., D. Romer, and D.N. Weil. 1992. "A Contribution to the Empirics of Economic Growth." *Quarterly Journal of Economics* CVII(2): 407-437.

MacKenzie, J.J., R.C. Dower, and D.D.T. Chen. 1992. *The Going Rate: What it Really Costs to Drive*. Washington, DC: World Resources Institute.

Montgomery, W.D., K. Johnson, and G.R. Fauth. 1993. *No Free Lunch: A Review of Technology-Based Studies on Costs of Controlling Carbon Emissions*. New York: DRI/McGraw-Hill.

Moroney, J.R. 1992a. "Energy, Capital and Technological Change in the United States." *Resources and Energy* 14: 363-380.

Moroney, J.R. 1992b. "Energy, Capital, and Growth." *Energy, Growth, and the Environment: Advances in the Economics of Energy and Resources* 7: 189-204.

Nichols, A.L. 1993. "Revealed Preference and the Net Benefits of Electricity Demand-Side Management." Unpublished paper presented at the Western Economic Association Meetings, June 20-24.

Norman, D.A. 1989. "Aggregate Energy Demand: Determination and Implications for Conservation Policy." Policy Analysis Department Research Study #046, American Petroleum Institute, April.

Norman, D.A. 1992. "Comments on America's Energy Choices." American Petroleum Institute, July 31.

Norman, D.A. 1993a. "Holding Oil and Aggregate Energy Consumption to Their 1990 Levels." American Petroleum Institute, April 22.

Norman, D.A. 1993b. "Energy Prices and Externalities." Policy Analysis Department Research Study #069, May.

Norman, D.A., and B. Tierney. 1995. "Household Energy Consumption in the United States: Lifestyles and Conservation Policy." Policy Analysis and Strategic Planning Research Study #079, July.

Preston, J.L., R.K. Adler, and M.A. Schipper. 1992. "Energy Efficiency in the Manufacturing Sector." Energy Information Administration/Department of Energy, *Monthly Energy Review* (December): 1-8.

Rasche, R.H., and J.A. Tatom. 1981. "Energy Price Shocks, Aggregate Supply and Monetary Policy: The Theory and International Evidence." In *Supply Shocks, Incentives and National Wealth,* edited by K. Brunner and A.H. Meltzer. Amsterdam: North-Holland Publishing Co.

Saunders, H.D. 1992. "The Khazzoom-Brooks Postulate and Neoclassical Growth." *The Energy Journal* 13(4): 131-148.

Schipper, L., R.B. Howarth, and H.S. Geller. 1990. "United States Energy Use from 1973 to 1987: The Impacts of Improved Efficiency." *Annual Review of Energy*: 455-504.

Schmalensee, R. 1994. "Environmental Regulation, Technology, and Living Standards." In *Balancing Economic Growth and Environmental Goals*. American Council for Capital Formation Center for Policy Research, Washington, DC.

Shin, D. 1990. "The Costs and Benefits of Federally Mandated Policies to Promote Energy Conservation: The Case of the Automobile Efficiency Standard." Policy Analysis Department Research Study #050, American Petroleum Institute, May.

Shin, D. 1991. "International Comparisons of Energy-Gross National Product Ratios." Policy Analysis Department Discussion Paper #068, American Petroleum Institute, June.

Solow, R.M.1956. "A Contribution to the Theory of Economic Growth." *Quarterly Journal of Economics* LXX: 65-94.

Sutherland, R.J. 1994. "Income Distribution Effects of Electric Utility DSM Programs." *The Energy Journal* 15(4): 103-118.

Tatom, J.A. 1982. "Potential Output and the Recent Productivity Decline." *Federal Reserve Bank of St. Louis Review* 64(1): 3-16.

Thomas, B. 1980. "Towards an Energy Interpretation of the Industrial Revolution." *Atlantic Economic Journal* 8(1): 1-15.

United States Department of Energy. 1988. *Oil Conservation Potential in the U.S. Economy*. Washington DC: Office of Policy, Planning and Analysis, Office of Policy Integration.

United States Department of Energy/Energy Information Administration. 1993. *Annual Energy Outlook 1993*, Washington, DC.

United States Department of Energy/Energy Information Administration. 1994. *Annual Energy Outlook 1994*, Washington, DC.

Viscusi, W.K., W.A. Magat, A. Carlin, and M.K. Dreyfus. 1994. "Environmentally Responsible Energy Pricing." *Energy Journal* 15(2): 23-42.

Wollstadt, R. 1990. "Can Energy Conservation Fully Replace Incremental Energy Production in a Growing U.S. Economy?" Policy Analysis Department Discussion Paper *v*061, American Petroleum Institute, March.

COMMENTARY

Jeffery C. Talbert

I. OVERVIEW

Energy conservation is possible from two broad perspectives, governmental policy, or the operation of free markets. Donald Norman's paper makes the case that a free market approach is superior to any governmental policy solution for slowing energy consumption. The key aspect of this argument is the relationship between energy use and economic growth. Since energy and growth are related, the paper argues that policy induced changes in energy consumption will have unwanted effects on economic growth. To explore this linkage, the paper reviews some flaws of proposed policies that attempt to control energy growth, discussing both the costs and benefits of conservation policies. The paper concludes that policy attempts to induce conservation necessitate substantial costs to society that outweigh their benefits.

The paper has two fundamental points. First, conservation policies are not desirable if we consider the declines in economic growth resulting from reduced energy consumption. And, second, if we

Advances in the Economics of Energy and Resources, Volume 9, pages 105-109.

choose to implement energy reduction policies, the free market should drive reduced consumption, not governmental regulations and policy. My comments will focus on these two areas, discussing the linkage between energy and growth, and focusing on the implications of governmental regulation policies.

II. THE INTERACTION OF ENERGY CONSUMPTION AND ECONOMIC GROWTH

Economic growth and energy consumption share an unusual relationship. Anecdotal stories describe how the modern industrial revolution was possible due to newer more powerful energy sources, and thus several studies have linked economic expansion with growing energy usage. Likewise, empirical time series work has found positive relationships between growth and consumption that reaffirms the findings of descriptive accounts. A missing component of this relationship is how different types of energy may influence this linkage.

For example, the change from wood to coal power in the nineteenth century is given as an example of an expanding energy source driving new economic growth. Did a similar growth pattern emerge from the start of the "Atomic Age" in the 1950s? And more importantly, will newly discovered energy sources deliver a new industrial revolution in the future? The nature of these relationships could have dramatic effects on future energy policy. For instance, should we invest in new energy technology looking for the next breakthrough (such as Liquid Metal Breeder Reactors, or Fusion Reactors)? Or, should we focus on sustaining current growth rates by ensuring an adequate supply of current technology energy for future needs. The decision between these two policies has important consequences for energy development, and most importantly fossil fuels.

Norman briefly discusses oil related energy as a special case, but does not explain the logic for these differences. The paper would benefit from a section that explores conservation effects on the various sources of energy that could help determine where to invest future energy resources. For example, the paper implies that alternative fuel sources would harm the petroleum industry, but does not distinguish between the different types of petroleum. Natural gas producers will likely benefit from alternative fuels mandates, such as CNG powered vehicles. A possible research question looks at the consumption/economic growth relationship in terms of different energy sources. Does energy source make a difference?

III. PROBLEMS WITH GOVERNMENT CONTROL OF ENERGY POLICY

While the paper leaves little doubt of the linkage between economic growth and energy consumption, it is weaker in its analysis of governmental conservation policies. Self-interests guarantee that most industries will view their markets as near perfect, requiring little governmental regulation. However, energy policy is a special market needing careful planning. Since energy is a finite resource, we are faced with certain long-term planning problems that short-term market forces are unable to address. Taken as a collective good, providing a stable, lasting supply of affordable energy is in the best interest of the nation and the energy industry. Therefore, government policies should ensure that limited resources are used as wisely as possible if the market is unable to attain this goal.

Compounding the problems associated with energy supply are those concerning externalities such as pollution. The aftermath of the industrial revolution provides evidence that markets will allow free-riders in terms of externalities like pollution. Clean air and water are clear examples where government intervention is necessary to prevent destruction of collective goods. Policymakers must decide if the market is capable of policing itself in terms of energy consumption, and if not, then enact national policies that are the least destructive to good market forces.

IV. TAXES OR FORCED REDUCTION?

Unlike heavy-handed governmental regulations such as price controls, market incentives for conservation can have positive effects on both economic growth and energy production. Two of the most often cited policy options for conservation are taxing energy and forcing a reduction in consumption. While the effect of taxes are subject to assumptions of price elasticity, they may produce positive collective goods (in addition to the usual negative aspects). For example, raising the fuel tax may discourage wasteful energy uses, finance governmental debt, encourage the development of alternative fuels, or promote domestic exploration of new energy sources. Some evidence suggests that such reductions in energy usage may slow economic growth, but only if we assume that the reduced activities are not replaced with alternative sources. In addition, it is often difficult to measure the related environmental benefits from such incentives.

The best example of forced reduction of energy consumption has been the CAFE requirements. Proponents of gasoline-based fuels argue that meeting the CAFE standards are too difficult, and will result in reduced satisfaction and vehicle safety. However, these studies do not consider the vast improvements in efficiency since the CAFE standards were first introduced. Vehicles are not only more fuel efficient, they are safer (new technologies such as air bags, side impact beams, and anti-lock braking), and in many cases have increased performance (from advances such as electronic fuel injection, and variable valve timing). Through the forced CAFE standards, automakers have learned to make vehicles much more efficient, which helps fuel economy as well as performance. The problem for policymakers is how to encourage innovation in efficiency, without creating unrealistic burdens on manufacturers. The requirement for zero-emission vehicles may present such a burden. Available technology used in current zero-emission vehicles has yet to yield an automobile that is both functional and affordable for consumers.

Another popular reduction in usage is through mass transportation. HOV lanes, light rail, and carpooling are all popular methods of mass transportation. Norman argues that few cities can encourage these mass transportation efforts efficiently, due to low population densities. However, reduced consumption is only one beneficial factor of mass transportation. Many cities depend on mass transit systems (San Francisco, Washington, DC, Atlanta, and New York) for various other reasons, such as to help reduce vehicle emissions, alleviate crowded downtown parking space, and relieve congested highways. Therefore, conservation is only one aspect of mass transit systems, and should not be considered the only benefit from their use. If we consider the additional benefits, concerns about reductions in lifestyle quality become less of a cost to conservation.

A final comment concerns the consequences of these policies on public welfare. Changes in the political system of the United States usually do not happen quickly, and often take years for any changes to take place. Thus, changes in energy policy will not be sudden, but rather slow incremental changes that will allow the market time to react. In fact, one reason for energy conservation is due to the sudden shocks and crisis of the 1970s. The Department of Energy was created to give the nation a national energy policy, and to prevent such sudden changes from crippling the nations supply of energy. While changes in the lifestyles of individuals due to energy conservation will undoubtedly be noticeable, they will be gradual enough to gain public approval. Most consumers accept some cost in return for clean air and water, and to guarantee an affordable lasting supply of energy. Since energy development is not a quick process, long-range planning is required to provide adequate resources when they are needed. Only government has the resources to make such investments in the future, as the market system could not afford such investments.

V. CONCLUSION

While energy conservation is needed to protect future energy reserves and slow pollution, it has damaging effects on economic growth. Donald Norman's paper reviews some of the problems associated with finding the proper balance between energy consumption and protecting future resources. If market forces are unable to protect these resources, the government will enact policies to encourage conservation and reduce energy consumption. Norman identifies some problems with using policy-induced reductions of energy consumption and recommends a free market approach to conservation. In addition, when considering energy conservation options we should also consider their potential cost, as any reduction in consumption will constrain economic growth. The best incentives would be those that allow the market adequate time to respond, and therefore have a minimal impact on economic growth. The real problem for policymakers is not whether to encourage conservation, but rather how the harmful side-effects of conservation can be minimized.

U.S. PETROLEUM SUPPLY:
HISTORY AND PROSPECTS

Edward D. Porter

ABSTRACT

In 1970 domestic crude oil production peaked. The subsequent decline in U.S. supply has been widely interpreted as attributable to either the cumulative exhaustion of a limited domestic resource base, or more plausibly to an increase in cost associated with pushing the frontiers of the resource base to progressively more expensive marginal properties. Of course, these are not mutually exclusive possibilities, insofar as the only reliable indicator of progressive depletion is precisely that of rising replacement cost.

There has been a great deal of recent literature which has documented the rise in replacement cost from the early 1970s through the early 1980s. Little attention to date has been focused on the behavior of supply and costs since that time. This paper addresses this more recent experience, in which supply has fallen, although at rates generally lower than expected, and reserves have been added, at rates generally higher than expected. While cost increases in the 1970s were

Advances in the Economics of Energy and Resources, Volume 9, pages 111-162.

consistent with the "rising cost" supply interpretation, their reversal in the 1980s was not. By 1990 the cost of reserve replacement, *and the level of reserve replacement actually occurring*, were roughly comparable to those 20 years earlier.

Over the next 15 years, using a model of petroleum supply developed at the API from this historical data, the prospect of continued decline in domestic supply predicted by a number of forecasters is confirmed, if current prices and policies are maintained over the period. By the year 2010, crude oil production is expected to fall nearly 3 mmbd below 1990 levels. However, this outlook is quite sensitive to variations in market conditions, technology, and government policy. In particular, opening of federal lands, such as ANWR and the OCS, could offset most of the expected decline, while introduction of new environmental regulations could seriously accelerate that decline. This supply outlook, combined with the prospect of growing demand, does imply a future of growing U.S. import dependence, although the rate of this dependence is not fixed by U.S. resource constraints but highly sensitive to U.S. policy choices.

I.   INTRODUCTION

For more than a century, U.S. crude oil supply grew rapidly. However, as seen in Figure 1, in 1970 production peaked, and then

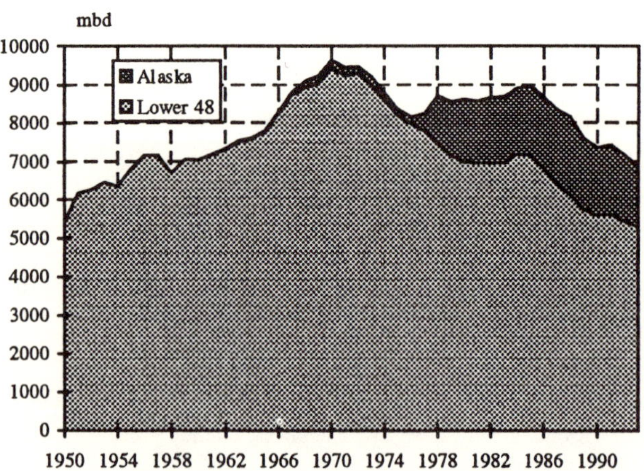

Figure 1.   U.S. Crude Oil Production

began a long decline, interrupted only briefly from 1975 to 1985 by the onset of production from the North Slope of Alaska combined with a short-lived stabilization of Lower 48 supply. Since 1986, the decline has resumed. By 1993, production in the Lower 48 had fallen about 44% from its 1970 peak.

The decline in supply experienced in the 1970s was quickly attributed to the imminent exhaustion of the domestic resource base, particularly that of the Lower 48 states, predicted in the early 1960s by M. King Hubbert.[1] But the 1980s contained a number of surprises on the domestic supply side. Most notably, in the first half of the 1980s, production from the United States began slowly rising again, contrary to most expectations. Despite the fact that this growth was small in absolute terms, it was enormous relative to what had been widely expected. In 1980, DOE was forecasting a drop in U.S. crude supply of over 1 mmbd by 1985.[2] In fact, domestic supply rose by about a half million barrels a day, so that less than 5 years into their long run forecast, and despite actual price levels nearly a third less than those upon which the forecast had been based, actual domestic supply was reaching levels 20% above the levels estimated, as seen in Figure 2.

This aggregate U.S. supply behavior was not strictly inconsistent with the Hubbert projections, insofar as Hubbert was concerned principally with the behavior of mature provinces, such as the Lower

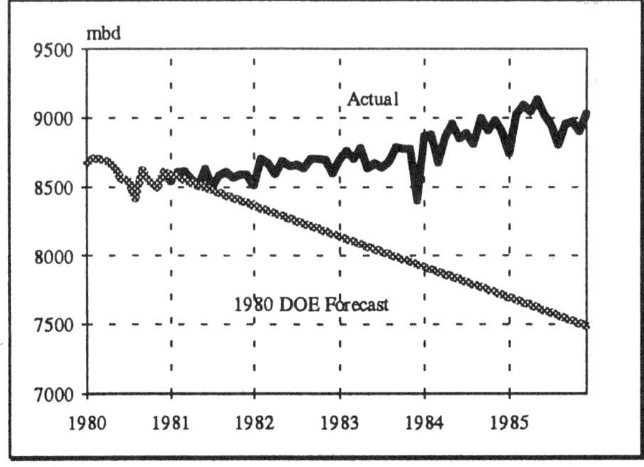

Figure 2.   U.S. Crude Oil Supply, 1980-1985

48, and a portion of this increase was attributable to production from new discoveries in Alaska. But what was strictly inconsistent with those projections was the fact that production from the Lower 48 states had itself stabilized and actually begun increasing by 1985. On the other hand, the observed behavior was hardly a clear confirmation of a strictly economic theory of supply either, insofar as the reversal occurred against a backdrop of steadily falling world oil prices. Rather, the failure of virtually all major forecasters in 1980 to anticipate U.S. crude supply as little as five years out to within 20% of the actual value simply provided a strong illustration of the rather severely limited understanding of the supply process that was informing public debate over energy policy in the prior decade.

In the event, little attention was paid to examining the reasons behind this major error, since the revival of domestic supply proved short-lived. In 1986, following the collapse of world oil prices, the decline of domestic supply resumed, at rates similar to those of the early 1970s. This new decline was interpreted as vindicating both geologists and economists by demonstrating both that supply responds to price, and that the inevitability of the natural decline embodied in the Hubbert curve could only be temporarily evaded.[3]

As the 1990s got underway, there again emerged a consensus that U.S. petroleum supply was once more locked onto an unalterable decline path determined by the advanced state of domestic resource depletion. Again, as in 1980, the Department of Energy is forecasting continued domestic supply decline, even in a market environment of rising real oil prices. The 1994 DOE Annual Energy Outlook expects U.S. petroleum supply to fall by about 2 mmbd between 1990 and the turn of the century.[4]

Similarly, in 1990 the Stanford Energy Modeling Forum (EMF) conducted an assessment of world oil markets, using a number of prominent oil market forecasting models.[5] While the EMF modelers agreed on the likelihood of decline, there was little consensus as to the likely magnitude of this decline. As seen in Figure 3, the decline estimated in the Stanford exercise over the next decade, for identical price scenarios, ranged from as little as 300,000 bd for one of the surveyed models to as much as 4.5 mmbd for another, with no clustering of results at any point in between.

This paper attempts to narrow the range of these possibilities with a careful examination of the trends in domestic activity over the 1966-

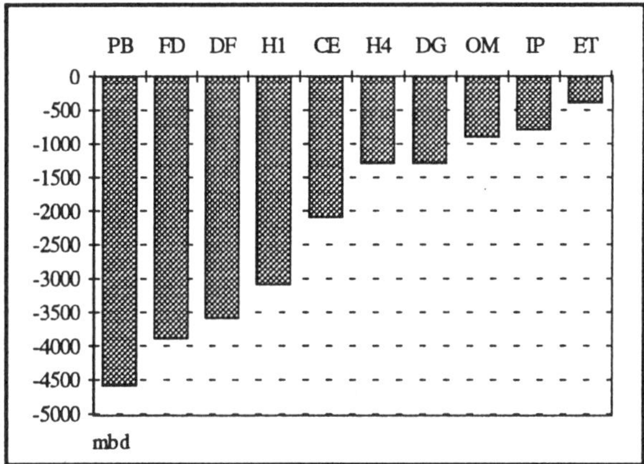

Figure 3.   EMF Estimated Changes in U.S. Supply,[6] 1990-2000

1993 period, and an assessment of possible scenarios for the next two decades.

II.   RECENT U.S. SUPPLY HISTORY

Since 1947, detailed data has been collected by the American Petroleum Institute, the Independent Petroleum Association of America, the Mid- Continent Oil and Gas Association, the Bureau of Mines, the U.S. Department of Commerce, and the U.S. Department of Energy documenting the course of U.S. drilling activity and costs, reserve accumulation, and supply. This data, particularly since 1966, provides a rich history of domestic supply activity in the post-World War II period. This section reviews briefly the recent historical experience.

A.   The Market Environment

The market environment within which the industry has operated over the 1966-1993 period has varied greatly along three principal dimensions—the price of oil, the structure of costs, and the nature of regulatory and taxation policy.

World Prices

During this 28-year history, prices of crude oil presented to the United States by the international market varied greatly. As shown in Figure 4, real oil prices (expressed in 1990 dollars) fell gradually to about $10 in the early 1970s, before rising sharply in two steps, tripling in 1974 following the Arab oil embargo, and nearly doubling in 1980 following the Iranian revolution and the outbreak of war between Iran and Iraq. From 1981 until 1985, real prices fell steadily, then collapsed to the teens in 1986. Since that time, except for the brief price spike in the fall of 1990 following the Iraqi invasion of Kuwait, prices "settled" into a range between $15-$20.

Principally because of the effects of domestic price controls (discussed in more detail later), domestic wellhead values remained well below these levels throughout the 1970s and early 1980s. Nonetheless, it was also the case that the range of wellhead values experienced since 1986 have been considerably higher than the levels of the early 1970s, similar to the actual average levels experienced under price controls between 1974 and 1978.

Costs

The second dimension along which the industry's environment changed drastically during this historical period was the costs it faced,

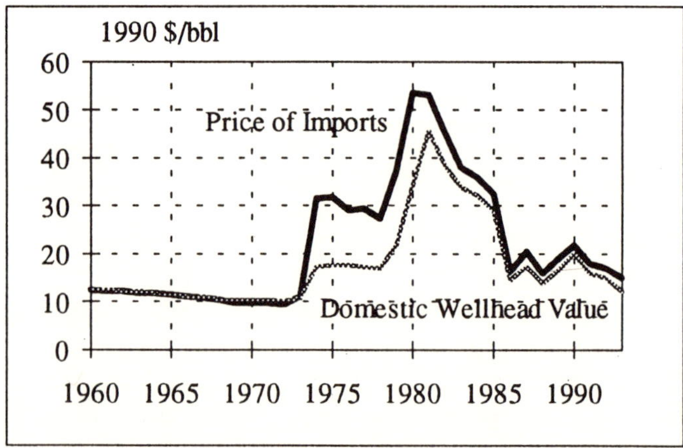

Figure 4.   World Crude Oil Prices

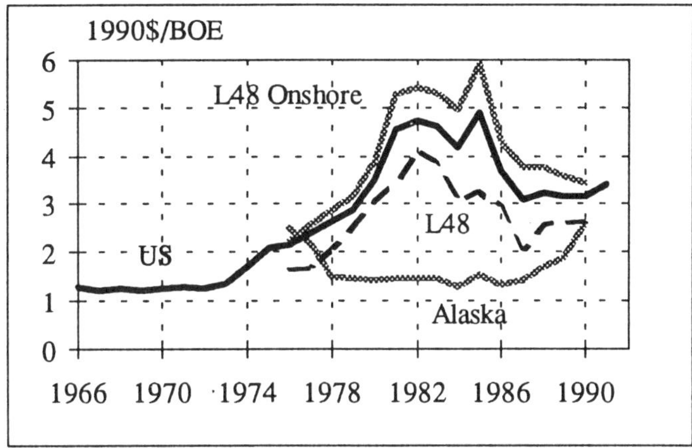

Figure 5.   U.S. Production Costs, 1966-1990

both in producing the resource from existing reserves, and the investment costs associated with adding new reserves. Figure 5 presents average production costs faced by the industry over the period. Prior to 1973, such costs remained at about $1 per barrel. In 1974, such costs began to rise toward a peak of nearly $5 per barrel in 1985, before falling to recent levels of about $3 per barrel.

Such costs have varied significantly by region, with the highest cost being the Lower 48 onshore, the lowest being Alaska. Movements in such costs reflect the influence of both fuel costs, which rise and fall with oil prices, and depletion of the natural drive mechanisms of the resource base, requiring pumping and the application of higher cost secondary, and tertiary production technology. Furthermore, there were even more significant changes in the capital cost associated with finding and developing new oil and gas reserve additions during this period. The largest component of such capital costs was drilling expenditures. As seen in Figures 6 and 7, oil and gas drilling costs per barrel of reserves added rose sharply between 1973 and 1983, particularly in the Lower 48 onshore, where oil drilling costs per barrel of reserves added increased sixfold and gas drilling costs more than tripled.

In both cases, however, the increase was a temporary phenomenon associated with the drilling boom. As drilling activity contracted sharply after 1985, so did drilling costs. By 1990, both oil and gas

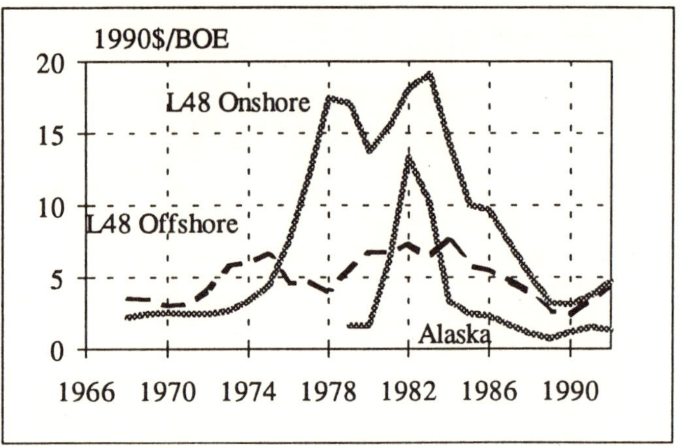

Figure 6.   U.S. Oil Drilling Costs

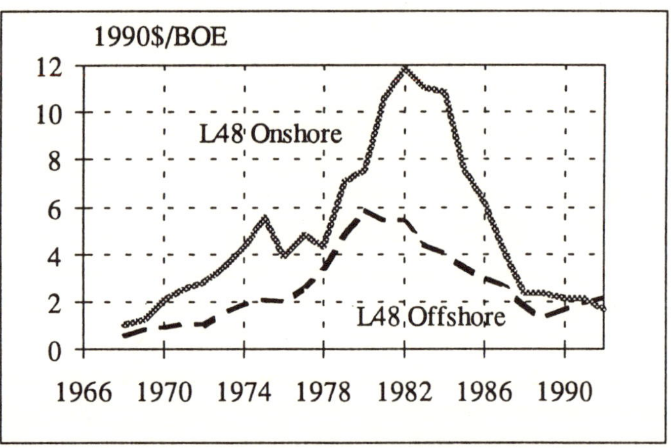

Figure 7.   U.S. Gas Drilling Costs

drilling costs per unit of reserves added were approaching levels typical of the early 1970s.

On both the basis of drilling cost and production cost,[7] the high cost area of the United States has generally been the Lower 48 onshore. While average well costs are typically an order of magnitude or more greater for Alaska and the offshore, the greater productivity of the younger resource base in those areas more than offsets such costs. Consequently, the popular impression that the costs of finding and producing OCS and Alaskan oil are higher is incorrect in any meaningful sense.[8] It has been the case for most of the period that the Lower 48 onshore area was the highest cost segment of the domestic resource base.

Taxation and Regulation

The price and cost data presented earlier, however, only partially capture the market environment faced by the industry in this historical period. That is, a large number of primarily federal policies served to distort the prices and costs actually being faced by the domestic industry. Import controls, frequent changes in the corporate income tax, multi-tiered price controls on oil, regulated gas prices, and the Crude Oil Windfall Profit Tax, all served to distort the structure of marginal revenues and marginal costs faced by the industry in this period, sometimes favorably, other times unfavorably, but often in ways which could be expected to significantly and systematically affect industry behavior in choosing both the level of production from existing reserves and the level of investment in new reserves.

Neither the world price of oil nor the domestic wellhead value of petroleum resources adequately capture the marginal revenues faced by domestic producers in this period. For crude oil, domestic marginal revenues never approached the level of world crude oil prices experienced in the early 1980s. Not only were domestic marginal revenues held well below world prices from 1974 until 1985, by price controls and the Crude Oil Windfall Profit Tax, those controls and taxes set up multiple tiers which discriminated among categories of the domestic resource base. Consequently, the marginal revenues derived from domestic production varied by location and age of the property being produced. In fact, the marginal revenue associated with the least favored production category, that of conventional non-stripper production from Lower 48 onshore properties already in production prior to 1972, was by 1978 (in real terms) no higher than it had been in 1966 (see Figure 8).

The decontrol of oil prices beginning in 1979 only partially addressed these issues. While wellhead values in the Lower 48 rose to nearly the price of imports, marginal net revenues peaked at less

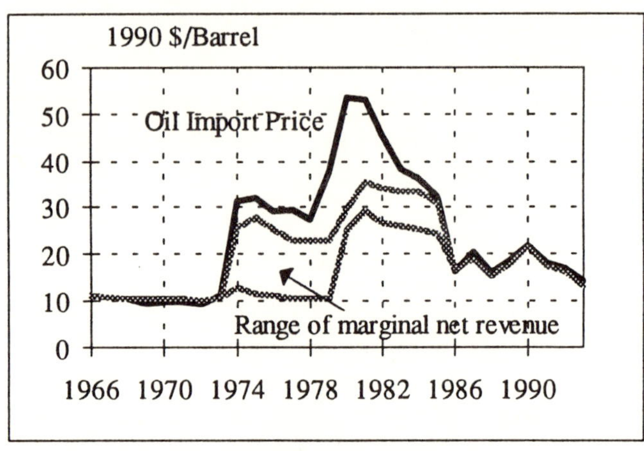

Figure 8.   Lower 48 Marginal Oil Revenues,[9] 1966-1993

than $35 in 1981, more than $15 per barrel less than the price of imports, due to the substitution of a Crude Oil Windfall Profits Tax (in the form of a multi-tiered excise tax) for the prior system of price controls. The marginal revenues for the least favored categories of oil under the WPT (again principally "old" oil from the Lower 48 onshore) never reached above $28 per barrel, and by 1985, prior to the collapse of world oil prices, were about $24 per barrel.

Apart from the Lower 48 states, marginal revenues from Alaskan North Slope production, which began in 1977, also never approached the level of import prices, although generally for different reasons only partially attributable to government policy. From 1980 until 1985, the Windfall Profits Tax both reduced net marginal revenues from the North Slope and created a range of revenues by discriminating between Sadlerochit formation production (taxed more heavily) and other North Slope production. Principally, however, the difference between Alaskan marginal revenues and world oil prices was attributable to the transportation cost which reduced the wellhead value of such oil delivered to the West Coast and the Gulf Coast. Even here, however, the magnitude of the difference was partially attributable to two federal policies which artificially inflated the transportation cost associated with such crude—namely the federal ban on export of Alaskan crude oil, which necessitated the marketing of such oil in the United States rather than more easily accessible markets in Asia, combined with the Jones Act, which (because the oil was bound for interstate commerce) necessitated the transport of such oil in higher cost U.S.-built tankers.

As seen in Figure 9, marginal revenues associated with crude oil production from the Alaskan North Slope peaked in 1981 at about $22 per barrel for oil from the Sadlerochit formation, and about $9 higher for other North Slope production, falling to about $20 in 1985. The 1986 international price collapse was especially severe for Alaskan marginal revenues, due to the largely fixed transportation charge. In 1986, marginal revenues (equal to wellhead value at that time insofar as the WPT was no longer binding) reached less than $7.50 per barrel. By 1990 such revenues had recovered to about $15 per barrel.

An even longer history of regulatory intervention served to keep natural gas prices also well below the BTU equivalent value of imported oil, as seen in Figure 10. Natural gas wellhead values peaked at less than $20 per BOE in 1982, and by 1990 had fallen to only about half the equivalent oil price.

However, the effects of government tax and regulatory policy were not limited to distortions of marginal revenues from oil and gas production during the historical period. Frequent changes in the provisions of the corporate income tax also affected both the value of after-tax net revenue which could be expected from a unit of such

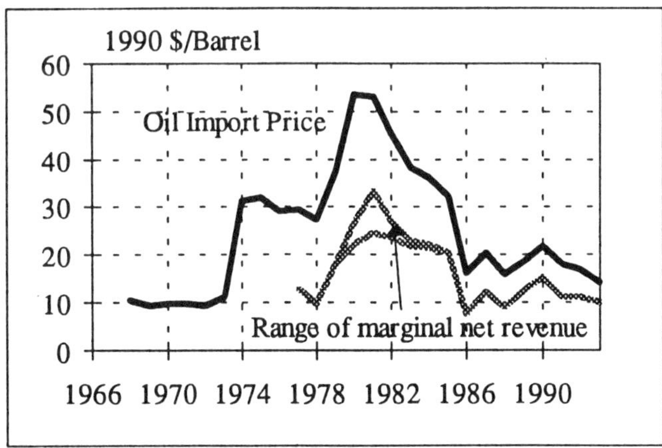

Figure 9. Alaska Marginal Oil Revenues

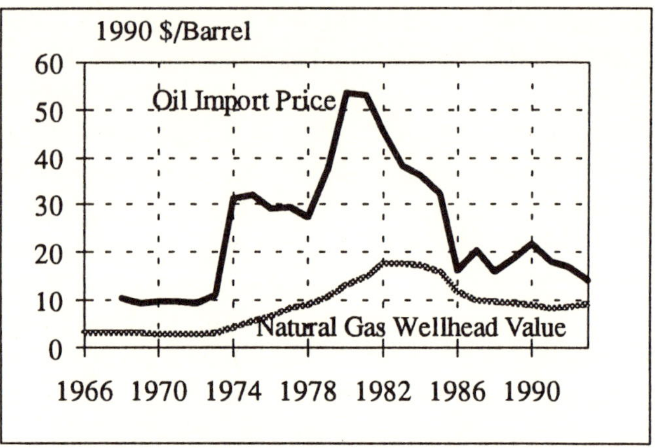

Figure 10.   U.S. Natural Gas Marginal Rekvenue

production, as well as the after-tax cost of capital investments in new reserves. As a consequence, such provisions affected the prospective profitability of investments in new reserves. Table 1 lists the major provisions of the corporate income tax affecting the petroleum industry over this period.

B.   Domestic Supply Activity

As the market environment changed from 1966 to 1993, the level of domestic supply activity responded. This activity consisted both of production and of drilling activity to replace the resources produced.

Production and Reserves

Prior to 1966, nearly 78 billion barrels of crude oil and over 56 billion barrels of oil equivalent of natural gas had been produced domestically in the United States, nearly 98% from the Lower 48 onshore. Over the next 28 years, nearly as much crude oil and more than twice as much natural gas was produced in the United States, as shown in Table 2. There were major shifts in the regional composition of supply during the period. Oil production shifted increasingly toward Alaska. New production from Alaska halted the

Table 1. Summary of Major Features of the Corporate Income Tax

		Majors	*Independents*
Corporate	1959-63:	52%	52%
Tax Rate	1964:	50%	50%
	1965:67:	48%	48%
	1968-69:	52.8%	52.8%
	1970:	49.2%	49.2%
	1971-78:	48%	48%
	1979-86:	46%	46%
	Post-1986:	34%	34%
Statutory	1959-69:	Maximum 27.5% of revenue	Maximum 27.5% of revenue
Depletion	1970-74:	Maximum 22% of revenue	Maximum 22% of revenue
Allowance	1975-83:	none	Max 22% of revenuefor 1000 b/d
	Post-1983:	none	Max 15% of revenue for 1000 b/d
Investment	Pre-1962	none	none
Tax	1962-65:	7% of tangible investment	7% of tangible investment
Credit	1966:	5.4% of tangible investment	5.4% of tangible investment
	1967:	5.7% of tangible investment	5.7% of tangible investment
	1968:	7% of tangible investment	7% of tangible investment
	1969:	2.1% of tangible investment	2.1% of tangible investment
	1970:	none	none
	1971:	5.3% of tangible invetment	5.3% of tangible investment
	1972-74:	7% of tangible investment	7% of tangible investment
	1975-85:	10% of tangible invetment	10% of tangible investment
	Post-1985:	none	none
Treatment	Pre-1983:	Fully expensed	Fully Expensed
of IDC's	1983-84:	80% expensed, 20% capitalized	Fully Expensed
	Post-84:	70% expensed, 30% capitalized	Fully Expensed

decline in U.S. crude production from 1977 until 1982. Gas production shifted increasingly offshore. By 1993, offshore production accounted for over a quarter of U.S. gas production.

In the Lower 48 onshore, which still accounted for over three fourths of total petroleum production during the period, there was a marked shift in production toward gas. In the years prior to 1966, gas production had amounted to less than three fourths that of oil, while in the past three years, gas production from the onshore Lower 48 states exceeded oil production by over 50%. This trend became especially apparent after 1985, as oil production resumed its decline and gas production stabilized.

There was a large drawdown of domestic petroleum reserves during the period, as seen in Table 3. Domestic petroleum reserves fell by

Table 2. History of U.S. Petroleum Production through 1990[10]

Production	Pre-1966	1966-70	1971-75	1976-80	1981-85	1986-90	1991-93	1966-93	Thru 1993
Crude Oil (Bil Bbl):	77.7	15.5	15.7	14.6	15.0	13.9	7.3	81.9	159.8
Lower 48 Onshore	75.6	13.8	13.4	11.3	10.0	8.5	4.4	61.4	137.0
Lower 48 Offshore	22.1	1.5	1.9	1.5	1.8	1.7	1.0	9.5	11.7
Alaska	0.0	0.3	0.4	1.8	3.2	3.5	1.9	10.9	11.1
Natural Gas (Bill BOE):	56.3	19.9	21.9	19.5	17.9	17.4	11.0	107.6	163.9
Lower 48 Onshore	55.2	17.4	17.8	14.6	12.8	12.3	7.9	83.0	138.2
Lower 48 Offshore	1.0	2.4	3.9	4.7	4.9	4.7	2.8	23.4	24.5
Alaska	0.0	0.1	0.1	0.2	0.3	0.44	0.3	1.3	1.3
Total (Bil BOE):	134.0	35.5	37.4	34.1	32.9	31.4	18.3	189.7	323.7
Lower 48 Onshore	130.8	31.2	31.3	25.9	22.8	21.1	12.3	144.6	275.4
Lower 48 Offshore	3.1	4.0	5.8	6.2	6.7	6.4	3.9	32.9	36.1
Alaska	0.1	0.3	0.5	2.0	3.4	3.8	2.1	12.2	12.3

Table 3.   U.S. Petroleum Reserves,[11] 1966-1994 (billions of BOE)

	1966	1970	1975	1980	1985	1990	1994
Crude Oil:							
United States	31.4	29.6	34.2	29.8	28.5	26.5	23.0
Lower 48 Onshore	29.2	26.4	21.9	18.0	17.5	16.5	14.1
Lower 48 Offshore	2.0	2.8	2.2	2.9	3.4	3.3	2.9
Alaska	0.2	0.4	10.1	8.9	7.6	6.7	6.0
Natural Gas:							
United States	57.0	55.0	46.8	40.6	40.7	35.4	34.2
Lower 48 Onshore	51.7	47.1	34.2	26.9	27.1	26.8	26.6
Lower 48 Offshore	4.9	7.0	6.9	8.0	7.5	6.8	5.6
Alaska	0.4	0.9	5.7	5.7	6.1	1.8	2.0
Total:							
United States	88.4	84.6	81.0	70.4	69.2	61.9	57.2
Lower 48 Onshore	80.9	73.5	56.1	44.9	44.6	43.3	40.7
Lower 48 Offshore	6.9	9.8	9.1	10.9	10.9	10.1	8.5
Alaska	0.6	1.3	15.8	14.6	13.7	8.5	8.0

over 31 billion barrels of oil equivalent during the period, with the decline in gas reserves constituting about three fourths of the total decline. As with production, there were significant regional shifts in the location of petroleum reserves during the period. With the Alaskan discovery booked in 1970, Alaska rose to nearly a quarter of domestic crude oil reserves, which peaked at nearly 40 billion barrels. However, after 1970, Alaskan reserves did not rise, and Lower 48 reserves continued to decline, at least until 1980.

After 1980, continued decline in overall reserves was attributable to continued deterioration of Alaskan reserves, which offset the stabilization of Lower 48 reserves. Lower 48 onshore crude oil reserves, which declined by nearly a third from 1966 until 1980, were virtually unchanged from 1980 through 1985. The turnaround in Lower 48 crude oil production in the first half of the 1980s reflected primarily increased intensity of use of the reserve base, not changes in the level of reserves themselves.

There were some similarities, and some differences, in the behavior of domestic oil and natural gas reserves over the period. First, both oil and gas reserves peaked at approximately the same time, and declined significantly over the period. Overall, gas reserves peaked at nearly 60 billion barrels of oil equivalent in the late 1960s before declining by about 26 billion barrels of oil equivalent by the end of

1993. Associated gas from the Alaskan Prudhoe Bay discovery booked in 1970 temporarily boosted domestic gas reserves, but, unlike oil, those reserves were eventually removed from the reserve base due to lack of transportation facilities. By the beginning of 1994, domestic gas reserves had fallen to about 34 billion barrels of oil equivalent, more than 40% below its peak level. Almost all of the decline in domestic gas reserves over the period occurred in the Lower 48 states, almost entirely between 1970 and 1978.

Reserve Replacement via Drilling Activity

Even a superficial examination of the data presented here makes it clear that the deterioration in reserve levels observed over the period is not simply the result of cumulative production. From 1966 through 1993, as was seen in Table 2, nearly 190 billion barrels of oil equivalent was produced from the domestic resource base, while reserves fell by only about 31 billion barrels. Consequently, about 84% of petroleum resources consumed over the period were replaced by new reserve additions made during the period.

As seen in Table 4, from the mid-nineteenth century until the beginning of 1966, over 109 billion barrels of oil and 113 billion barrels of oil equivalent of natural gas had been developed in the United States, over 95% in the Lower 48 onshore areas. Between 1966 and the end of 1993, another 73 billion barrels of oil and 85 billion barrels of oil equivalent of natural gas reserves had been added.

Over the period, the composition of these additions has changed somewhat, in two respects. First, there has been a somewhat greater concentration of gas resources in the total than had been true earlier. More significantly, there has been a marked shift in the regional distribution of these resources from the Lower 48 onshore to Alaska and the Lower 48 offshore. During the period from 1966 to 1993, such areas contributed about 22% of total reserve additions. Nonetheless, the most "mature" areas of the Lower 48 continued to be major contributors to the reserve accumulation process. Over 46 billion barrels of crude oil and over 58 billion barrels oil equivalent of natural gas reserves were added from the Lower 48 onshore areas since 1966.

These additions replaced nearly 90% of the oil and nearly 80% of the gas produced during the period, but the replacement rates were substantially lower in the 1970s, particularly in the Lower 48 onshore, where replacement fell to as low as 32% for gas and to less than 60%

Table 4. History of U.S. Reserve Accumulation

	Pre-1966	1966-70	1971-75	1976-80	1981-85	1986-90	1991-93	1966-93	Thru 1993
Gross Reserve Additions:									
Crude Oil (Bil Bbl):	109.1	23.2	9.3	11.7	13.6	11.5	4.0	73.3	182.4
Lower 48 Onshore	104.8	10.5	8.0	8.8	9.8	7.0	2.1	46.2	151.0
Lower 48 Offshore	4.1	2.4	1.0	2.4	2.3	1.6	0.8	10.5	14.6
Alaska	0.2	10.3	0.3	0.5	1.5	2.9	1.1	16.6	16.8
Natural Gas (Bil BOE):	113.2	20.4	9.7	14.6	17.8	12.9	9.6	85.0	198.2
Lower 48 Onshore	106.9	10.2	5.7	9.2	12.7	13.0	7.2	58.0	165.0
Lower 48 Offshore	5.9	5.0	3.7	5.0	4.5	3.9	2.0	24.1	30.0
Alaska	0.4	5.2	0.3	0.4	0.6	-4.0	0.4	2.8	3.2
Total (Bil BOE):	222.3	43.6	18.9	26.3	31.4	24.4	13.6	158.3	380.5
Lower 48 Onshore	211.7	20.7	13.7	18.0	22.5	20.0	9.3	104.2	316.0
Lower 48 Offshore	10.0	7.4	4.7	7.4	6.8˙	5.5	2.8	34.6	44.6
Alaska	0.6	15.5	0.5	0.9	2.1	-1.1	1.5	19.4	20.0
Replacement Rate:									
Crude Oil (%):	140.3	149.3	59.1	80.0	90.6	82.7	55.0	89.5	114.1
Lower 48 Onshore	138.6	76.3	59.6	77.8	98.1	82.0	47.9	75.2	110.2
Lower 48 Offshore	195.3	158.7	53.6	155.9	126.0	91.7	76.3	110.1	124.4
Alaska	500.0	3872.2	68.7	27.7	46.8	84.7	59.7	151.8	151.6
Natural Gas (%)	201.1	102.3	44.3	75.1	99.4	74.1	86.7	78.9	120.9
Lower 48 Onshore	193.7	58.5	31.9	63.3	99.4	105.3	90.8	70.0	119.4
Lower 48 Offshore	567.3	204.7	94.6	106.9	92.7	83.2	70.7	103.0	122.7
Alaska	757.4	945.5	226.0	194.4	1227.1	-107.5	136.8	221.7	240.9
Total (%)	165.9	122.9	50.5	77.2	95.4	78.0	74.0	83.4	117.5
Lower 48 Onshore	161.9	66.3	43.8	69.6	98.8	94.9	75.5	72.1	114.8
Lower 48 Offshore	318.6	187.1	81.4	119.0	101.8	85.5	72.2	105.0	123.6
Alaska	639.1	4828.7	110.3	44.3	60.3	-27.6	69.1	159.0	162.4

for oil from 1971 to 1975. Notably, however, the rates of replacement in the Lower 48 onshore recovered dramatically in the first half of the 1980s, when over 99% of gas production and over 98% of oil production was replaced with new reserve additions, suggesting stabilization of supply, which in fact was observed. In the last several years, however, replacement rates in the Lower 48 onshore have fallen sharply, particularly for oil. From 1991 to 1993, less than half of crude production in the Lower 48 was replaced by new reserve additions.

One possible factor in explaining the sharp drop in reserve replacement in the 1970s is the behavior of the costs of such replacement. The cost of adding reserves to the domestic petroleum resource base is principally the real drilling cost associated with an incremental barrel of petroleum reserve additions. As seen in Figure 11, this cost rose sharply in the late 1970s and early 1980s, but fell rapidly in the latter half of the 1980s. By 1990, this cost was approaching its 1970 level, where it has remained for the past several years.

Table 5 summarizes the composition of drilling cost during the period from 1966 to 1990. As seen in the table, there were massive declines in drilling productivity in the 1970s, attributable to sharp declines in both drilling rates per rig and finding rates per successful foot drilled. By 1985 drilling rates had more than recovered to their 1970 level, though finding rates had continued to decline. In the latter half of the 1980s, all components of productivity—drilling rates, success rates, and especially finding rates, rose as rig activity declined. As a result, by 1990 the cost of adding an incremental

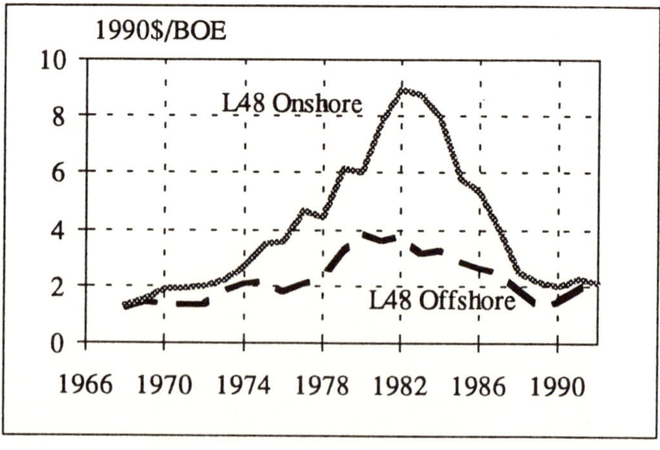

Figure 11.   U.S. Drilling Cost[15]

Table 5. Components of U.S. Lower 48 Drilling Costs, 1970-1990

		1970	1980	1985	1990	Average Annual Inccrease (%/Yr)			
						1970-80	1980-85	1985-90	1970-90
Lower 48 Onshore									
GRA Drilling Cost	(90 $/BOE)	1.89	6.02	5.82	1.98	12.3	-0.7	-19.4	0.2
Oil	(90 $/Bbl)	2.06	8.68	6.60	2.46	15.5	-5.3	-17.9	0.9
Gas	(90 $/BOE)	1.66	4.78	5.06	1.72	11.2	1.1	-19.4	0.2
Rig Cost	(mil 90$ / rig year)	7.2	12.2	15.3	12.3	5.4	4.7	-4.2	2.7
Rig Productivity	(mil BOE / rig year)	3.261	1.734	2.254	5.338	-6.1	5.4	18.8	2.5
Drilling Rate	('000 ft / rig year)	130	108	154	164	-17.0	51.4	1.3	1.1
Success Rate	(%)	55.1	66.7	67.9	69.3	21.0	3.9	0.4	1.2
Finding Rate	(BOE / successful foot)	45.4	24.0	21.6	47.0	-47.1	95.7	16.8	0.2
Oil	(Bbls / successful foot)	36.6	14.2	16.4	32.0	-61.3	125.5	14.4	-0.7
Gas	(BOE / successful foot)	67.8	35.5	31.2	63.0	-47.7	77.6	15.1	-0.4
Lower 48 Offshore									
GRA Drilling Cost	(90 $/BOE)	1.37	3.87	2.89	1.47	10.97	-5.68	-12.68	0.35
Oil	(90 $/Bbl)	2.40	4.22	3.86	1.84	5.81	-1.79	-13.80	-1.33
Gas	(90 $/BOE)	0.73	3.70	2.32	1.32	17.62	-8.94	-10.63	3.01
Rig Cost	(mil 90$ / rig year)	21	31	21	19	4.0	-7.0	-1.9	-0.3
Rig Productivity	(mil BOE / rig year)	13.0	6.8	6.3	11.4	-6.3	-1.4	12.4	-0.7
Drilling Rate	('000 ft / rig year)	104	59	66	63	-5.4	2.0	-0.7	-2.4
Success Rate	(%)	65	61	56	42	-0.8	-1.6	-5.4	-2.1
Finding Rate	(BOE / successful foot)	191	189	173	422	-0.1	-1.8	19.6	4.0
Oil	(Bbls / successful foot)	103	157	119	284	4.2	-5.3	18.9	5.2
Gas	(BOE / successful foot)	399.2	210.7	234.9	523.1	-6.2	2.2	17.4	1.4

barrel of petroleum reserves onshore in the Lower 48 states was only about 10 cents per barrel higher than it had been in 1970. Offshore, patterns were similar.

In summary, the past data indicates that there have been changes in the composition of drilling activity which are associated with the progressive development of the resource base. In particular, there has been a steady erosion in the share of activity devoted to exploration as opposed to development as potential exploratory targets have been progressively exhausted by past exploration or prohibited by policy constraints. Similarly, there has generally been an increase in the share of drilling activity devoted to the development of gas rather than oil resources.

However, the data provide no evidence of a steady upward progression in the cost of resource development in the United States with progressive depletion, even in the Lower 48 onshore areas. While the data point rather starkly to severe declines in productivity of drilling effort associated with rapid expansion in the rate of that effort, they also point out that these effects have been of minor long-term significance to resource development cost over the period. By 1990, at levels of activity comparable to those two decades earlier, the cost of adding a barrel of petroleum resources to the domestic reserve base was only slightly higher than it had been more than two decades earlier, despite the fact that an additional 144 billion barrels of oil equivalent had been developed from that resource base in the interim.

III.   LESSONS FROM THE PAST: DETERMINANTS OF U.S. PETROLEUM SUPPLY

The data presented here establish that the industry's market environment changed radically several times throughout the period, with enormous fluctuations in world prices, domestic resource costs, and government policy. Moreover, they establish that the industry has undergone major changes in the nature of its supply activity, changing the regional and resource composition of its production, and the level and composition of its efforts to replace the reserves depleted by such production. But the data and trends themselves do no more than suggest the ways in which changes in the market environment have been connected to the observed changes in industry behavior. This section attempts to examine, in a slightly more formal way, the nature of these empirical relationships, in order to provide a basis on which to assess future supply prospects.

A.   Alternate Theories of Supply

Of course, the data does not itself unambiguously identify a theory of supply upon which to base judgments of future domestic supply prospects and the effects of public policies on those prospects. To do so requires an interpretation of the data.

A fundamental anomaly in the domestic supply data that has plagued industry analysts since the early 1970s is the fact that supply grew steadily in an environment of stable or even declining world prices, but peaked and began to decline just as those world prices began rising. Clearly, current production was not simply an increasing function of current price alone. In particular, there are two complications. First is the dynamic nature of the industry. Supply today is largely determined by investments made five to ten years ago, as today's investment has implications far into the future. In harsh frontier areas, such lags between input and output are often even longer. Second, there is the notion of the exhaustibility of the resource, which needs to be incorporated into any plausible characterization of the supply process.

However, there are many possible characterizations of such "exhaustibility." Like the images created by the blind men describing the elephant, each from his particular perspective, as a tree or a rope, a variety of characterizations have sprung up to explain one or more of the anomalies described in the previous section. This section examines each of these principal characterizations of supply in light of this history, and presents some empirical relationships that capture the essence of the major trends observed over the recent past.

Supply as Depletion of a Fixed Stock

The simplest, and perhaps the most popularized, characterization of domestic petroleum supply activity is that of a process of depleting a largely fixed stock of proved reserves. In such a formulation, nature alone (or primarily) determines the amount of recoverable resource, and supply choices consist solely (or principally) of decisions regarding the rate at which to deplete this fixed stock. In its purest form, this is the characterization of supply from a fixed stock examined by Hotelling.[16] Reserves, in this view, are simply the remaining portion of this original endowment, and decrease monotonically with cumulative production. Moreover, the simplest formulation of the Hotelling model yields strict positive implications for the qualitatitive pattern of supply over time from these resources. In particular, producers will choose to supply production along an intertemporal path over which net profit rises at just the rate of interest, or in other terms, there is an unobserved "user cost" to the producer which represents the opportunity cost of foregone future sales attributable to current production from the fixed resource base. At constant prices and with rising marginal costs, this necessarily implies a pattern of declining production over time.

Empirical support for this simple view is provided by the fact that proved reserves have generally declined over the period, from about 90 billion barrels of oil equivalent in the late 1960s to less than 60 billion barrels at the beginning of 1994. Moreover, production rates have also fallen more or less in line with declining reserves, as was seen earlier. But even a slightly closer inspection of the data reveals that this popular characterization of the supply process as one of depleting a fixed stock at a declining rate is seriously at odds with the empirical evidence.

If the fixed stock view were accurate, the sum of cumulative production and proved reserves (what is generally termed ultimate recovery) would have been generally constant over time, and the observed reduction of roughly 30 billion barrels of proved reserves from 1966 until 1994 should be approximately equal to the amount produced over that period. In fact, over that period nearly 190 billion barrels of oil equivalent had been produced, more than six times the observed reduction in reserve levels over the period. As seen in Figure 12, the reason for this is that the estimate of ultimate recovery in any given year has by no means been constant over time. Rather, estimates of ultimate recovery have grown steadily throughout the period, rising by nearly 160 billion barrels of oil equivalent.

Reserve Replacement from Shrinking Target

A more sophisticated view of the supply process recognizes the possibility of reserve replenishment via discoveries and development, but characterizes such efforts as being inevitably subject to rapidly diminishing returns due to the well-known skewness of the field size

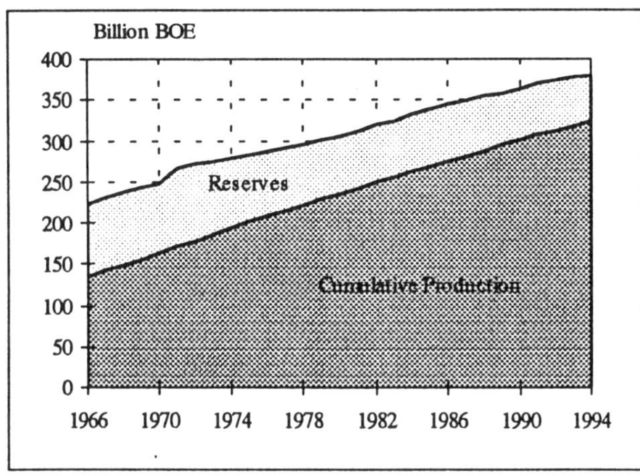

Figure 12. U.S. Ultimate Petroleum Recovery

distribution in any fixed geographic area, and the resultant tendency for the largest fields to be discovered first, leaving progressively smaller fields to be added by further discoveries and the reserve growth associated with those discoveries.

This approach, most notably associated with the work of Hubbert, but with many variations on the basic theme he provided, has been the most common approach used empirically to model domestic petroleum supply.[17] Generally, in this approach drilling uncovers fields of varying size, with the largest fields in a given area typically located first, progressively smaller fields located thereafter. Once discovered, a field's reserves "grow" with progressive development, at diminishing rates, converging toward a limit on its ultimately recoverable resources that may not be approached for 50 years or more from the date of discovery. The characteristics of this approach are twofold—the diminishing field size distribution leading to falling exploratory productivity, and the pattern of development fixed by a deterministic development schedule dependent on only the size of the initial discovery and the "age" of the discovery (years from the initial discovery date).

Prices and market conditions in such models may have significant impacts, but generally these are limited to the influence of price in affecting the level of drilling activity, which in turn affects discovery levels directly and the development of those discoveries in subsequent years. Generally, however, there is no mechanism by which a change in market conditions affects the development of incremental reserves *from discoveries made in years prior to the change.*

Such a formulation provides a convenient rationale for a distinction, made often in the economic literature, between "old" and "new" oil, with the price responsiveness of supply largely concentrated in the latter, while supply from the former is largely fixed by historical choices. Such a formulation provided a rationale for the multi-tiered structure of price controls and excise taxes in the United States from 1974 until 1985. Such tiers were structured in part to minimize the adverse supply effects associated with affecting income transfers (in the price control program) or raising revenues (in the case of the Windfall Profits Tax) by placing the largest burden on that portion of the resource base thought to be the least responsive to price. In principle, such an approach would not have been wholly without merit on grounds of economic efficiency, *if in fact this were a plausible characterization of the supply process.* The popularity of this characterization stems from both its appeal to a widely known empirical fact—the declining size of discoveries over time, and the broad consistency of its predictions for declining drilling productivity with the data observed through the mid-1980s.

As seen in Figure 13, the heyday of exploration in the United States was already long past well before 1966. Using data on ultimate recovery of crude oil by date of field discovery,[18] at the end of 1988 the distribution of cumulative reserve additions (ultimate recovery) was as shown. Discoveries (measured as ultimate recovery, not as reserves booked in the year of discovery) peaked at nearly 40 billion barrels in the 1930s, over four times the level discovered in the 1970s, despite sharply higher drilling levels in the 1970s.

Superficially, this appears to imply the inevitability of declining drilling productivity, such as that observed from the early 1970s until the mid-1980s. That is, the declining quantities of ultimate recovery added from post-1940 discoveries would dramatically drive down discovery rates per foot drilled even if drilling activity remained constant in later years (rather than increase).

However, on closer inspection it is clear that such an interpretation requires either a serious misinterpretation of the data or an unconventional notion of productivity. That is, the data presented here represents *the cumulative additions to reserves from fields*

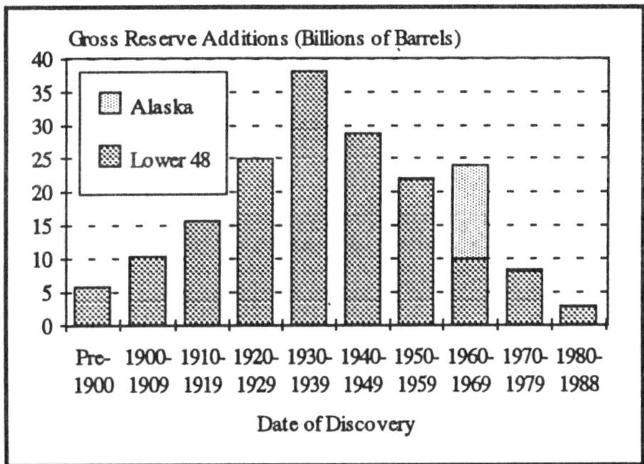

Figure 13. Ultimate Recovery by Discovery Year[19]

discovered in the years indicated, from the date of discovery until the date of the estimate, not the reserves added in the year of the discovery. Attributing this cumulative total to the drilling of the discovery well, rather than to the cumulative drilling effort which added the reserves over time, does give rise to an inevitable decline in the size of reserves attributable to those wells, but this is a peculiar, and certainly a nonconventional concept of productivity. A more conventional notion of productivity would assign new reserves to the drilling responsible for their addition. This is the definition used in the data presented earlier in the paper, which showed a fall, and more recently a dramatic rise, in productivity.

In fact, reserves from a particular discovery are typically added by drilling activity completed over a period of many years. Over time, the "fixed" stock of potential exploratory targets shrinks, and average field size may decline. However, the remaining known oil in place, the target of potential new development drilling, will not typically shrink. Estimated reserves from past discoveries "grow" as this development drilling is completed. Despite the fact that older fields tend to grow much more slowly than younger ones, the fact that older fields are so much larger than younger ones causes even their slower growth to dominate the more rapid growth from the smaller young fields. As seen in Figure 14, in the 22 years from 1967 through 1988,

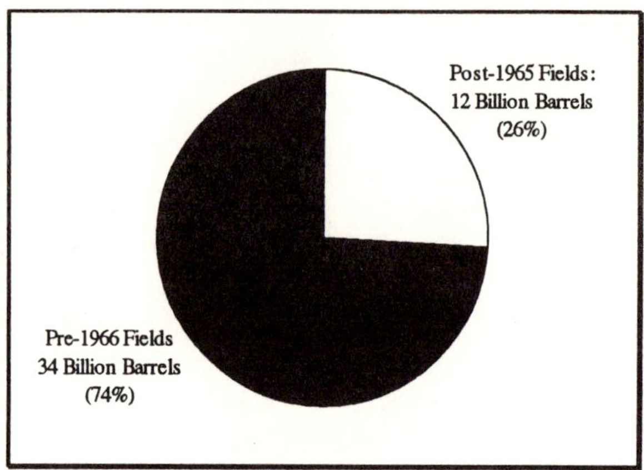

Figure 14. Cumulative Additions to
Crude Oil Reserves, Lower 48, 1967-1988

nearly three fourths of total reserve additions were from fields discovered prior to 1966.

Moreover, of these pre-1966 fields, it was not the youngest that provided the bulk of reserve additions. Rather, the overwhelming share of additions from these older fields originated in the oldest of those fields. Figure 15 presents the distribution of gross reserve additions made in the 1967-1988 period by date of field discovery. More than half of the gross reserve additions of crude oil made in the Lower 48 states between 1967 and 1988 originated in fields discovered prior to 1940, and nearly a quarter originated from fields discovered prior to 1920.

Finally, the data point clearly to the fact that the rates of reserve growth from these older fields do not decline monotonically with the age of the field, as is widely assumed in the literature on reserve growth from older fields.[20] As seen in Figure 16, the pattern of U.S. reserve additions in the Lower 48 states was dominated by the behavior of additions from the fields discovered prior to 1966, which declined steadily from the late 1960s through the late 1970s, but then revived through the first half of the 1980s. Contrary to the popular interpretation that any supply response to price would be limited to "new" oil, the data suggests quite the opposite. The rate of reserve additions from the older fields moved quite vigorously in response

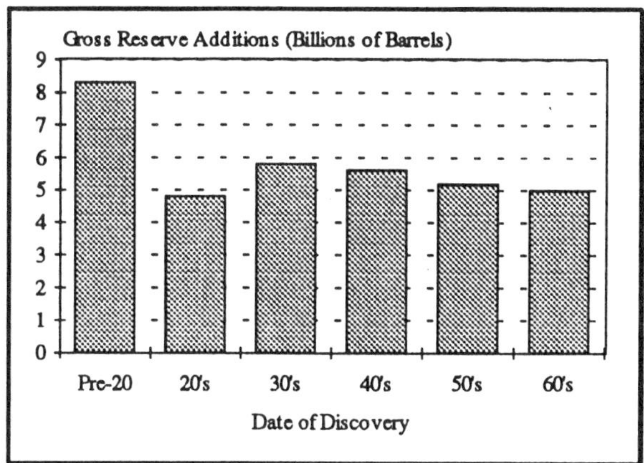

Figure 15. Lower 48 Cumulative Oil
Reserve Additions from "Old" Fields, 1967-88

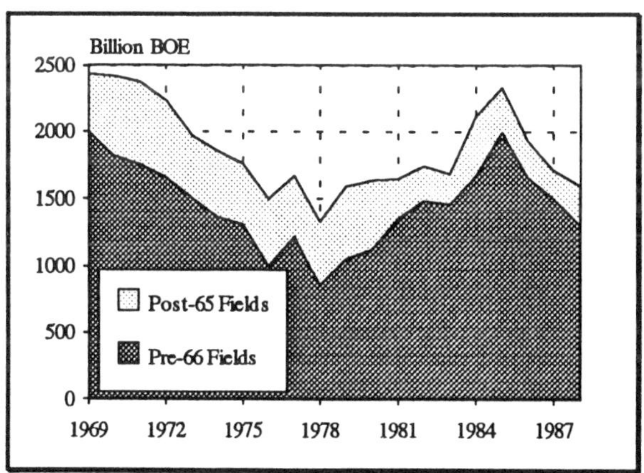

Figure 16. Crude Oil Gross Reserve Additons,[22] Lower 48

to market changes, while that from the newer fields was relatively
unaffected.[21]

The explanation for this behavior is simply that in the aggregate,
exploration and development proceed simultaneously, not
sequentially. Fields do not have a fixed life determined by the initial
size of reserves found by the discovery well or even some fixed

multiple of that discovery size. Rather, a discovery opens access to a stock of oil in place which is typically many times larger than the initial reserves added in the year of discovery. Typically, subsequent reserve additions only approach one third or less of this resource stock during primary and secondary recovery from the field, leaving a large inventory of resources in place which potentially can be eventually converted to reserves. Given that the magnitude of this inventory is so much larger than that associated with smaller discoveries in newer fields, small changes in the rates of recovery attributable to either improved price expectations or technology can dominate the reserve additions generated by recent discoveries. This importance of older fields is the mark of a mature petroleum province such as the Lower 48—particularly the onshore Lower 48—because most fields are known, the source of reserve additions becomes increasingly development rather than exploration activity, and continued reserve growth depends increasingly on the ability to increase the intensity of use of the older fields.

However, a fixed characterization of supply generally misses these features of the mature area, and as a consequence is inconsistent with both the productivity data presented earlier and the data on reserve growth shown here. The data also suggest strongly that policies informed by such a characterization, such as the multi-tiered price controls of the 1970s, were misguided. The direction of such controls imposed on the Lower 48 was to favor exploration of new areas rather than development of the old. Given the state of maturity of the domestic resource base, this was precisely the wrong policy direction, as it served to divert drilling activity systematically away from the areas of greatest resource potential (old fields) by favoring areas of much smaller resource significance (new fields). In doing so, such controls may themselves have played a significant role in the rapid deterioration of drilling productivity witnessed during the 1970s.

Scarcity and Resource Cost

Each of these characterizations of supply appear to be seriously at odds with one or more key pieces of empirical evidence drawn from the observed supply behavior of the recent past. Such problems have led to the more eclectic characterization of the supply process by Adelman (1990,1991), in which resource scarcity is not deterministically defined by reserve estimates or some broader volumetric measure of recoverable resources, nor by costs which inexorably rise with depletion. Rather, in his view the only reliable indicator of scarcity is rising observed costs of replacing current production, and such increases are neither inexorable nor inevitable, as in the previously examined charcterizations, but rather are the outcome of a tug of war between technological progress and diminishing returns. In this view, the rapidly changing features of the market environment described earlier, along with geology and technological change, are central determinants of supply behavior.

B. An Empirical Supply Model

The data here suggest the ambiguous tug of war between diminishing returns and technical progress that Adelman has suggested.[23] Of the three approaches discussed, his is the only one sufficiently flexible to allow for the observed patterns in the data of costs which both rise and fall with cumulative development.

In this section, a sequence of models is presented, starting with a simple benchmark describing the levels of investment and production that would originate in a market free of the distortions of taxes and regulation, then extending this framework to progressively include more realistic features capturing the essence of the taxation and regulatory distortions actually present during the historical period, culminating finally in an empirically plausible representation of U.S. domestic supply with which to assess future domestic supply prospects.

Efficient Levels of Production and Investment

In the absence of taxation and/or regulation, the levels of investment and production chosen in the market would represent an efficient program of development. Consequently, examination of the determinants of output and investment in such a hypothetical setting, while not realistic, provides a useful hypothetical reference point for examining the effects of taxation and/or regulation.

Investment in petroleum reserve additions is motivated by the *expected* prospective net income generated by production from the incremental reserves associated with such investment. Because the production from an investment in a barrel of reserves added today is spread over time, its value in situ is not simply the current wellhead price, but a fraction of that price, depending on the expected production path over time and the discount rate.

In particular, if a barrel of new reserves added today can be expected to be producing at an exponentially declining rate, λ, over time, so that at some point s years from today, the amount produced from a barrel of reserves added at time t is

$$q(t + s) = \lambda e^{-\lambda s} \tag{1}$$

At an expected price of P, then, the expected present value of the intertemporal stream of revenues from an incremental barrel of new reserves, v, can be written as[24]

$$v(t) = \int_t^T P(1-\delta)\, \lambda e^{-\lambda s} e^{-rs} ds \tag{2}$$

where T is the terminal date of production from the reserve, δ is the proportion of price consumed by extraction costs, and r is the discount rate. Expression (2) may be approximated over the producing life of the incremental reserve unit by the expression

$$v(t) = (1-\delta)(\frac{\lambda}{\lambda + r})P \tag{3}$$

That is, the value of revenues from an incremental barrel of reserves will be some fraction of the current price, which will decline as the rate of discount increases (since the future production from those reserves will be valued less the higher the discount rate).

If the marginal cost of adding reserves rises with the level of reserves added, $G[t]$, and the level of cumulative reserve additions, $Z[t]$, but falls over time with technical progress, then

$$c_G(t) = c_G[t,\ G(t),\ Z(t)] \tag{4}$$

where
$$\begin{aligned} c_{Gt} &\leq 0 \\ c_{GG} &\geq 0 \\ c_{GZ} &\geq 0 \end{aligned}$$

Investment in new reserves will expand to the point, $G^*(t)$, that the expected value of an incremental barrel of such reserves just equals the cost of adding that incremental unit of reserves, or, as shown in Figure 17,

$$v(t) = c_G[t,\ G(t), Z(t)] \tag{5}$$

Effects of Regulation and Taxation

The effects of regulation on the level of investment, or at least the types of regulation typically imposed in the 1970s, which held wellhead prices far below world levels, was fairly clear. It depressed $v(t)$, and thereby reduced the level of investment which would otherwise have occured.[25]

The effect of the corporate income tax, however, is more complex. First, there are more levers available in the tax (the rate, the qualifications for expensing versus capitalization, eligibility for and rate of the investment tax credit, depreciation rules, etc.). Second, the mechanisms at work are more subtle, insofar as they may affect either the structure of revenues associated with a prospective investment, after tax costs, or (typically) both.

With the corporate income tax at rate u, for instance, the after-tax value of a barrel of prospective reserves, $v'(t)$, is

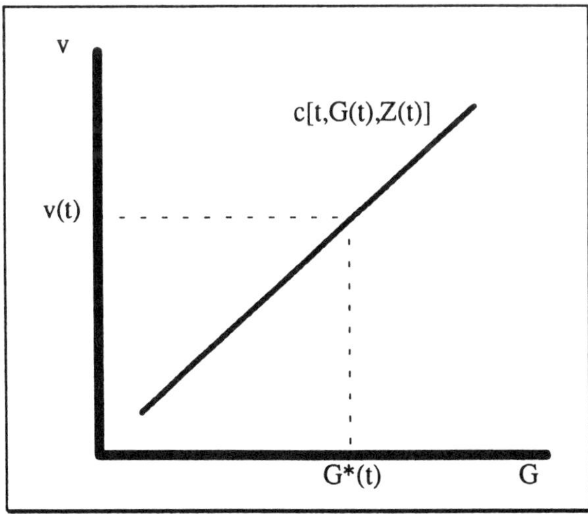

Figure 17.   Optimal Investment in Reserve Additions

$$v'(t) = (1-u)(1-\delta)(\frac{\lambda}{\lambda + r})P = (1-u)v(t) \qquad (6)$$

But the corporate tax also affects after-tax costs. That is, since costs are deductible, the relation between pre-tax cost, c, and post-tax cost, c', is given by

$$c'_G(t) = \left[1 - u\left[\gamma + D(1-\gamma)\right]\right]c_G(t) \qquad (7)$$

where γ is the share of capital cost fully expensible, and D is the present value of a dollar of capitalized costs, which depends on the discount rate and depreciation rules.

First, it should be recognized that the distortionary effect of the corporate tax on investments in new reserves stems entirely from the treatment of capital costs as less than fully expensible. If all capital costs were fully expensible ($\gamma = 1$) in equation (7), the profitability of prospective investments would be unaffected by the rate of the corporate tax, since both sides of equation (5) are multiplied by the same proportion ($1-u$).

That is, such a tax would be on pure profits. Total profits would of course be lower the higher the tax rate, but the tax would reduce prospective revenue by the same proportion as deductibility reduced current capital cost, so that the prospective profitability of the investment, would be unaffected. Such a tax is said to be neutral insofar as it would not change the marginal private incentives to invest in new capacity. As seen in Figure 18, with full expensing of capital cost, the corporate tax lowers pre-tax v to v', but lowers pre-tax cost c by the same amount. As a consequence, the resulting level of investment in new reserves, G^*, is precisely the same with the tax as without the tax.

Of course, the actual corporate tax does not allow for full expensing of capital cost, and as a consequence the tax does distort investment choices in a manner which, in and of itself, unambiguously discourages investment. This occurs as a consequence of the fact that the tax reduces prospective revenues by proportionately more than after-tax capital costs. As seen in Figure 18, the level of investment with the tax with partial expensing, G', is unambiguously lower than without the tax. The disincentive to investment will increase with the tax rate, the percentage of cost which is capitalized, the discount rate, and the time over which the capitalized portion of cost must be recovered.

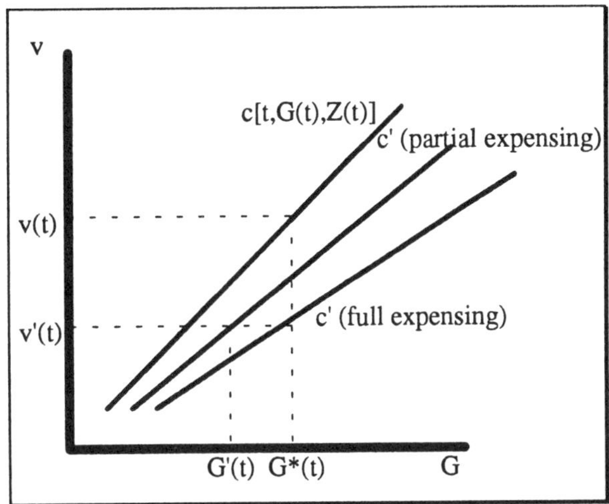

Figure 18. Effects of Corporate Income Tax on Investment

However, there are two features of the corporate tax which have in the past served to offset, at least partially, these disincentive effects. First, the depletion allowance acted to raise v' and the investment tax credit served to reduce c'. In principle, large enough allowances and credits could fully correct, or even more than fully correct, the disincentives associated with partial expensing (leading to overinvestment). However, even when such corrective measures were in effect, they were offset by two other factors which themselves worked to discourage investment: namely severance taxes and the Crude Oil Windfall Profits Tax.[26]

In practice, the addition of these other factors changed the relationships between post-tax revenues and price and post- and pre-tax costs to

$$v'(t) = [(1-roy-sev-wpt-\delta)(1-u) + u(dep)]\left[\frac{\lambda}{(\lambda + r)}\right]P \qquad (8)$$

where roy = royalty rate
        sev = severance tax rate
        wpt = WPT rate (oil only)
        dep = statutory depletion rate

and

$$c'_G(t) = [1-u[\lambda + D(1-\lambda)]-itc]c_G(t) \qquad (9)$$

where itc = investment tax credit rate. In summary, the net effect of severance taxes, the WPT, and the corporate tax all worked to lower v' below v. At the same time, deductibility served to reduce c' below c, but the limitations on deductibility worked to keep the reduction proportionately less than that associated with revenues. The depletion allowance and the investment tax credit worked to offset these disincentives, leaving the net effect of taxes on distorting the level of investment in petroleum reserves an empirical question.

However, the concepts presented here suggest such an empirical measure. That is, if the ratio between pre- and post-tax costs is written as

$$f(t) = [1-u[\lambda + D(1-\lambda)]-itc] \qquad (10)$$

then

$$m'(t) = \frac{v'(t)}{f(t)} \qquad (11)$$

can be interpreted as the marginal effective post-tax price of a barrel of reserve additions at time t, whereas the pre-tax marginal effective price at time t is

$$m(t) = v(t) \qquad (12)$$

Thus, the distortionary influence of taxes and regulations on the value of domestic reserve additions may be measured as the ratio of $m'(t)$, computed using actual prices and taxes, to $m(t)$ computed using unregulated prices and tax rates set to zero. An index of actual $m'(t)$ was computed at actual wellhead values and tax rates. Then, a corresponding pre-tax, pre-regulation index, $m(t)$, was computed on the assumption that all wellhead values were unregulated and all tax rates were zero. A ratio of unity would indicate the absence of distortionary effects of regulation and taxation. A value greater than 1 indicates that the net effect of government policy is to stimulate investment, while a value less than unity indicates that the distortions

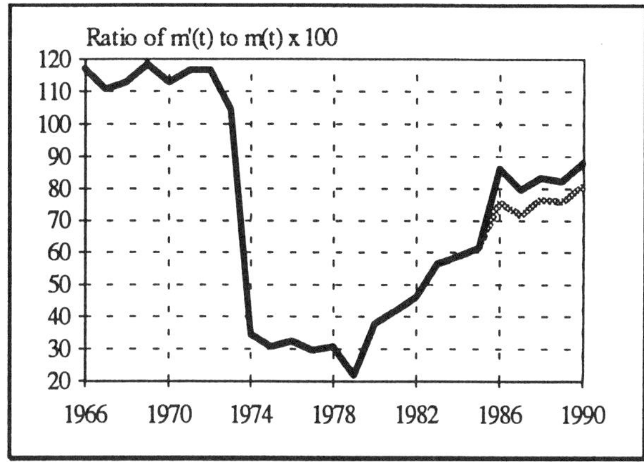

Figure 19. Index of Policy Distortions of Domestic Lower 48 Oil Reserve Values (Ratio of M'(t) to m(t))

work to discourage investment. The ratio of these indices for the Lower 48 during the historical period are shown in Figure 19.

It appears from the calculation that the net effect of taxation was stimulative at the margin to oil investment prior to 1974 (principally due to statutory depletion), but by the late 1980s had become a disincentive, reducing reserve values from 10%-25% below undistorted levels.[27] In the interim, however, the combined effects of regulation (prior to 1980) and the WPT (from 1980 to 1985), provided a massive disincentive to investment in domestic reserves, by preventing the value of domestic in situ resources as much as 80% below levels consistent with those which would have occurred at unregulated prices.

The Determinants of Domestic Supply

The decision to invest in incremental domestic reserves is not solely a function of the marginal after-tax value of reserves, $m'(t)$, however. Rather, it is a comparison of $m'(t)$ with the costs associated with such investment that is the determining factor, as suggested previously. These costs will depend on the resource base, the state of technology, and the market for drilling services. Because each of these factors often vary considerably by region, the U.S. model is specified as consisting of three submodels corresponding to three regions—the Lower 48 onshore, the Lower 48 offshore, and Alaska.

In each region, the core of the model is found in a set of three equations, representing the production function for cumulative gross reserve additions as a function of cumulative drilling activity, the demand for drilling services, and the supply of drilling services.

Reserve Production Functions

In each region there has been a strong relationship between the level of cumulative reserves added over time, $Z(t)$, and the cumulative footage drilled in search of those reserves, $H(t)$. Consequently, a relationship was specified of the form

$$Z_t(t) = \alpha_{1i} e^{\Theta_{1t}} H_{1T}(t)^{\beta_{1t}} \tag{13}$$

where $Z(t)$ is cumulative reserves added (since 1966) and $H(t)$ is cumulative footage drilled (since 1966), and Θ_1 is an autonomous rate of change in drilling productivity, attributable to technical progress,[28] and the subscript i refers to the region (Lower 48 onshore, Lower 48 offshore, or Alaska). Figure 20 presents the actual and fitted values for both oil and gas in the largest region, the Lower 48 onshore.[29]

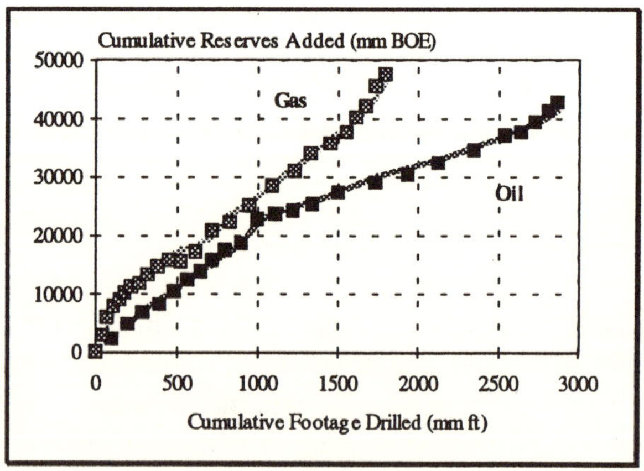

Figure 20. Cumulative Reserves Added as A Function of Cumulative Footage Drilled, Lower 48 Onshore

The estimated parameters for the production function relationship of equation (13) are shown in Table 6.[30] These fitted relationships for oil and gas in the Lower 48 onshore region are shown by the solid lines in Figure 20.

Two features of these relationships stand out. First, in most cases there is strong evidence of diminishing marginal returns to drilling over the historical period. This shows up as β_1 coefficient values of less than unity. Nonetheless, there is little measurable effect of autonomous technical change in the production function estimated over the full historical period, as indicated by the zero values on most of the Θ_1's. However, as was seen previously, and is apparent in Figure 20, there is strong evidence of a more than offsetting effect of technical change in the past five years, as the marginal productivity of drilling has returned to rates roughly resembling those of the late 1960s. The problem is largely the lack of sufficient information in the dataset to meaningfully distinguish with confidence between the competing effects of technological progress and the diminishing returns associated with depletion.[31]

The relationships in Table 6 determine the level of reserves which will be added for a given level of current drilling activity in each region. It should be noted that the derivative of equation (13) with respect to time equals the level of gross reserve additions at time t, or

Table 6. Estimated Production Function Parameters (t-statistics shown in parentheses)[32]

Region		α_1	Θ_1	β_1	R^2
L48 Onshore	Oil	5.840 (17.2)	0	0.6001 (13.2)	.99
	Gas	4.86 (15.7)	0	0.7816 (16.9)	.99
L48 Offshore	Oil	-22.45 (-1.9)	.0136 (2.2)	0.9179 (18.9)	.99
	Gas	6.509 (231)	0	0.718 (97.0)	.99
Alaska	Oil	5.45 (60.6)	0	0.336 (8.7)	.99
	Gas	7.596 (66.3)	0	0.996 (12.3)	.97

$$\left(\frac{\partial Z_i(t)}{\partial t}\right) = G_i(t) = \Theta_{1i} Z_i(t) + \beta_{1i} \frac{Z_i(t)}{H_i(t)} F_i(t) \tag{13'}$$

where footage drilled, $F(t)$, is by definition

$$F_i(t) = \left(\frac{\partial H_i(t)}{\partial t}\right) \tag{13''}$$

Consequently, the level of reserves added in any period for any particular level of drilling is given by equation (13'). Such additions will depend on the state of resource depletion, Z, technology, and the level of drilling activity occurring.

Determinants of Drilling Activity

Drilling demand in each region depends on the structure of prices, costs, taxes, and the productivity of drilling activity. In particular, producers are expected to choose the level of drilling activity such that the marginal value of the last foot drilled (in terms of the value of reserves added) just equals the cost of drilling that foot. This simple condition, for the production technology of (13), implies that

$$v_i'(t)\beta_{1i}\left[\frac{Z_i(t)}{H_i(t)}\right] = f_i(t) w_i(t) \tag{14}$$

where $w(t)$ is the cost per foot drilled in the market for drilling services. Since $w(t)$ rises with the level of drilling activity,

$$w_i(t) = \alpha_{2i} e^{\Theta_{2i}t} F_i(t)^{i/\beta_{2i}} \tag{15}$$

where Θ_{2i} is the rate of autonomous change in drilling cost[33] over time, and β_{2i} is the elasticity of the supply of drilling services. The level of drilling services occurring at time t is the solution to equations (14) and (15), which may be written in reduced form as

$$F_i(t) = A_i e^{B_i t}\left[\frac{Z_i(t)}{H_i(t)} m_i'(t)\right]^{\beta_{2i}}, \tag{16}$$

where $\quad A_i = \left[\dfrac{\beta_{1i}}{\alpha_{2i}}\right]^{\beta_{2i}}$

$$B_i = -\beta_{2i}\Theta_{2i}$$

The estimated parameters are shown in Table 7.[34,35]

Equations (13′) and (16) define the supply curve of gross reserve additions in each region as a function of prices, taxes, and technical change.

Production and Reserve Accumulation

Reserves, $R(t)$, are accumulated via reserve additions and depleted by production, according to the identity

$$R_i(t) = R_i(t-1) + G_i(t-1) - Q_i(t-) \tag{17}$$

where $Q(t)$ is current production.

Production is determined as an exogenous fraction of reserves, or

$$Q_i(t) = p_i^r(t)R_i(t) \tag{18}$$

Table 7. Estimated Drilling Demand Parameters
(t-statistics shown in parentheses)

Region		$log(A)$	β_2	R^2
L48	Oil	2.44	0.465	.80
Onshore		(3.0)	(3.0)	
	Gas	1.82	0.58	.88
		(2.4)	(3.4)	
L48	Oil	-2.10	0.263	.81
Offshore		(-1.8)	(2.4)	
	Gas	-1.97	0.560	.72
		(-2.5)	(4.5)	
Alaska	Oil	-0.56	0.359	.76
		(-0.4)	(1.8)	
	Gas	-8.57	0.645	.25
		(-2.6)	(1.7)	

where $pr(t)$ is an exogenously specified production to reserve ratio.[36] Cumulative production at time t, $X(t)$, is given by

$$X_i(t) = X_i(t - 1) + Q_i(t) \qquad (19)$$

and ultimate recovery at any time t, $Z(t)$, is simply the sum of all prior gross reserve additions (which equals the sum of cumulative production and current proved reserves), or

$$Z_i(t) = Z_i(t - 1) + G_i(t) \qquad (20)$$

Together, equations (13′), (16), and (18), along with identities (13″), (17), (19), and (20) comprise the full supply model in each of the three regions.

IV. PROSPECTS FOR U.S. SUPPLY

In order to assess the prospects for domestic supply over the next two decades in light of the major uncertainties in each of the three areas discussed here, a set of scenarios was developed in which the principal determinants of supply are allowed to vary over a plausible range along each of three dimensions: world price, the rate of technical progress in reducing drilling cost, and the government supply policies adopted over the period. These scenarios were evaluated using a U.S. supply model calibrated to the historical data presented earlier.[37]

A.   A Reference Scenario

As a first step in assessing future prospects, the model was simulated over the period to 2010 under an assumed reference case scenario. In this scenario, crude oil prices remain constant in real terms at about $20 per barrel (in 1990 dollars) through 2010, and gas prices remain constant in real terms at approximately half this level. This is not meant to be a forecast, but simply a reference point. As such, it has two useful characteristics. First, it is a reasonably close approximation to conditions of the recent past (since 1986). Second, it is reasonably close to the average wellhead values experienced over the historical period examined earlier, so that the behavior simulated by the model over the forecast period is well within the range of historical experience over which the model has been calibrated. This facilitates meaningful comparisons of the simulated supply behavior over the next 20 years with that experienced over the past 20 years.

Production

In this reference scenario, U.S. crude oil production falls by about 3 million barrels per day by the year 2010, as seen in Figure 21.

As seen in Table 8, about half of the decline in crude oil production is from the Lower 48 onshore, while the other half is principally Alaska.

The overall decline expected over the 20 years from 1990 to 2010 is expected to be more severe than that of the 20 years from 1970 to 1990, despite the fact that the highest cost portion of the resource base, the Lower 48 onshore, is expected to decline more slowly in the future than in the past (due principally to improved drilling economics). This accentuates the importance of Alaska and the OCS, the lowest cost portions of the ' domestic resource base, which historically provided an offset to onshore Lower 48 decline, but are instead expected to aggravate the decline in the future, due to artificial constraints on land access which prevail in this scenario.

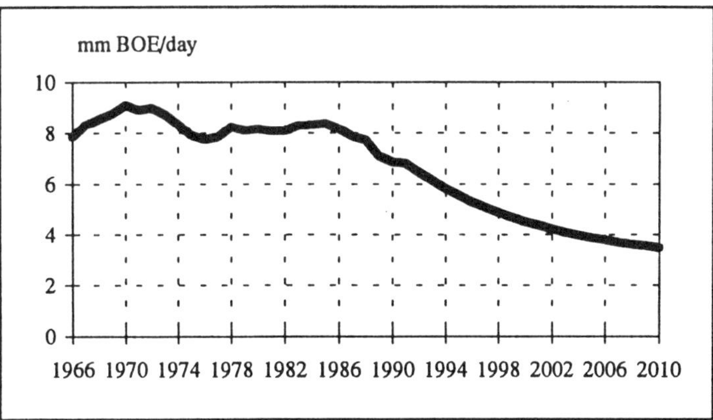

Figure 21. U.S. Crude Oil Production, 1966-2010

Table 8.   U.S. Petroleum Supply, "Reference" Scenario (mmboe/day)

	1970	1990	2010	Change 70-90	Change 90-10
Crude Oil					
U.S.	9.1	6.9	3.5	-2.2	-3.4
L48 Onshore	7.8	4.2	1.9	-3.6	-2.3
L48 Offshore	1.0	0.8	1.0	-0.2	0.2
Alaska	0.2	1.8	0.6	1.6	-1.2
Natural Gas					
U.S.	12.2	9.9	5.8	-2.3	-4.1
L48 Onshore	10.2	6.9	4.1	-3.3	-2.8
L48 Offshore	1.9	2.8	1.4	0.9	-1.4
Alaska	0.1	0.2	0.3	0.1	0.1
BOE					
U.S.	21.3	16.8	9.3	-4.5	-7.5
L48 Onshore	18	11.1	6.0	-6.9	-5.1
L48 Offshore	2.9	3.6	2.4	0.7	-2.2
Alaska	0.3	2	0.9	1.7	-1.1

Reserve Replacement

The declines in production in this scenario occur because at the prices and tax rates included in this scenario, investment in new reserves continues to fall short of production. As seen in Table 9, over 60 billion barrels of oil and gas reserves are added during the period, but over 90 billion barrels are produced during the same period.

This rate of reserve replacement (about 67%) is slightly below the 75% replacement experienced during the past 20-year period. As seen in Table 10, crude oil reserves fall by nearly 13 billion barrels over the 20-year period, while natural gas reserves fall by about the same amount, a slightly greater drawdown of reserves than occurred in the past 20 years.

B.   Effects of Price

As was emphasized earlier, this scenario does not represent a forecast, but a reference point. As such, it is useful to examine how this outlook changes with alternative price assumptions. In particular, two alternatives were examined, corresponding to oil prices of $25 (25% above the previous case), and $15 (25% below the previous case and gas prices following the same proportional

Table 9. U.S. Reserve Replacement, History and Reference Scenario

	Cumulative Production (Billion BOE)		Cumulative Reserve Addns. (Billion BOE)		Replacement Rate (%)	
	1971-1990	1991-2010	1971-1990	1991-2010	1971-1990	1991-2010
Crude Oil						
U.S.	59.1	35.5	46.3	21.4	78.3	60.1
Lower 48 Onshore	43.2	20.9	33.7	10.8	78.0	51.7
Lower 48 Offshore	7.0	6.6	7.5	7.4	107.1	112.1
Alaska	8.8	8.0	5.2	3.2	59.1	40.0
Natural Gas						
U.S.	76.7	54.9	55	39.3	71.7	71.6
Lower 48 Onshore	57.6	39.4	40.6	26.9	70.5	68.2
Lower 48 Offshore	18.2	13.7	17.1	10.2	94.0	74.5
Alaska	0.9	1.7	-2.7	2.3	-300.0	135.3
BOE						
U.S.	135.8	90.4	101.3	60.8	74.6	67.3
Lower 48 Onshore	100.8	60.3	74.3	37.7	73.7	62.5
Lower 48 Offshore	25.2	20.3	24.6	17.6	97.6	86.7
Alaska	9.7	9.7	2.5	5.6	25.8	57.7

Table 10.   U.S. Petroleum Reserves (billions of BOE)

	Reserves			*Change*	
	1970	*1990*	*2010*	*70-90*	*90-10*
Crude Oil					
U.S.	29.6	26.5	13.6	-3.1	-12.9
L48 Onshore	26.4	16.5	7.3	-9.9	-9.2
L48 Offshore	2.8	3.3	4.1	0.5	0.7
Alaska	0.4	6.7	2.3	6.3	-4.4
Natural Gas					
U.S.	54.9	35.4	21.9	-19.5	-13.4
L48 Onshore	47.1	26.8	16.1	-20.3	-10.7
L48 Offshore	7	6.8	3.4	-0.2	-3.4
Alaska	0.9	1.8	2.4	0.9	0.6
BOE					
U.S.	84.5	61.9	35.5	-22.6	-26.4
L48 Onshore	73.5	43.3	23.4	-30.2	-19.9
L48 Offshore	9.8	10.1	7.5	0.3	-2.6
Alaska	1.3	8.5	4.7	7.2	-3.8

variation). Figure 22 presents the sensitivity of the 20-year outlook for petroleum production[38] to these alternative price assumptions.

Table 11 presents the details of the sensitivity analysis. The most notable feature of these scenarios is the fact that even at the highest of the range of prices considered, there are substantial declines in supply.

C.   Effects of Government Policy

Finally, the sensitivity of supply prospects to changes in government policy is examined. The principal reason for the persistent tendency for supply to decline over time in these scenarios is the fact that the most attractive frontiers of the domestic resource base, Alaska and the OCS, have been systematically restricted from further oil and gas development. On the other hand, these are not the only restrictions on domestic resource development under consideration. A number of regulatory constraints have been suggested in recent years with the potential of further aggravating the demise of the domestic resource base.

Consequently, this section examines the effects on the domestic supply outlook of two variants on the policy environment. In the first case, the Arctic National Wildlife Refuge (ANWR) is opened to development. In the second, a number of new environmental

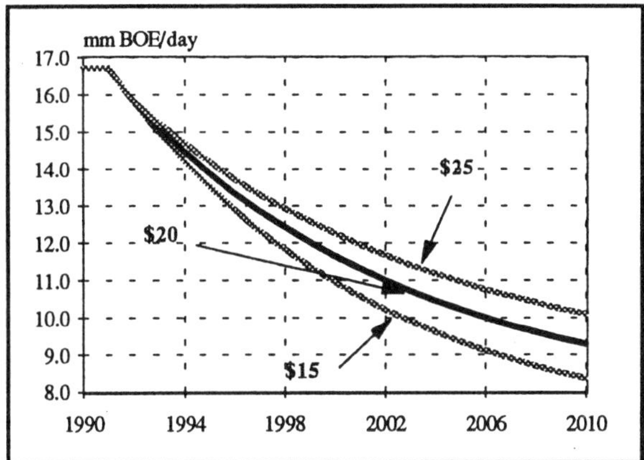

Figure 22.   U.S. Petroleum Production, Alternate Price Scenarios

Table 11.   Sensitivity of Supply Outlook to Price mmboe/d

| | 2010 Production | | |
	$15	$20	$25
Crude Oil			
U.S.	3.2	3.5	3.7
Lower 48 Onshore	1.7	1.9	2.0
Lower 48 Offshore	1.0	1.0	1.1
Alaska	0.5	0.6	0.6
Natural Gas			
U.S.	5.1	5.8	6.4
Lower 48 Onshore	3.7	4.1	4.5
Lower 48 Offshore	1.2	1.4	1.5
Alaska	0.2	0.3	0.3
BOE			
U.S.	8.4	9.3	10.1
Lower 48 Onshore	5.4	6.0	6.5
Lower 48 Offshore	2.2	2.4	2.6
Alaska	0.7	0.9	1.0

restrictions are imposed on the traditional areas of drilling in the Lower 48 onshore, corresponding roughly to the categorization of a number of materials associated with exploration and production operations as hazardous wastes similar to those contained in Subtitle C of the Resources Conservation and Recovery Act (RCRA).[39]

The upper line in Figure 23 presents the domestic oil supply outlook under the assumption that 9.2 billion barrels of oil are

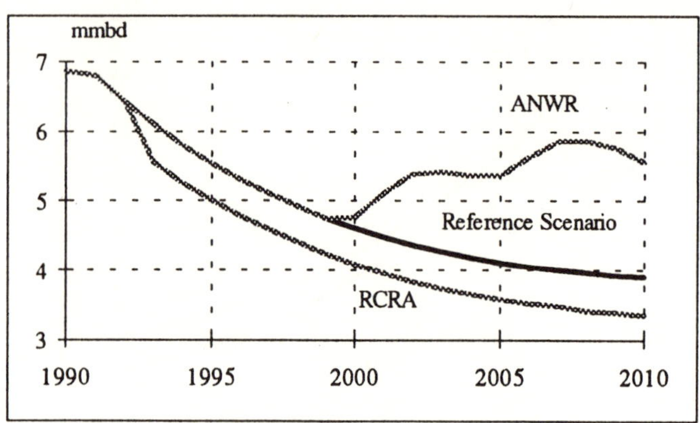

Figure 23.   Effects of Government
Policy on Domestic Oil Supply Outlook

discovered within the ANWR coastal plain.[40] It is apparent from the figure that ANWR alone offers the potential for offsetting as much as two thirds of the decline expected in the "status quo" scenario. The bottom line in the figure corresponds to the outlook with tightened RCRA regulation beginning in 1992. By 2010 there is more than a 2 mmbd difference in supply between the supply enhancement scenario including ANWR and the supply restriction scenario including tightened RCRA regulation.

V.   POLICY IMPLICATIONS AND ISSUES

The analysis presented here carries a mixed message for U.S. energy policy.

On one hand, there is little evidence to support the simplistic interpretation of supply as either the depletion of a fixed reserve stock or an encounter with inexorably rising replacement costs. Furthermore, there is little to support the view of the imminent demise of the domestic industry seen by some forecasters. Forecasts of the halving of domestic supply within the decade foreseen by some forecasters appear unduly pessimistic. On the other hand, the outlook for domestic supply is not good. A continuation of existing market conditions and existing policies can be expected to produce a shrinking domestic upstream industry between now and the year 2010.

Moreover, the implications of this review and outlook for government policy are quite different from the implications drawn from the two traditional interpretations of supply mentioned above. That is, if supply were drawn from a largely fixed reserve base, or if the cost of reserve replacement rose inexorably, any policies designed to enhance domestic supply would be either futile or at best prone to inefficiency. However, the interpretation presented here implies quite the opposite.

That is, the depletion effect (diminishing returns to drilling activity) observed in the forecast is by no means uncontrollable. In the past, it has been controlled or arrested by two factors—movement of exploration to new frontier areas, such as Alaska and the OCS, and technological progress in reversing such cumulative effects in traditional producing areas, such as the Lower 48 onshore. In the future, government policy combined with a rapidly changing external environment threatens to hinder both factors.

In terms of movement to new frontiers, most such movement domestically is sharply restricted by government policy, not natural or economic constraints. Such restrictions of domestic investment to the highest cost portions of the domestic resource base (the Lower 48 onshore) make domestic investment uncompetitive with a multitude of foreign supply opportunities which have in recent years opened up in a score of countries throughout the world.

Moreover, in terms of sustaining the technical progress necessary to offset diminishing returns to drilling in the Lower 48 onshore, these limitations offer to threaten the complementary roles traditionally played by the international majors and independents in developing the domestic resource base. Traditionally, the majors have been the source of the bulk of industry research and development, which has diffused through the domestic industry by the concurrent involvement of majors and independents in development of the domestic resource base. As the domestic prospects attractive to major firms are progressively placed off limits, while international opportunities abound,[41] this traditional diffusion mechanism for technical change is seriously threatened.

For both reasons, the prospects for stability of domestic petroleum supply are not particularly good. Given the prospect of rising demand, this supply outlook does portend a future of growing U.S. import dependence. However, it does not imply that the rate of future growth is determined exclusively by geology and the progressive exhaustion of domestic resources. Rather, it suggests that the degree of future import dependence is highly controllable, insofar as the principal reason for the pessimism in the supply outlook is largely a matter of policy choice rather than fundamental resource scarcity.

NOTES

1. From the early years of the petroleum industry in the mid-nineteenth century, until after World War II, there were periodic episodes of official concern that the exhaustion of the domestic resource base was imminent. Each of these incidents was followed by a surge of new supply which made the predictions often appear ridiculous, sometimes only a few years following their publication. After World War II, these pessimistic assessments began to turn in the other direction, with assessments that domestic supply could continue rising for many years. By the early 1960s, however, M. King Hubbert, in a series of papers, offered a prediction that domestic supply was in fact imminent, with the peak less than a decade away. While initially ridiculed, his prediction turned out to be accurate, leading to a series of official downward revisions of domestic resource potential.

2. Moreover, DOE was by no means alone in this assessment. A study of world oil markets in 1980 and 1981 conducted by the Stanford Energy Modeling Forum (EMF6) contained estimates of such supply by ten prominent energy forecasting models. All estimated a decline in U.S. supply between 1980 and 1985, from as little as 300,000 b/d to as much as 1.6 mmbd. See Energy Modeling Forum (1981).

3. See Cleveland and Kaufmann (1991) for one exposition of this view, within the context of a hybrid model allowing for economic influences on the Hubbert constraints.

4. This is the reference case scenario presented by DOE (1994), in which real crude oil price (in 1992 $) rises from $18 in 1992 to $21 in 2000 and $28 in 2010.

5. See Stanford Energy Modeling Forum (EMF) (1991).

6. The ten models used in the EMF11 exercise, identified by abbreviation in Figure 5, were as follows:
PB University of Pennsylvania/Boston University
FD Federal Reserve Bank-Dallas
DF Decision Focus, Inc.
H1,4 Harvard Oil Market Simulation Model(s)
CE Canadian Energy Research Institute
DG Dermot Gately, New York University
OM US DOE, EIA, Oil Market Simulation Model
IP International Petroleum Exchange, MIT
ET Alan Manne, Stanford University

7. Cost is measured as the three-year moving average of drilling costs per barrel of oil equivalent (BOE) of reserves added.

8. Of course, the cost per foot or per well is far higher in either Alaska or the OCS, but the productivity of the effort in terms of BOE's produced per well or foot more than offsets these differences.

9. Marginal net revenue is represented as wellhead value net of WPT. The top boundary of the envelope represents the marginal revenues corresponding to the highest level of controlled prices and the lowest level of WPT rates (generally newly discovered oil), while the bottom boundary of the envelope represents that corresponding to the lowest level of controlled prices and the highest WPT rates (generally production from old fields). This is a simplification of the regulatory structure in place during the period, but generally captures the structure of marginal revenues faced by the bulk of Lower 48 production.

10. Natural gas includes dry gas and natural gas liquids.

11. Expressed as of January 1 of each year indicated in the table.

12. Natural gas is defined here to include dry gas plus natural gas liquids.

13. Total through 1990 may differ from the sum of components due to 1977 revisions of reserve data by DOE from previous data prepared by API. Total through 1990 includes DOE 1977 revisions, but reserve additions by year for the 1976-1980 period do not.

14. Replacement rate is the proportion of production during the period indicated that has been replaced by new reserves added during that period.

15. Costs are reported here as the three-year moving average of drilling costs incurred per barrel of reserves added. Drilling costs from Joint Association Survey. Reserves from API (pre-1977), EIA.

16. See Hotelling (1931).

17. See, for instance, U.S. Department of Energy (1991), USGS (1971, 1990), Oak Ridge National Laboratory (1989, 1990), Cleveland and Kaufman (1991), among others. An exposition of Hubbert's work is given in Hubbert (1962).

18. This data was compiled by API from 1966 until 1979, and has recently been updated by the U.S. Department of Energy for the years 1977 until 1988. The data presented here is that of API through 1979, and that of DOE for 1980 to 1988.

19. This is ultimate recovery of crude oil by discovery year as estimated in 1988. See DOE (op. cit.). Ultimate recovery is the sum of all reserves added up through 1988 (equal to the sum of reserves plus cumulative production at year end 1988).

20. See, for instance, Root (1981), in which reserve growth is estimated to grow steadily over time, at a declining rate, toward a level ultimately approaching about seven times the initially estimated discovery. The U.S. DOE (1991) updates Root's work, but still assumes monotonic growth at declining rates, ultimately reaching about ten times the initial estimate of the discovery.

21. The relatively low responsiveness of new field gross reserve additions is more pronounced than is apparent here, due to the presence of multi-tiered price controls and the WPT during much of this period. Fields with discovery dates as old as 1965 and earlier were generally among those treated least favorably by such controls, and witnessed relatively smaller price changes than those of the newer fields.

22. Expressed as a three-year moving average.

23. Nonetheless, this is not strictly consistent with the approach suggested by Adelman (1994). In the formulation here, there is no distinction made between exploration and development investment, or between discoveries and other reserve additions. Adelman dismisses the inclusion of exploration investment in the replacement cost, insofar as exploration yields information, not reserve additions. An alternative specification more consistent with this notion would include all

reserve additions as a function of development activity alone. Future development of this model will explore such a specification.

24. See Adelman (1990, 1991, 1992) for a discussion of this formulation.

25. This may be a great oversimplification, however. The fact that price controls did not apply uniformly, but were applied differentially across segments of the resource base, may have had serious consequences for the productivity of domestic drilling activity. That is, by diverting activity away from old fields toward newer discoveries with far smaller resource potential, while simultaneously raising the costs of development (via the drilling services market) the controls themselves may have been a major source of the temporary collapse in the productivity of drilling activity in the 1970s. This prospect is beyond the scope of the current paper, but will be investigated more fully in a separate study.

26. And, while not included explicitly here, since 1986 the Alternative Minimum Tax also works to discourage investment by introducing a possibility that a larger portion of incremental capital must be capitalized than would be the case under the normal tax. The structure and applicability of the AMT has changed several times since 1986 already, and further changes are included in recent legislation now before Congress.

27. The range of values shown after 1986 reflects the uncertainty introduced by the Alternative Minimum Tax. The lower bound is computed under the assumption that *no* capital expenditures can be expensed. The upper bound is computed for rules applicable to the normal tax.

28. This represents an autonomous increase in the effectiveness of drilling at adding reserves. In terms of the data presented earlier, this is the sum of the rates of autonomous increase in success rates and finding rates. Improvements in seismic technology and/or the effectiveness of drilling technology to "capture" reserves (such as horizontal drilling) are the types of change included here.

29. The estimated relationships included a dummy variable equal to 1 in the years 1966 to 1976, reflecting the fact that the reserve accumulation data in those years originated with the API, while in later years it is from EIA.

30. The Alaskan production functions each include a dummy variable. In the case of oil, the dummy represents years before the Prudhoe discovery, in the case of gas it represents years in which Prudhoe gas reserves were carried by DOE as part of U.S. proved reserves.

31. Where Θ was estimated in the equation, it was typically insignificant. However, its inclusion generally caused a large drop in both β and its associated t statistic, suggesting that insofar as both technical change and depletion move simultaneously, it is impossible to statistically separate the two effects solely on the basis of the data used here.

32. Where OLS estimates of the parameters indicated the presence of serial correlation, a first order autocorrelation correction was applied. See Appendix to Porter (1992) for details of this estimation.

33. Specifically, in terms used previously, this is the autonomous decrease in costs attributable to increasing drilling rates per rig year. It measures factors which reduce the cost of drilling holes in the ground (stronger bits, for example) rather than the effectiveness of those holes.

34.   Where OLS estimates indicated serial correlation, a first order autocorrelation correction was applied.

35.   Again, it must be noted that there were no statistically significant technical change terms that could be identified with the available data. However, again this cannot be taken as indicative of no significant technical change occurring, but rather as indicative of an inability to statistically distinguish such an effect with the available data.

36.   This is a shortcoming of the current model specification, insofar as it precludes a short-term supply response to price which is evident in the historical data. Endogenizing the production reserve ratio will be an aim of future model development.

37.   See Porter (1992) for model description.

38.   Petroleum shown in Figure 22 includes both oil and gas.

39.   See Gruy (1991) for a detailed description of the scenaios developed to analyze this alternative. In this particular case, the scenario is represented by an initial loss of reserves equal to 4 billion boe onshore due to shutdown and revisions associated with initial compliance, followed by a permanent increase of $7/foot in incremental onshore drilling costs.

40.   For a detailed description of the ANWR development scenario behind these numbers, see WEFA (1990).

41.   See Randol (1991), and Sowell (1993) for descriptions of the motivation and extent of the exodus of the petroleum industry from the United States.

REFERENCES

Adelman, M. 1992. "Finding and Development Costs in the United States, 1945-1986." In *Advances in the Economics of Energy and Resources* (volume 7) edited by John R. Moroney. Greenwich, CT: JAI Press.

Adelman, M. 1990. "Mineral Depletion, with Special Reference to Petroleum." *Review of Economics and Statistics* (February): 217-230.

Adelman, M. et al. 1991. "User Cost in Oil Production." *Resources and Energy* 13.

Adelman, M. 1994. "Economic Thoughts on Sustainable Development." Paper presented at Texas A&M University, Colloquium on Energy Use and Sustainable Economic Growth, College Station, Texas, November.

American Petroleum Institute. *Reserves of Crude Oil, Natural Gas Liquids, and Natural Gas in the United States and Canada.* Washington, DC. Annual until 1979.

American Petroleum Institute. *Survey of Oil and Gas Expenditures.* Washington, DC. Annual since 1983.

American Petroleum Institute. 1985. *Well Completions and Footage Drilled in the United States, 1970-82.* Washington, DC.

Cleveland, C., and R. Kaufmann. 1991. "Forecasting Ultimate Oil Recovery and Its Rate of Production: Incorporating Economic Forces into the Models of M. King Hubbert." *Energy Journal* 12 (2).

Energy Modeling Forum. 1981. "World Oil." EMF Report 6, Stanford University.

Energy Modeling Forum. 1991. "EMF 11: International Oil Demand and Supply." Stanford University, April.

Gruy Engineering Corp. 1991. "Estimates of RCRA reauthorization Economic Impacts on the Petroleum Extraction Industry." July 20.

Hotelling, H. 1931. "The Economics of Exhaustible Resources." *Journal of Political Economy* 39.

Hubbert, M.K. 1962. "Energy Resources." *National Academy of Sciences* Publication 1000-D.

Oak Ridge National Laboratory. 1989. "Replacement Cost Integration Program: Model Description." Report to DOE, March.

Porter, E. 1992. "U.S. Petroleum Supply: History, Prospects, and Policy Issues." American Petroleum Institute, Research Study Number 64, August.

Randol, W.L. 1991. "Assessing the Domestic Operations of International Oil Companies: Explaining the Exodus of Capital." First Boston, Equity Research Report, September 5.

Root, D. 1981. "Estimation of Inferred Plus Indicated Reserves for the United States." In *U.S. Geological Survey Circular 860*, edited by Dalton et al.

Sowell, E. 1993. "Trends in the Geographic Allocation of Upstream Capital and Exploration Expenditures by Leading Companies." American Petroleum Institute, Policy Analysis Department, January.

U.S. Department of Commerce, Bureau of the Census. *Annual Survey of Oil and Gas*. Annual 1973 to 1982.

U.S. Department of Energy. *U.S. Crude Oil, Natural Gas, and Natural Gas Liquids Reserves*. Washington, DC. Annual since 1977.

U.S. Department of Energy. 1991. *U.S. Oil and Gas Reserves by Year of Field Discovery*. Washington, DC, August.

U.S. Department of Energy, Energy Information Administration. 1994. *Annual Energy Outlook*. Washington, DC.

WEFA. 1990. *The Economic Impact of ANWR Development*. Bala Cynwyd, PA.

COMMENTARY

J. Bryan Maggard

I. SUMMARY

The thesis of this paper is that the current decline of U.S. petroleum production rates is not primarily determined by resource constraints. Instead, the rate of petroleum production decline is very sensitive to market considerations and U.S. governmental policy decisions. The author illustrates this through the use of a detailed econometric forecasting model of U.S. petroleum supply.

The effects of market considerations are demonstrated by deviations from a scenario in which crude oil prices remain constant at the 1990 value of approximately \$20/STB (in 1990 dollars). Under the constant price scenario, U.S. petroleum production rate is expected to fall approximately 7.5 MMBOE/D by the year 2010. Under the assumption that real crude oil prices increase by 25% to \$25/STB, the model predicts only a 6.6 MMBOE/D decrease in petroleum production rate. However, under the assumptions that real crude oil prices drop by 25% to \$15/STB the predicted decrease in U.S. petroleum production rate is approximately 8.3 MMBOE/D by the year 2010.

Advances in the Economics of Energy and Resources, Volume 9, pages 163-167.

Two examples showing the effects of U.S. governmental policy decisions on U.S. oil supply are presented. The constant price scenario mentioned, predicts a decrease in U.S. oil supply of 3 MMSTB/D by the year 2010. The first policy scenario considers the effect of classification of many materials associated with petroleum exploration and production as hazardous waste under RCRA. Under this increased regulation, the decline in U.S. oil supply is predicted to be 3.5 MMSTB/D. The second policy scenario considers the opening of ANWR to petroleum exploration and production operations. Under the ANWR scenario, the decline in U.S. oil supply is expected to be only 1.2 MMSTB/D by the year 2010.

II.   COMMENTS ON EMPIRICAL SUPPLY MODEL—NOMINAL DECLINE RATE

An Empirical Supply Model is used in performing the predictions presented in this paper. As a petroleum engineer, I will make several comments regarding the equations used to calculate production rate from incrementally developed petroleum reserves.

The Empirical Supply Model uses an exponential decline equation to calculate production rates. The nominal exponential decline rate, λ, is calculated as the ratio of the initial production rate to the incremental reserves associated with a well(s). The advantage of using this particular value for nominal exponential decline rate is that the cumulative production per BOE of incremental reserves asymptotically approaches 1 BOE of produced reserves. The disadvantage of using this particular nominal exponential decline rate, λ, is that it does not reflect reality. Actual decline rates depend more on the total petroleum resource than on the quantity of reserves.

Consider a typical oil well undergoing exponential decline. Because all prior capital investment was made after performing marginal economic valuation, previous investment will not be considered in determining when the well will be abandoned. Instead, the well will be abandoned when the recurring operating expenses exceed the net revenue rate for the well. The production rate associated with abandonment of a well is commonly called the *Economic Limit* (q_{final}). This is the production rate at which it becomes uneconomic to continue production operations (i.e. NPV of continued production operations becomes negative).

Table 1. Error in λ for a Well with a True
Nominal Exponential Decline Rate of 0.5

$q_{initial}/q_{final}$	*Reserves, STB*	λ	%$_{Error}$
1000.	729770.	0.5005	0.11
100.	72320.	0.5051	1.1
10.	6575.	0.5556	11.0

As predicted by the "shrinking target" theory, newly discovered and developed petroleum reservoirs become smaller and of poorer quality. A symptom of this is that the average ratio of initial production rate to final production rate decreases. This causes the nominal exponential decline rate of the Empirical Supply Model, λ, to be too large, resulting in lower production rates used in the econometric model. Deviations in λ for a typical oil well with true nominal exponential decline rate of 0.5 are shown in Table 1. The worst case shown, with a production rate ratio ($q_{initial}/q_{final}$) of only 10, shows an error in λ of 11%. Such an oil well with a true nominal exponential decline rate of 0.5, an initial production rate of 10 STB/D and an Economic Limit of 1.0 STB/D has reserves of approximately 6.6MSTB, making it economically feasible in areas with low drilling costs. It should be noted that the majority of oil wells currently in operation in the United States produce less than 10. STB/D.

III. COMMENTS ON EMPIRICAL SUPPLY MODEL—HYPERBOLIC DECLINE OF GAS WELLS

An exponential decline is usually appropriate for estimating production rates from oil wells. However, production rates from gas wells usually decline much more slowly. With wellhead revenues from U.S. gas production exceeding the wellhead revenue from U.S. oil production in 1993, it is becoming more important to consider a realistic equation for calculation of production rate decline for gas wells.

For gas wells, a hyperbolic decline is commonly used in predicting production rates and calculating reserves. The equation form is

$$q(t) = \frac{q_i}{(1 + b\, D_i t)^{1/b}}$$

The physical properties of gas can cause this hyperbolic production decline due to the changes in gas compressibility as a reservoir is produced. The Figure 1 illustrates the hyperbolic nature of production decline for a typical gas well. These production performance data were generated using a numerical petroleum reservoir simulator, and reflect the physical properties of gas. It can be seen that the actual production rate decline is much slower than an exponential decline. Use of an exponential decline equation in the calculation of gas production rates in the Empirical Supply Model results in gas rates that are too low, and reducing the NPV of gas production in the model.

In addition to the hyperbolic nature of gas well production decline due to gas properties, even larger hyperbolic exponents, b, can be observed for production from multilayered gas reservoirs. Fetkovich (1980) recommended using values of b as high as 0.9 for multilayered gas reservoirs. Reserves calculations for many multilayered gas reservoirs are made using hyperbolic decline curves with exponents, b, as high as 0.9.

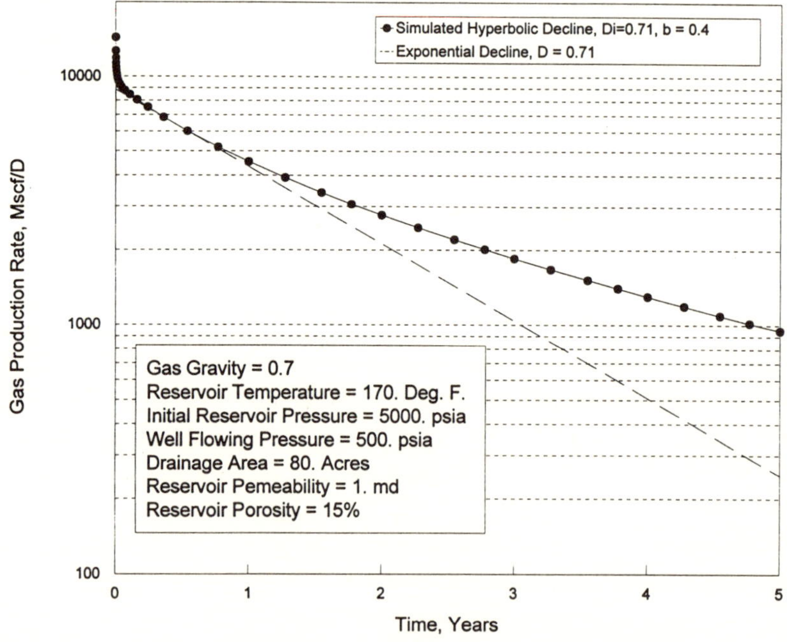

Figure 1. Hyperbolic Decline Due to Gas Properties

IV. COMMENTS ON POLICY IMPLICATIONS AND ISSUES

The author demonstrated that government policy has a profound impact on U.S. petroleum production (supply). It was demonstrated that the depletion effect on the development of new reserves is not unmanageable. However, it is my opinion that the loss of infrastructure may also have a profound effect on U.S. petroleum production in the future.

Traditionally, the major oil companies have been the source for research and development of oilfield technology. However, the current picture is bleak. Most of the R&D branches of major oil companies currently have no major involvement (or new investments) in either theoretical research, or in the development of new technology. Instead, they are involved in the transfer of previously developed technology to field operations.

Traditionally, the smaller independent petroleum producers have relied on the trickling down of technology from the major oil companies downward through the industry. With little new technology being developed, this is changing. While some efforts are being made to switch the development of new technology to universities, funding seems to be difficult to come by.

The lack of investment in theoretical research and development of new technology could lead to a domestic petroleum industry that is less efficient in the world market. This coupled with the mature character of the U.S. resource base is a serious threat to the entire industry.

REFERENCE

Fetkovich, M.J. 1980. "Decline Curve Analysis Using Type Curves." *JPT* (June): 1065-1077.

TRENDS IN U.S. NATURAL GAS PRODUCTION

Robert A. Wattenbarger and Mauricio E. Villegas

ABSTRACT

The trends of U.S. gas production rates are quite different than for oil since the early 1970s. The Hubbert model does not explain the gas rate decline up to the mid-1980s. Increases in gas rates since 1986 are responding to lower prices, clearly indicating that gas production is currently limited by demand, not supply. The gas industry is still in a period of excess producing capacity.

Advances in the Economics of Energy and Resources, Volume 9, pages 169-196.
Copyright © 1995 by JAI Press Inc.

ISBN: 1-55938-922-2

I.   INTRODUCTION

Natural gas has become increasingly important to "oil and gas" producers in the United States in recent years. Gas was once considered to be somewhat of a nuisance to oil producers—a by-product that created operational problems and added little to profitability. In many cases excess associated gas was vented, or "flared." This same practice was repeated worldwide. But recently demand has steadily grown and gas prices have steadily improved. In 1993, the wellhead revenue of gas exceeded the wellhead revenue of oil for the first time in the United States (IPAA, 1994; *Oil & Gas Journal* and *World Oil*, various issues). At the same time, the president of the Independent Producers Association of America claimed that independent producers are making over 80% of their profit from gas (*Oil & Gas Journal* and *World Oil*, various issues). Major producers are also stating that their company priorities in the United States are oriented toward gas (*Oil & Gas Journal* and *World Oil*, various issues). The U.S. oil and gas industry is gradually becoming the "gas and oil" industry.

A look at some of the recent (since 1970) gas data is puzzling. There are often not direct relationships between gas production rate and prices. The gas industry is complicated by long-term sales contracts, government regulations and incentives, seasonal demand, underground storage, and its relationship with the oil industry. The purpose of this paper is to present some of the trends in the gas industry from the production viewpoint. Data is presented and comments are made on some of the trends. Some comparisons are made to oil industry data. A future challenge will be to develop models for the purpose of analyzing and forecasting gas production rates.

II.   LONG-TERM GAS PRODUCTION TRENDS

Figure 1 shows the U.S. gas production rate since 1918 (Degolyer and MacNaughton, 1992). These data are also tabulated in Table 1. Oil production rate is also included on an equal BTU basis, meaning that the vertical scale is proportional to the amount of energy being produced. The gas data are for marketed gas which does not included vented gas or gas reinjected into oil reservoirs for pressure

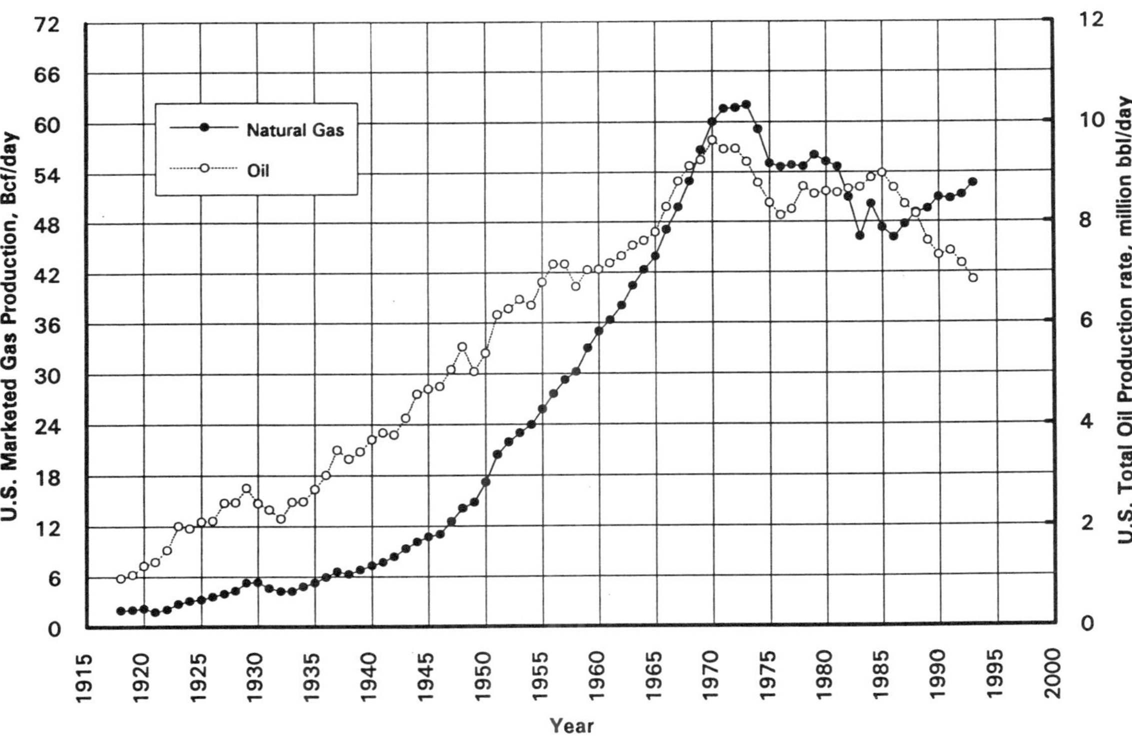

Source: DeGolyer and Macnaughton, 1992.

Figure 1. Gas and Oil Production rate since 1918 (vertical scale on equivalent BTU basis)

Table 1. U.S. Production Rates

Year	Marketed Gas (Bcf/day)	U.S. Crude Oil with Alaska (Millon bbl/day)	Gas Production (Bcf/day)	
			Tight Gas	Offshore
1918	1.973	0.975		
1919	2.055	1.037		
1920	2.192	1.214		
1921	1.808	1.294		
1922	2.082	1.527		
1923	2.767	2.007		
1924	3.123	1.956		
1925	3.260	2.092		
1926	3.589	2.112		
1927	3.973	2.469		
1928	4.301	2.470		
1929	5.260	2.760		
1930	5.315	2.460		
1931	4.630	2.332		
1932	4.274	2.151		
1933	4.274	2.481		
1934	4.849	2.488		
1935	5.260	2.730		
1936	5.945	3.013		
1937	6.603	3.505		
1938	6.301	3.327		
1939	6.795	3.466		
1940	7.288	3.707		
1941	7.699	3.842		
1942	8.356	3.799		
1943	9.342	4.125		
1944	10.164	4.597		
1945	10.740	4.695		
1946	11.041	4.751		
1947	12.548	5.088		
1948	14.110	5.535		
1949	14.849	5.046		
1950	17.205	5.407		
1951	20.438	6.158		
1952	21.945	6.274		
1953	23.014	6.458		
1954	23.945	6.342		0.193
1955	25.781	6.807		0.299
1956	27.616	7.171		0.342
1957	29.260	7.170		0.418
1958	30.219	6.710		0.613
1959	33.014	7.054		0.860
1960	34.986	7.055		1.118
1961	36.301	7.183		1.236
1962	38.027	7.332		1.726

(continued)

Table 1. (Continued)

Year	Marketed Gas (Bcf/day)	U.S. Crude Oil with Alaska (Millon bbl/day)	Gas Production (Bcf/day)	
			Tight Gas	Offshore
1963	40.411	7.542		2.082
1964	42.356	7.635		2.301
1965	43.945	7.804		2.551
1966	47.151	8.295		3.726
1967	49.781	8.810		4.655
1968	52.932	9.121		6.355
1969	56.712	9.238		7.522
1970	60.055	9.637	2.500	9.007
1971	61.616	9.463	2.554	9.838
1972	61.726	9.467	2.650	10.641
1973	62.055	9.208	2.629	10.894
1974	59.181	8.774	2.792	11.634
1975	55.093	8.375	3.043	11.410
1976	54.663	8.154	3.294	11.823
1977	54.863	8.245	3.424	12.320
1978	54.723	8.707	3.504	14.066
1979	56.085	8.552	4.045	14.918
1980	55.288	8.621	4.409	14.746
1981	54.674	8.572	4.681	15.196
1982	50.910	8.649	4.649	14.975
1983	46.258	8.688	4.168	12.972
1984	50.148	8.903	4.893	14.302
1985	47.315	8.971	4.973	12.690
1986	46.189	8.680	4.748	12.571
1987	47.762	8.349	4.917	13.913
1988	49.090	8.151	4.963	14.168
1989	49.575	7.626	5.160	14.298
1990	50.942	7.335	5.440	15.094
1991	50.773	7.417	5.478	12.780
1992	51.266	7.171		
1993	52.619	6.842		

maintenance. The long-term trend shows an exponential-like growth of gas production rate until 1970. Then the rate growth slowed and actually peaked in 1973. Since that time the trend has not been so simple. There have been periods of rate growth and periods of rate decline.

What kind of analysis can be made of gas production rate data? How can gas rate trends be explained and possibly forecasted? We will first look at the oil rate trends.

A.   Long-term Trend for Oil Rate

This same question has been raised for the United States in the past. In earlier days, there was no systematic method for analyzing the data. However, M. King Hubbert (1956), then with the United States Geological Survey, made an analysis and forecast in 1956 of U.S. oil production trends which proved to be remarkably accurate. He forecasted that U.S. oil production rate would peak in 1970. His forecast shocked the industry which had become accustomed to ever increasing oil production rates. It seemed to most industry executives and observers that the end of oil production rate increases was nowhere in sight. History proved Hubbert's forecast to be accurate in one important aspect: the U.S. oil production rate did peak in 1970.

Hubbert's forecast was based on a simple production model. In 1956, he simply fit a nearly symmetrical production rate curve to existing data such that the area under the curve (ultimate oil recovery) was equal to geological estimates of ultimate oil recovery for the United States. His assumption of a symmetrical production curve was based on observations of the development of other resources and the observation that the U.S. oil production rate had seemed to increase exponentially during its growth period and his expectation that it would decrease exponentially during the latter stages of development. There was no proof that the rate of increase and the rate of decline would be equal, but this assumption of symmetry simplified his analysis and seemed plausible. Although Hubbert had a geological background, he used accepted industry estimates for the ultimate oil recovery for the United States. He used values of 150 billion bbl and 200 billion bbl to provide scenarios to bracket the uncertainty of this value. It was his 200 billion bbl scenario that accurately forecasted the peak year in oil production rate.

Later he updated his work in several papers (Hubbert, 1962, 1967, 1980). In these papers he put his method on a more mathematical curve-fitting basis, the "Hubbert model," but confirmed his original estimates of ultimate recovery. Figure 2 is a recent fit of the U.S. oil production rate (Wattenbarger, 1994a, 1994b), with and without Alaska. The early oil production rate fit the Hubbert model fairly well, before 1970. However, many rate fluctuations have caused significant departures from the smooth shape of the Hubbert model. After oil rate peaked in 1970, the oil rate departs considerably from the Hubbert model. The Arab oil embargo and the resulting energy

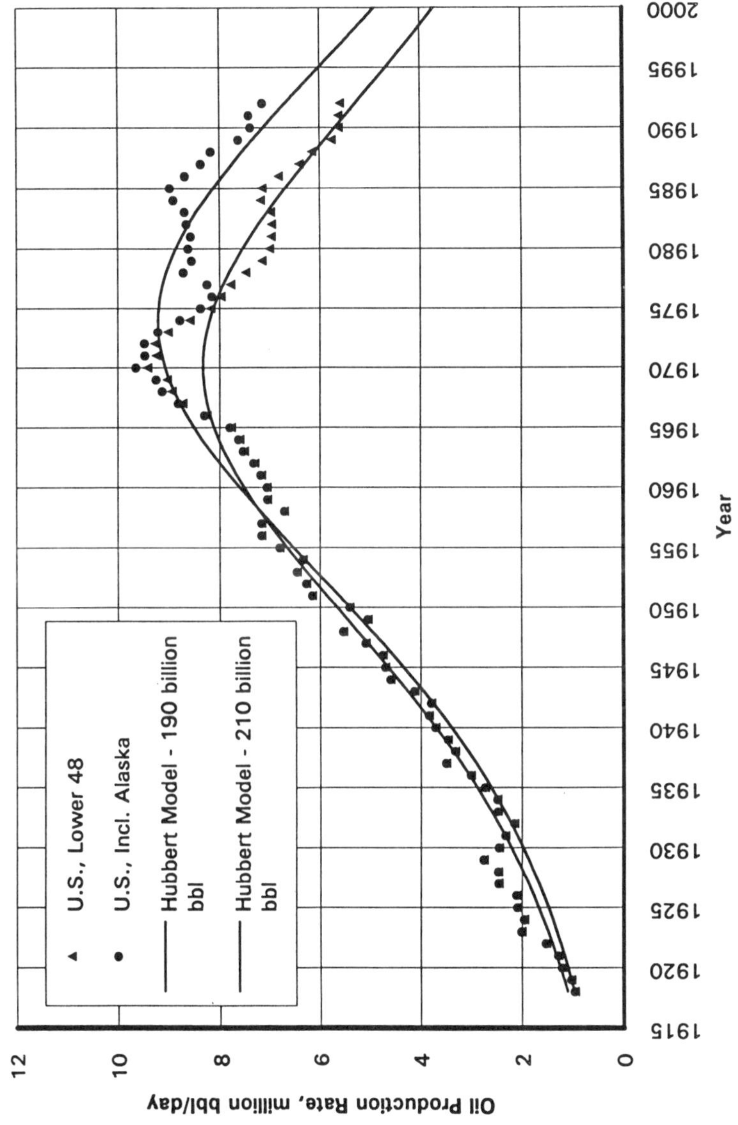

Figure 2. Oil Production Rate Recently Fitted with Hubbert's Model

Source: DeGolyer and Macnaughton, 1992.

175

crisis had considerable effects on the oil rate. Remarkably, the ultimate recovery of the Hubbert model (Figure 2) is still in the range of Hubbert's estimates.

The Hubbert model is based mainly on physical concepts and does not specifically take into account changes in the political and economic climate. Kaufmann (1991) developed a model that was based on Hubbert's model but took certain political and economic factors into account. He managed to fit the recent fluctuations in oil rate quite well for the "lower 48." So we may observe that the Hubbert model seemed to be useful in estimating ultimate oil recovery fairly well and was also useful in forecasting oil rates until oil rates peaked in 1970. After 1970, political and economic factors seem to become more important.

B.   The Hubbert Model for Gas

In his 1956 work, Hubbert also conducted an analysis of U.S. marketed gas production. He estimated natural gas reserves of 850 Tcf with a maximum production rate of about 38 Bcf/d occurring in 1970 and declining thereafter. He updated this work several times, once in 1962 (958-1,053 Tcf, 53 Bcf/d in 1977), then in 1972 (1,050 Tcf, 65.8 Bcf/d in 1975) and again in 1980 (870 Tcf, no maximum rate reported). Now, with fourteen additional years of natural gas production history, we have updated the Hubbert model.

Figure 3 shows the actual gas production rate compared to the Hubbert model. This shows a least squares fit of the Hubbert model to actual production rate data from 1918 through 1993. This least squares fit was constrained so that the maximum predicted rate would peak in 1973 at 62.05 Bcf which is the actual peak of the U.S. gas production rate. A value of $Q_{inf} = 860$ Tcf was determined with this curve fit. Although this value of ultimate recovery is almost identical to Hubbert's 1956 estimate, it can be seen that the recent gas rate trend does not fit the Hubbert model at all. Gas production rate has been increasing since 1986. As a matter of fact, the cumulative gas production (775 Tcf in 1992) plus proved gas reserves (165 Tcf in 1992) is 940 Tcf, surpassing 860 Tcf.

Figure 4 shows the difference between actual gas production and that predicted with the Hubbert model in Figure 3. It is clear that the error seems to be getting worse with time. The Hubbert model just does not seem to be useful for U.S. gas production.

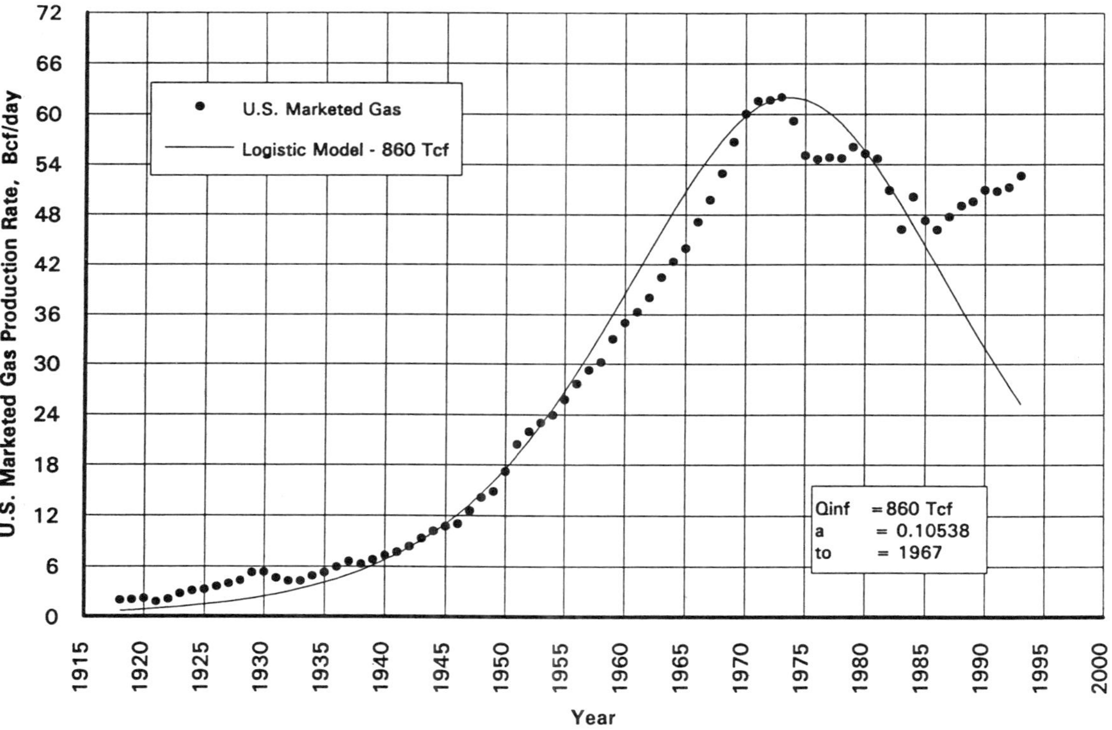

Figure 3.   Hubbert Model Fit to U.S. Gas Production Rate

177

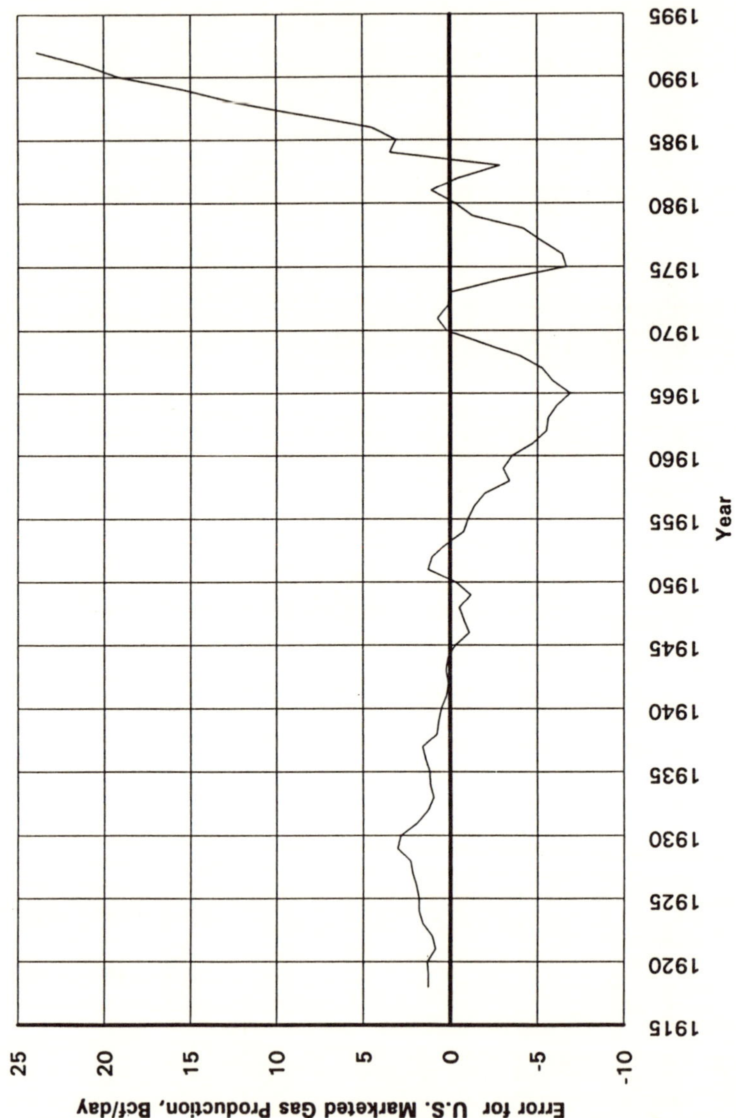

Figure 4. Error in Hubbert Model for U.S. Gas Production Rate

178

III. ULTIMATE GAS RECOVERY

The Gas Potential Committee was formed in 1964 (Potential Gas Committee, 1993). This is a committee of experts who estimate and publish the "potential gas resource" every two years. This is equivalent to ultimate gas recovery when combined with cumulative production and proved reserves. They apply various geological and statistical techniques to estimate various categories of gas resources in specific regions of the United States. Their work and their reports are very complete. This estimate is much higher than Hubbert's estimate and undoubtedly is much more accurate than Hubbert's curve fit with a simple mathematical model.

The total gas resource is comprised of cumulative production, reserves, and "potential gas resources." The potential gas resources includes expansion of reserves in existing fields plus gas which will be produced from undiscovered fields. Figure 5 shows their periodic estimates from 1968 through 1992. Throughout this period of time cumulative production plus reserves has matured considerably, while there has been considerable upheaval in the industry. Their estimate of total gas resources, or ultimate recovery, has remained remarkable steady through the years at about 1,900 Tcf.

Many other estimates of ultimate recovery have been made by others. For example, Gas Research Institute estimates that potential gas resources are 1,102 Tcf with current technology and 1,390 Tcf with advanced technology which is not yet available (Potential Gas Committee, 1993; Gas Research Institute, 1994a). This would make their estimate of ultimate gas recovery about 2,042 Tcf to 2,330 Tcf.

A. Proved Gas Reserves

Figure 6 shows the U.S. gas and oil proved reserves from 1973 to 1992 (IPAA, 1994). These data are also tabulated in Table 2. Both gas and oil show the declining reserves pattern of a mature industry. (Proved reserves represent the "certain" remaining production from existing producing fields. This value is usually conservative at any particular time.) The gas proved reserves is also included in Figure 5.

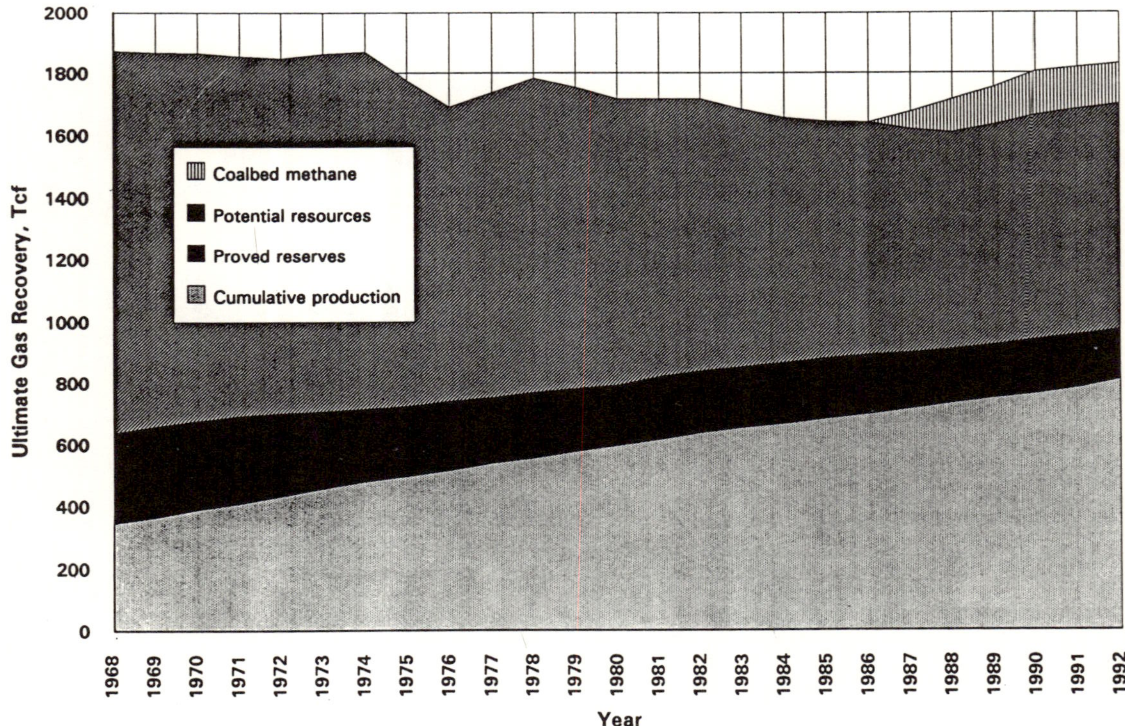

Source: Potential Gas Committee, 1993.

Figure 5. Estimates of Ultimate Gas Recovery for the U.S. Estimates made by the Potential Gas Committee

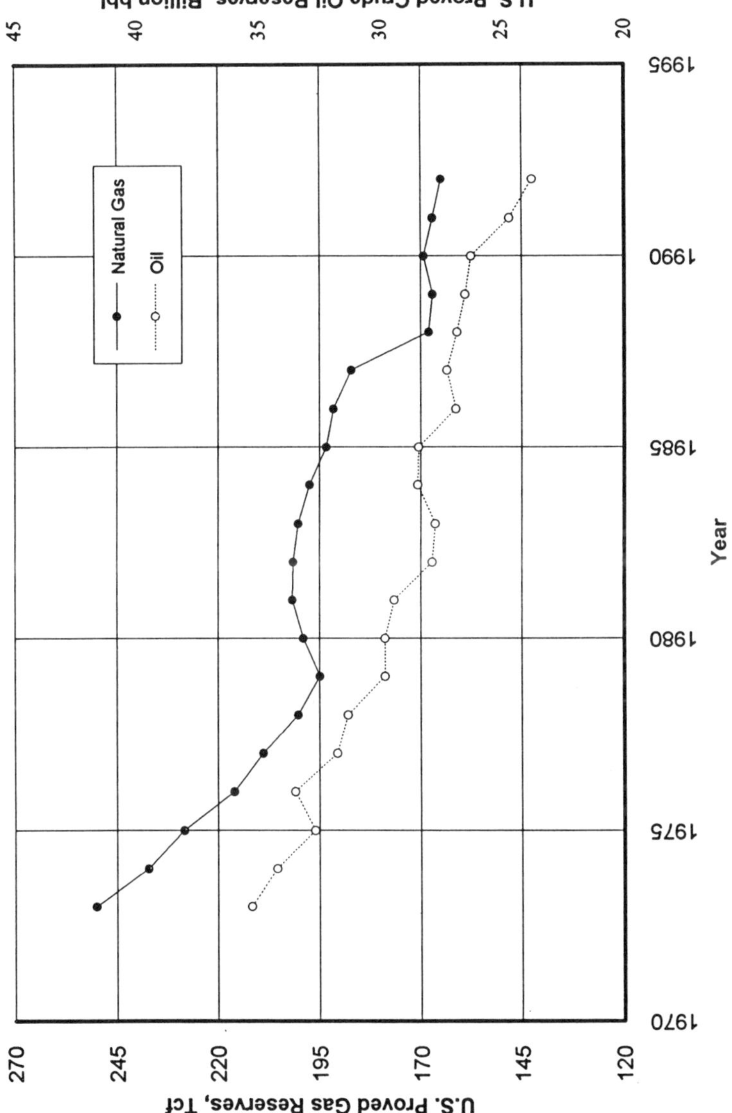

Figure 6. U.S. Gas and Oil Proved Reserves

Table 2.   U.S. Natural Gas and Crude
Oil Prices, Revenues, and Proven Reserves

| | Price in 1993$ | | Wellhead Revenues | | Proven Reserves | |
| | Gas | Oil | Gas | Oil | Dry Gas | Crude Oil |
Year	$/Mcf	$/bbl	Billion 1993 $/year		Tcf	Billion bbl
1973	0.640	11.390	13.908	38.281	250.000	35.300
1974	0.830	19.000	17.192	60.848	237.100	34.250
1975	1.140	19.360	21.929	59.181	228.200	32.682
1976	1.380	19.450	26.355	57.731	216.000	33.502
1977	1.760	19.040	33.727	57.299	208.900	31.780
1978	1.870	18.540	35.758	58.921	200.300	31.335
1979	2.230	23.930	43.848	74.697	194.900	29.810
1980	2.750	37.400	53.358	117.358	199.000	29.805
1981	3.120	50.010	59.845	156.470	201.700	29.426
1982	3.650	42.270	65.043	133.442	201.500	27.858
1983	3.690	37.300	59.387	118.283	200.300	27.735
1984	3.630	35.280	63.402	114.337	197.500	28.446
1985	3.300	31.690	54.298	103.766	193.400	28.416
1986	2.490	16.030	39.987	50.786	191.600	26.889
1987	2.070	19.130	34.405	58.296	187.200	27.256
1988	2.020	15.040	34.548	44.746	168.000	26.825
1989	1.930	18.140	33.410	50.493	167.100	26.501
1990	1.870	21.960	33.305	58.793	169.300	26.254
1991	1.730	17.450	30.618	47.241	167.100	24.682
1992	1.850	16.400	33.004	42.926	165.000	23.745
1993	2.020	14.230	37.002	35.537		

Each year the amount produced is subtracted from the proved reserves (added to cumulative production). During the same year extensions in reserve estimates in existing fields plus reserve estimates in new fields are added to the proved reserves. Figure 6 shows that the United States is not "replacing reserves" for either gas or oil.

Another way to look at proved reserves is to calculate a proved reserves/annual production ratio. This is called the "reserve life index." This is shown in Figure 7 for the period from 1973 to 1992. In recent years this value has dropped below 10 years. Some observers view this as a sign of an efficient gas producing system while others view this as limited reserves. This trend in reserve life index has been generally down except for the period in the early 1980s which is sometimes called the "gas bubble."

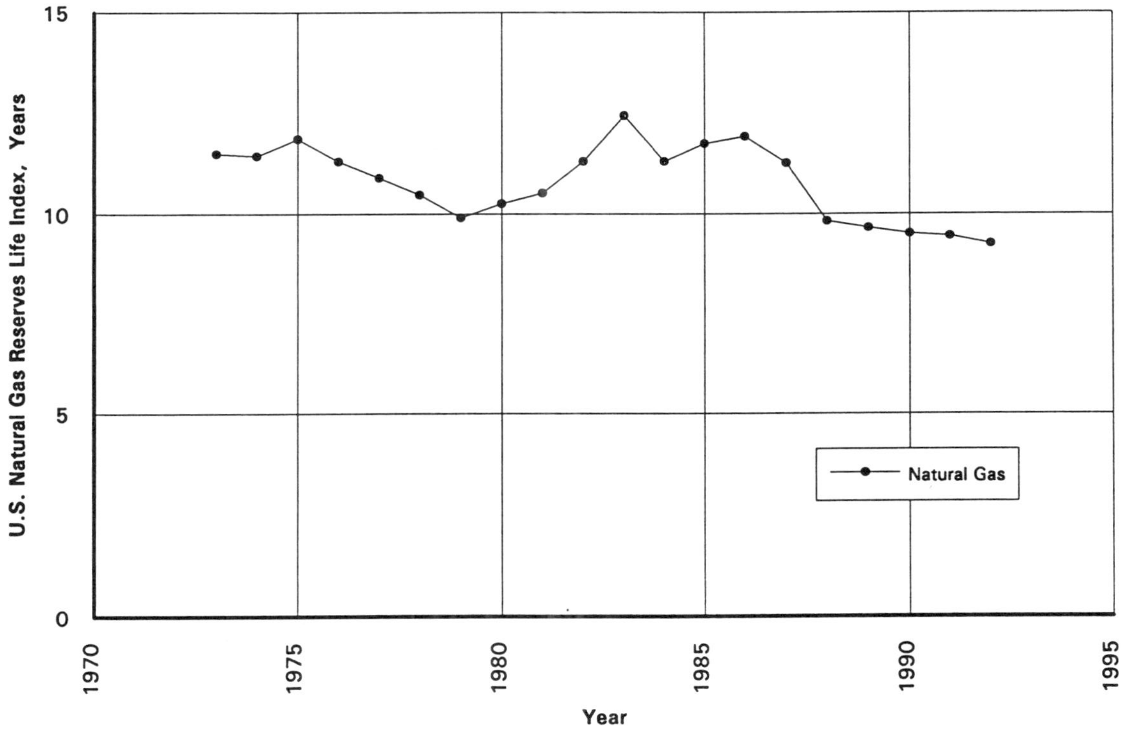

Figure 7. U.S. Gas Reserve Life Index

IV.   U.S. GAS TRENDS SINCE 1970

The trends for gas and oil production were fairly straightforward until 1970. Both production rates were almost monotonic while the gas and oil industry continued to grow. Since 1970, however, the trends in both production rates have fluctuated and have been more complicated. Figure 8 shows an expanded scale of the period from 1970 through 1993.

A.   The Trend in Wellhead Gas Prices and Revenue

Figure 9 shows the gas and oil prices from 1973 to 1993 in terms of 1993$. For both gas and oil, these prices are averaged for actual sales for each year (IPAA, 1994). Since gas sales tend to be more affected by long-term contracts than oil sales, this introduces a time lag in gas prices responding to changes in oil prices (to the extent that they are related). For example, oil price peaked in 1981 but gas price peaked in 1984. The long-term contracts also tend to have a smoothing effect on gas prices compared to oil prices.

An interesting trend is the change in gas price relative to oil price. This can be shown on an equivalent energy basis as a ratio of gas price/BTU to oil price/BTU. This trend is shown in Figure 10. Although there is considerable fluctuation in this ratio from 1973 to 1993, it is clear that the trend is upward for gas. Gas was 26% as valuable as oil in 1974 but was 82% as valuable as oil in 1993. These are wellhead prices.

The cost of gas production is generally lower than for oil production. This probably means that gas production has become more profitable than oil production.

An important aspect of the gas and oil industry is the wellhead revenue to the producer. The trend in revenue from 1973-1993 is shown in Figure 11 and tabulated in Table 2. This clearly shows that gas has gone through a period of increasing importance. In 1974, gas revenue was only 29% of oil revenue at the wellhead. In 1993, gas revenue was greater than oil revenue for the first time in history. This event gained considerable attention in the industry (IPAA, 1994; *Oil & Gas Journal* and *World Oil*, various issues). The president of the Independent Producers Association of America claims that independent producers are making over 80% of their profit from gas (*Oil & Gas Journal* and *World Oil*, various issues). Major producers

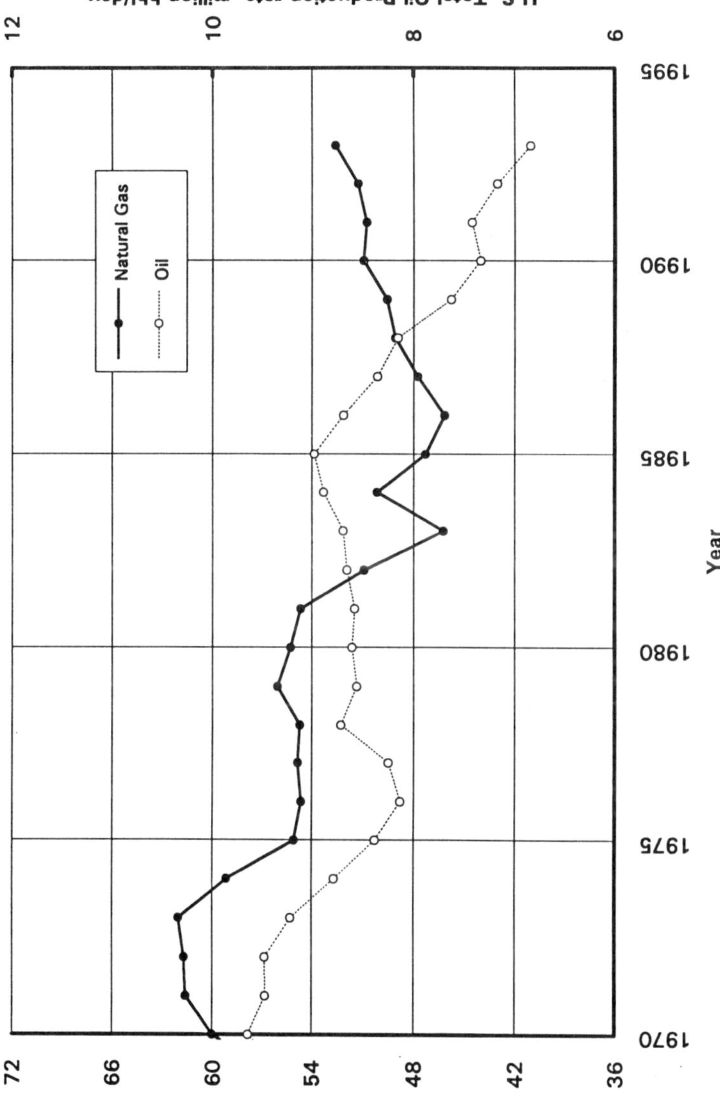

Figure 8. Gas and Oil Production Rate Since 1970 (vertical scale on equivalent BTU basis)

185

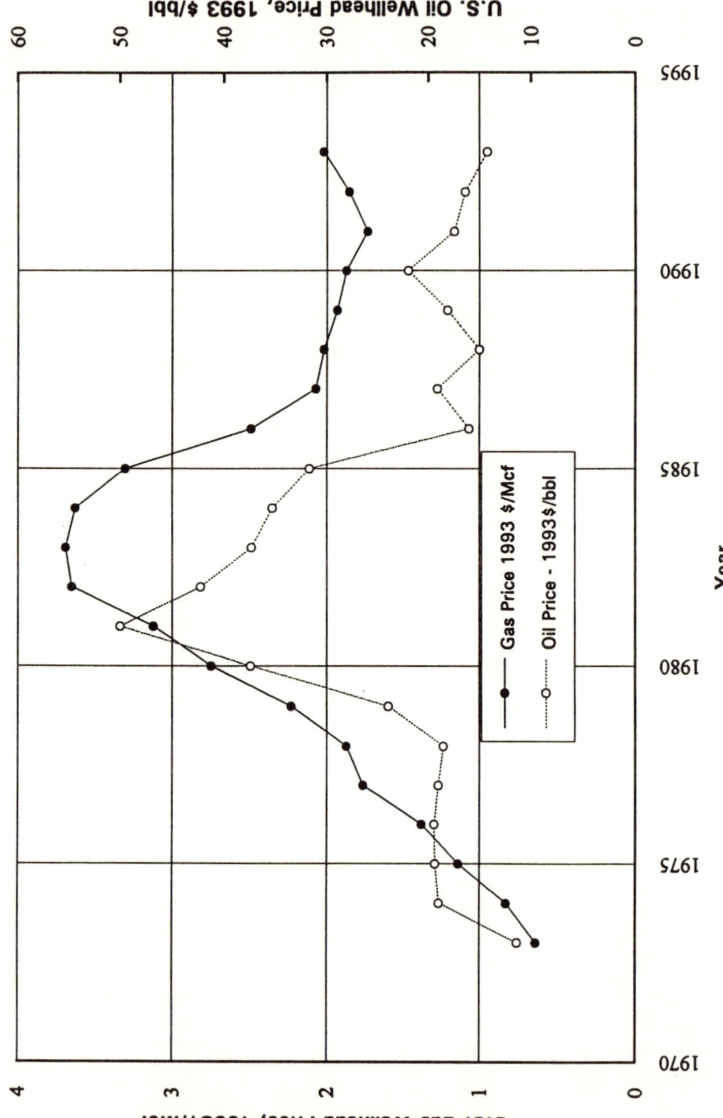

Figure 9. Recent Gas and Oil Prices, 1973-1993

Source: IPAA, 1994.

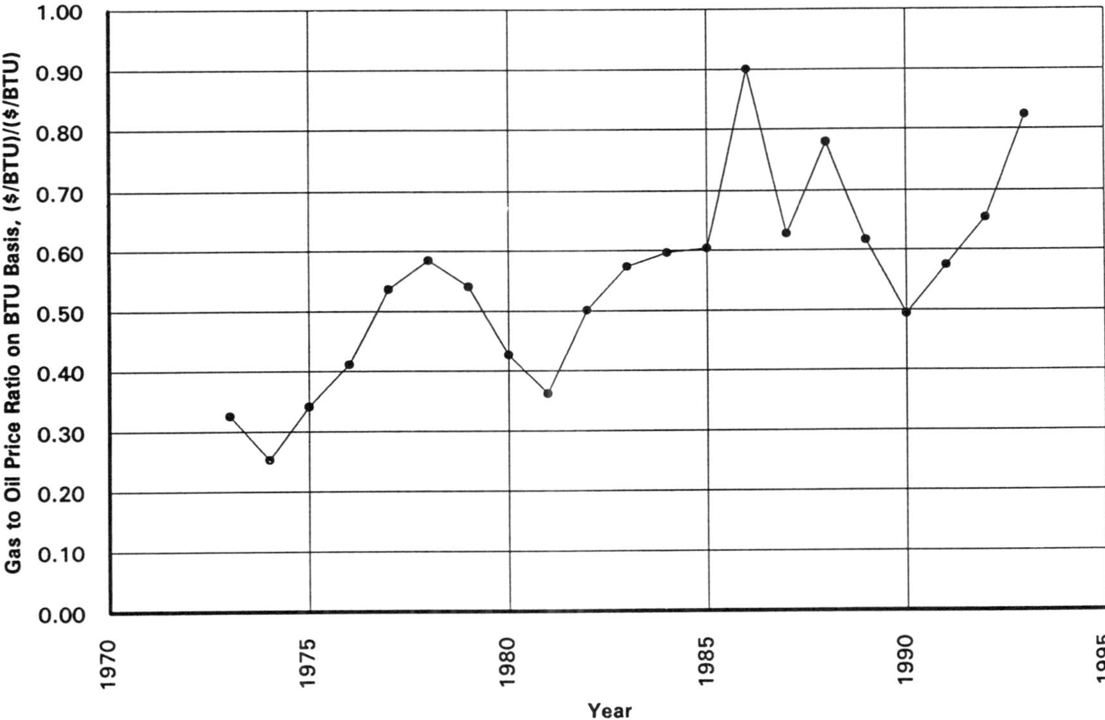

Figure 10. Gas/Oil Price Ratio (on equivalent BTU basis)

are probably different because they have been selling their less profitable oil properties while retaining the highly profitable large oil fields. Nonetheless, the majors are stating that their company priorities in the United States are oriented toward gas (*Oil & Gas Journal* and *World Oil*, various issues).

B. The 1970-1973 Period

Gas production continued to increase during this period even though oil production peaked in 1970. The rate of increase had slowed from pre-1970 increases. A contributing factor might have been the decline in associated gas corresponding to the decline in oil production. Gas prices were low and the gas market continued to increase at a steady rate (see Figure 10). Then, in the winter of 1972-1973, the weather was extremely cold and shortfalls in gas delivery occurred. One of the authors remembers living in Denver when the public schools were closed because of the shortage of deliverable gas. This was one of the first public signs that the system was strained. Later in 1973, the Arab oil embargo occurred.

C. The 1973-1975 Period, a Drop in Rate

The Arab oil embargo on sales to the United States started in October 1973 and was lifted in March 1974. This was a period of declining gas consumption—the first noticeable decline in U.S. history. The slow-down in the U.S. economy undoubtedly caused part of this declining consumption. However, there was also a considerable amount of "fuel switching" away from gas because of shortfalls during the 1972-1973 winter (Holditch, 1994). Of the drop in gas production, about 7 Bcf/d can be attributed to the reduction in associated gas from oil production (33%) and the rest was reduction from gas well production (67%). It is interesting to observe that between 1973 and 1975 the rates of flared and vented gas were reduced by half and have remained about constant since then (0.3 Bcf/d).

The drop in gas consumption caused concern in the gas industry; both from the standpoint of the limited deliverability capacity as well as the loss of markets. Out of this concern, the Gas Research Institute (GRI) was formed. GRI was funded by gas companies and was responsible for stimulating gas markets, stimulating gas production capacity, and providing analysis of the gas industry.

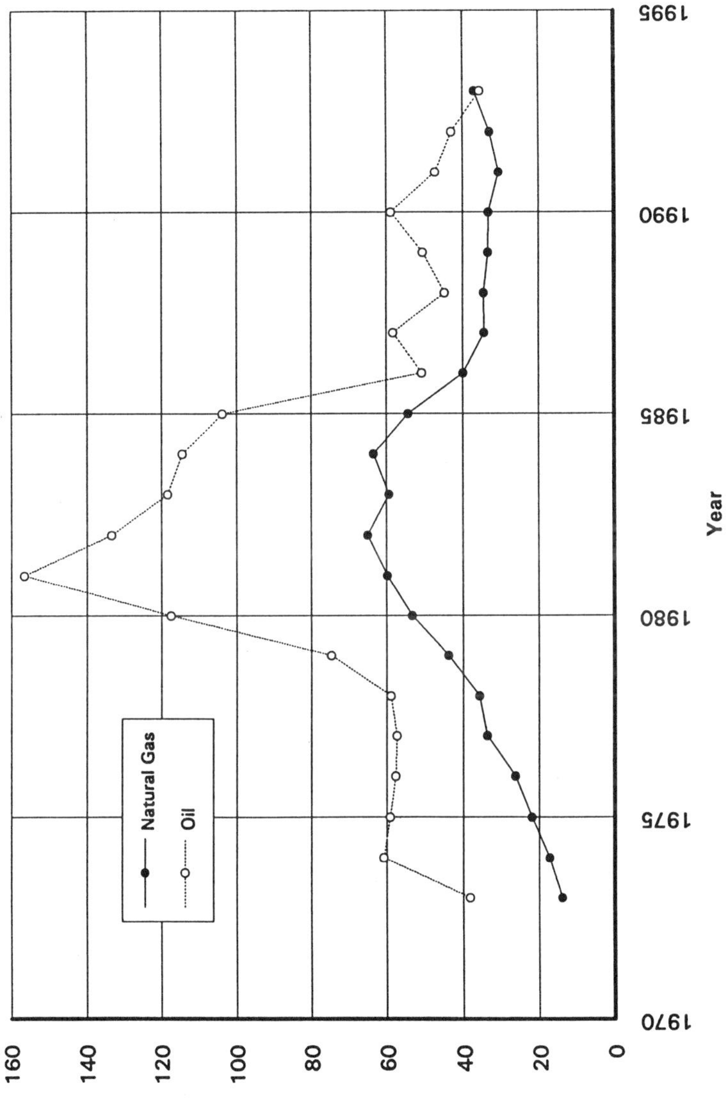

Figure 11.   Wellhead Revenue for Gas and Oil

Source: IPAA, 1994.

D.   The 1975-1979 Period, Slow Growth

Production slowly grew during this period of time. Oil prices were rapidly increasing but not gas prices. This was a period of prosperity for the producers. Long-term gas sales contracts were common with "take or pay" clauses which guaranteed continued revenue for the producers (the "buyer" pipeline companies had to pay the producer some agreed revenue during periods of time when the gas was not needed). Interstate gas prices were regulated.

E.   The 1979-1986 Period, the "Gas Bubble"

This was a disastrous period for many "buyer" pipeline companies and producers. The Iranian revolution lead to a chaotic oil market in 1979—the "second oil price spike." Oil prices increased dramatically and a "boom" in the U.S. gas and oil industry reached unprecedented proportions. The oil prices peaked in January, 1981 and started downward; finally plunging to a low in 1986. The gas prices followed with a time lag (for average prices) since most gas prices were fixed in long-term contracts.

Gas demand began falling, resulting in slightly lower gas production rates until 1981, then rapidly dropping gas production rates after 1981. This period of time was disastrous for many producers and pipeline companies—it is often referred to as the "gas bubble," implying that gas reserves and production capacity were high while gas demand was low. The "gas bubble" can be seen in Figure 7 as an increased life index. An unusual financial burden was placed on many pipeline companies who had committed to long-term "take or pay" contracts at high prices.

F.   The 1986-present Period, Steady Rate Increase

Oil production rate began dropping in 1986 when the oil prices fell. This trend has continued through 1993 with each year having a lower oil production rate. Very little exploration for oil has been done during this period. In contrast, gas production rates bottomed out in 1986 and have increased every year since. A number of factors may be contributing to this gas trend. Some of these will be discussed later. Whatever the reasons, it can be said that this period of increasing gas rate and decreasing oil rates is unprecedented.

V. FACTORS IN THE CURRENT GAS PRODUCTION TREND

During the period 1986 to 1993, gas production rate has increased by 6.5 Bcf/day. This increase is the result of a number of factors. We will now consider some of the factors that may be affecting this current gas production trend.

A. Effects of Government Policy/Incentives

The Natural Gas Policy Act of 1978 was implemented to increase the supply of natural gas through incentives to the operators. Certain categories of "nonconventional gas" were designated that were excluded from price control. Tax credits were also allowed for this gas. The categories for nonconventional gas were "tight gas" (less than 0.1 millidarcy permeability), shale gas, coalbed methane, and other high cost gas such as "deep gas." The response was immediate. Gas qualifying for this exemption began selling as high as $9.00/Mcf. Many long-term contracts were signed with "take or pay" clauses which obligated the buyer to buy certain quantities whether the buyer needed it or not. This led to considerable turmoil in the gas industry as gas demand fell in the early 1980s. Many buyers simply could not pay for the contracted gas. Bankruptcies and law suits were common.

For years the U.S. government has controlled "interstate" gas prices. This was gas that was sold into interstate pipelines which was most of the produced gas. The government released all new gas from price control in January, 1985. This has been a big factor leading to the current trend of increasing gas rates. Tax credits incentives allowed for nonconventional gas are an additional stimulus (Holditch, 1994).

In some ways, gas is considered to be the fuel of the future. It has environmental advantages over oil in its production, transportation, and consumption. The current Presidential administration has declared its emphasis on the use of natural gas and will continue to encourage its extended use and development (White, 1993).

B.   Demand

The demand for natural gas has steadily improved since 1986. This reversed a trend in gas demand which was caused largely from fuel switching in the industrial and electrical utility sectors during the previous fourteen years (Energy Information Administration, 1994). Most producers see the effects of demand through gas prices and also seasonal variation in demand. It is common gas sales from a gas field to be curtailed during part of the year because of slack demand.

Figure 12 shows the monthly gas production rate for a particular field over a period of 22 years. It can be seen that many of the years have a month or so of low production because of slack demand. This might occur in the middle of the summer, but often occurs at other times when an excess in gas producing capacity and gas storage is recognized. The annual curtailment has generally improved over recent years. The example field happens to be a tight gas field and considerable new drilling took place in 1991 and 1992, accounting for the recent rate increases. However, this example also shows less curtailment in recent years. Current production is still only about 80% of production capacity due to market conditions.

C.   Nonconventional Gas

The gas price incentives and tax credit incentives have led to an increase in nonconventional gas production. Figure 13 shows how tight gas production has increased. These data are also tabulated in Table 1 (Gas Research Institute, 1994b). The increase from 1986 to 1991 has only been 0.7 Bcf/day. But in 1991, tight gas production accounted for almost 11% of the U.S. gas production and coalbed methane accounted for another 2%. These unconventional sources of gas are a significant share of U.S. gas production and will probably grow in significance in the future. It has been said that coalbed methane alone is replacing conventional reserves (*Oil & Gas Journal* and *World Oil*, various issues). Figure 5 shows coalbed methane separately.

Also shown on this graph is offshore gas production (not necessarily nonconventional) which has not shown much of an increase in the current trend period.

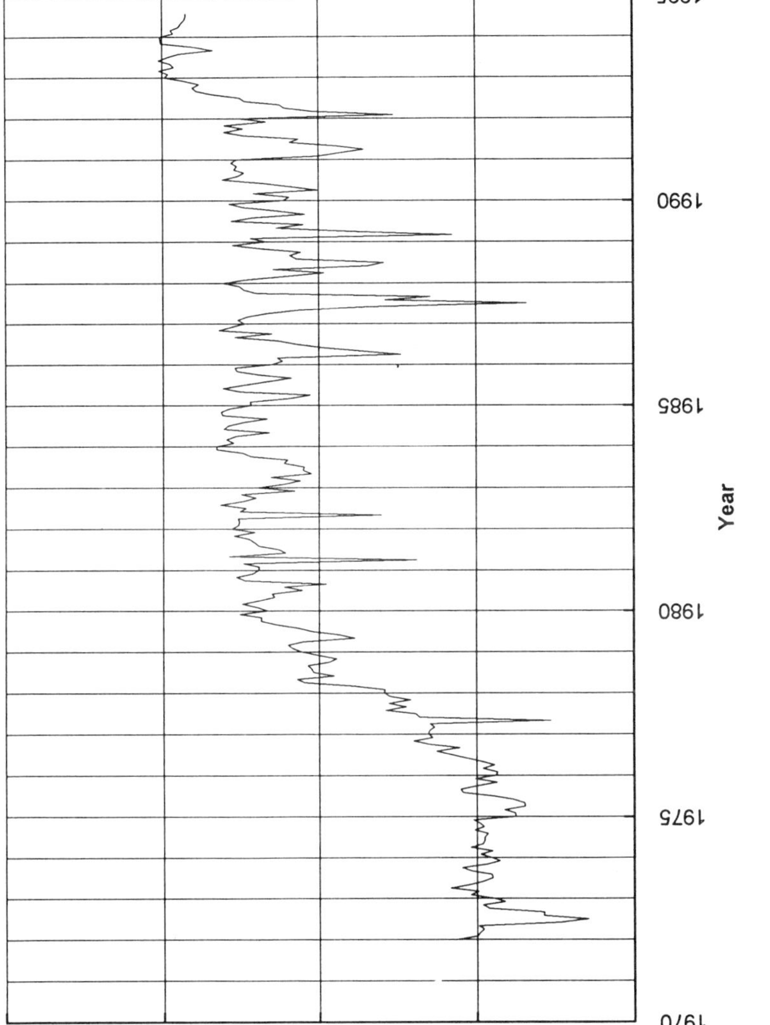

Figure 12. Gas Production Rate in a Typical Field, Showing Periods of Slack Demand

193

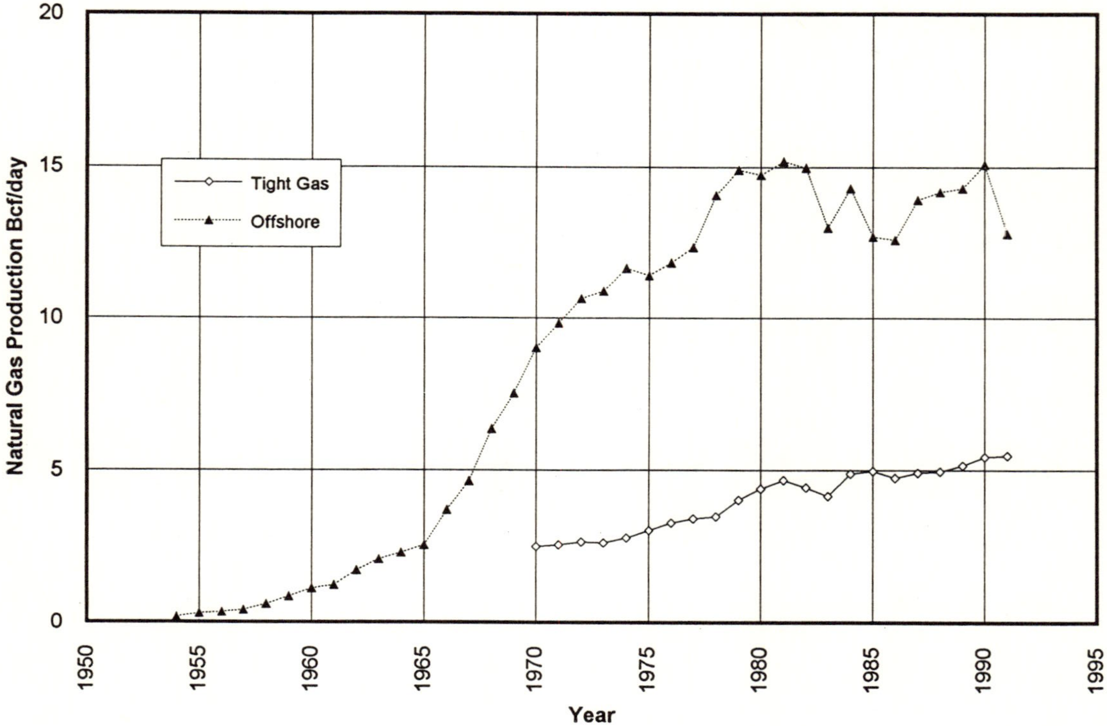

Figure 13. Offshore Gas Production and "Tight Gas" Production

VI. SUMMARY

We have presented data for the U.S. gas and oil industry. The focus has been on the period from 1970 to the present. Many of the trends are puzzling compared to the rather simpler trends before 1970. As a way of summarizing our observations, we itemize the following:

1. The Hubbert model is probably more useful for oil than for gas.
2. The period since 1970 is complicated by a number of political and economic events which have affected gas and oil production.
3. The 1979-1985 period was characterized by high oil and gas prices. This increased oil production rates because producers had a market for oil and had price and tax incentives. This increased oil production reduced oil imports. However, the high gas prices reduced gas demand, leaving gas producers with shut in wells while production was curtailed during the "gas bubble" years.
4. The 1986-present period is characterized by low oil and gas prices. Oil production rates are decreasing because of resource depletion. However, gas seems to be demand constrained. Low gas prices are increasing gas demand. Curtailment of gas production has been reduced, letting gas producers produce their wells closer to capacity.
5. The market for gas has improved considerably since 1986 because of low prices and environmental concerns.
6. Gas is now more important than oil to operators.
7. Nonconventional sources of gas are becoming increasingly important but are not a major factor in increasing gas production rates.
8. The future is much brighter for gas than for oil.

NOTES

a = Parameter of Hubbert's model
bbl = Barrels
Bcf = Billion standard cubic feet of gas

BTU = British Thermal Unit, a measure of energy
Mcf = Million standard cubic feet of gas
Tcf = Trillion standard cubic feet of gas
t_o = Arbitrary reference time at which Q_o is taken, years
Q_{inf} = Ultimate gas recovery, Tcf
1993\$ = Dollars adjusted for inflation to a 1993 reference

REFERENCES

DeGolyer and MacNaughton. 1992. *Twentieth Century Petroleum Statistics*, Dallas, December.

Energy Information Administration. 1994. *Annual Energy Review*. Washington DC.

Gas Research Institute. 1994a. *IN FOCUS–Tight Gas Sands* (volume 10, 1), June, Las Vegas, NV.

Gas Research Institute. 1994b. *The Long-term Trends in U.S. Gas Supply and Prices–1994 Edition of the GRI Baseline Projection of U.S. Energy Supply and Demand to 2010: Gas Research Insights*. Chicago, IL, May.

Holditch, S.A. 1994. Personal Communication, October.

Potential Gas Committee, Potential Gas Agency. 1993. *Potential Supply of Natural Gas in the United States, December 31, 1992*. Golden, CO, May.

Hubbert, M.K. 1956. "Nuclear Energy and Fossil Fuels." Pp. 17-25 in *Drilling and Production Practice*. Dallas: Texas American Petroleum Institute.

Hubbert, M.K. 1962. "Energy Resources." A report to the Committee on Natural Resources, National Academy Sci.-Natl. Research Council, Pub. 1000-D, 141 p.: Reprinted 1973 by Natl. Tech Information Service, U.S. Dept. of Commerce, no. PB-222401.

Hubbert, M.K. 1967. "Degree of Advancement of Petroleum Exploration in United States." *The American Association of Petroleum Geologists Bulletin* 51 (11): 2207-2227.

Hubbert, M.K. 1980. "Techniques of Prediction as Applied to Production of Oil and Gas." Proceedings of a Symposium Held at the Department of Commerce, Washington DC, June 18-20.

Independent Petroleum Association of America (IPAA). 1994. *United States Petroleum Statistics: 1993 Data*. Washington, DC, March.

Oil & Gas Journal and *World Oil*. Various issues.

Kaufmann, R.K. 1991. "Oil Production in the Lower 48 States." Pp. 111-127 in *Resources and Energy* (volume 13). Elsevier Science Publishers B.V.

Wattenbarger, R.A. 1994a. "Oil Production trends in the CIS." *World Oil* (June): 91-97.

Wattenbarger, R.A. 1994b. "Oil Production Trends in the Former Soviet Union." In *Advances in the Economics of Energy and Resources* (volume 7), edited by J.R. Moroney. Greenwich, CT: JAI Press.

White, W. 1993. "An Address at the Corpus Christi Energy Conference, September..

COMMENTARY

James M. Griffin

For environmental reasons, it is hoped that natural gas will play an increasing role in future U.S. energy supply. But is this realistic? Interestingly, Wattenbarger and Villegas are hesitant to reach such conclusions. They appear guardedly optimistic by noting that Hubbert's (1962) mechanistic decline curve does not appear to work well for natural gas, because since 1986, U.S. gas production has increased whereas Hubbert's model would forecast a steady decline. They also note that natural gas is now relatively more important as a profit center for the industry and conclude that the future for gas is "much brighter for gas than for oil." They are reticent to draw more specific conclusions than these.

In analyzing trends in U.S. natural gas production, Wattenbarger and Villegas (1994) adopt the conceptual lens of the petroleum engineer to address this important question. In contrast, the conceptual lens of the economist leads me to approach this problem from a quite different perspective. Behind every data point of gas production, the economist visualizes a supply and demand curve while the petroleum engineer is likely to focus on the technical factors governing natural gas production.

Advances in the Economics of Energy and Resources, Volume 9, pages 197-201.

Natural gas supply has been heavily researched by economists dating back to the early econometric models by Erickson and Spann (1971), and MacAvoy and Pindyck (1975). Unfortunately, these researchers would have done well not to have oversold the power of their economic lens. Too much was promised and too little was delivered. Moreover, given the high quality of U.S. data, the problems cannot be laid at the foot of "data quality," Quite simply, econometric models have great difficulty when the random component is large vis-à-vis the role played by economic factors. The huge random component is illustrated by the large year-to-year variations in U.S. natural gas discoveries. To the extent that large random shocks are spuriously correlated with price movements, the price elasticities of supply may be severely biased.

Besides the effect of price, the econometric modeler faces the tough choice of how to model decreasing returns from exploration. Does one assume as does Kaufman, Balcer, and Kruyt (1975) that pool sizes are log-normally distributed or does one let the data speak for themselves? The latter approach, while less restrictive, faces the problem of spurious correlation with the large random error. Yet another problem is characterizing the ability of improved seismic in discovering new gas fields. Economist are by training ill-equipped to formulate variables reflecting technological improvements and instead often fall into the trap of using a time trend. Misspecification of the role of technological change in turn is likely to bias the other responses of price and decreasing returns. Given the highly random nature of the data and the difficulty in formulating variables to reflect decreasing returns and technological advances, it should not be surprising that the forecast performance of these models has been quite poor.

The differences in conceptual lens between the economist and the petroleum engineer are best illustrated by M. King Hubbert's application of the logistic curve to correctly forecast in 1962 the peak in U.S. oil production eight years later. Hubbert adopted the logistic function to provide estimates of ultimate recoverable reserves (Q_∞). According to this function; current production (Q_t) is determined by the following deterministic model:

$$Q_t = \frac{Q_\infty}{1 + \alpha e^{-\beta^{(t-t_0)}}} \tag{1}$$

Unknown parameters include Q_∞, θ, β, and t_0 which are chosen based on the ability to fit the data. Transforming equation (1) and taking natural logarithms, one obtains

$$\ln\left[\frac{Q_\infty}{Q_t} - 1\right] = \ln\alpha - \beta(t\text{-}t_0) \qquad (2)$$

By performing a grid search over different values of Q_∞ and t_0, Hubbert used equation (2) to fit estimates of α and β by least squares. The logistic function has the nice property of generating finite reserves. Moreover, production follows a symmetric, bell-shaped curve as shown in Figure 2 of Wattenbarger and Villegas. Its beauty is its simplicity. According to Hubbert, prices and technological advances may play minor roles, but the process of physical exhaustion of a fixed reserve stock is the key empirical driver. John Ryan's (1975) critique of Hubbert's methodology exemplifies the problems economists have with deterministic, curve fitting exercises. Ryan's first objection to this analysis is that a variety of Q_∞ and t_0 coefficients will provide approximately the same fit with estimates of Q_∞ ranging from 175 to 250 billion barrels. The second and more fundamental objection is that this a purely deterministic relationship in which prices and technology play no role. Resource economics teaches that higher prices move resources from the noneconomic to the economically recoverable category. Likewise, in other areas of mineral economics, technological advance has had a profound effect in offsetting the tendency toward Malthusian poverty. Despite Ryan's defense of economic orthodoxy, historical observation has judged Hubbert well at least for U.S. oil production. Cleveland and Kaufman (1991) compare Hubbert's simple model for oil with other models and conclude that it outperforms other rivals.

Especially perplexing is Figure 3 in which Wattenbarger and Villegas show how poorly the Hubbert methodology predicts gas production after 1986. Note that gas production increases steadily over the period 1986-1993, while the logistic curve would predict gas production in 1993 at *half* its observed rate. Clearly, the logistic curve fails badly.

But can the conceptual lens of the economist provide an explanation? As shown in Figure 8 of Wattenbarger and Villegas, while gas production was expanding over the period 1986-1993, average gas contract prices were declining by 20% in real terms. At

first, one might conclude that economics suffers even a worse malady
than the Hubbert model because it appears to violate the law o
supply. Assuming the demand curve is shifting outward over thi
period and the supply curve is stable, prices should rise at highe
production. Instead prices are falling which would imply that th
supply curve is *negatively* sloped! Since negatively sloped suppl
curves reject the laws of scarcity, perhaps some other explanatio
is consistent with the data.

A second possible explanation for this apparent anomaly is tha
technological advances shifted the supply schedule downward an
to the right over this period. With a stable demand schedule, price
fall as production increases. If this interpretation of the data is correc
then finding cost reductions enabled greater production at lowe
prices. But we should expect to see this confirmed by lower findin
costs.

There is, however, a third and far less optimistic explanation fo
the future. The period 1983-1986 was characterized by a "gas bubble"
so that at the average long term contract price, there was insufficien
demand, causing gas to be shut in. Only after these artificially hig
contract prices were renegotiated downward, did gas once again begi
to flow. Thus the 1986-1983 upward trend in gas production ma
simply be a demand side phenomenon coupled with widesprea
contract renegotiation. If this explanation holds, the productio
increase of the 1986-1993 period was a temporary phenomenon an
production will likely resume a downward path.

Even though the lens of the economist does not offer a shar
forecast of the future, they are important in identifying the ke
empirical phenomena and moving us beyond fitting the Hubber
curve. Specifically, both decreasing return and technologica
improvements should manifest themselves in the volume of ga
discoveries and their finding costs. This suggests that the nex
extension in the Wattenbarger and Villegas paper should be t
analyze trends in volumes discovered and their corresponding findin
costs. Presumably, this analysis should separate onshore 48 state
from offshore, since the latter is likely to reflect frontier exploratio
and not be subject to the same extent of decreasing return
phenomena as onshore prospects. To the extent that for the onshor
48 states both finding rates and costs are relatively constant, the
this would justify considerable enthusiasm for the future of the U.S
natural gas industry.

REFERENCES

Cleveland, C.J., and R.K. Kaufman. 1991. "Forecasting Ultimate Oil Recovery and Its Rate of Production: Incorporating Economic Forces into the Models of M. King Hubbert." *Energy Journal* 12(2): 17-45.

Erickson, E.W., and R.S. Spann. 1971. "Supply Response in a Regulated Industry: The Case of Natural Gas." *Bell Journal of Economics* (Spring): 94-121.

Hubbert, M.K. 1962. "Energy Resources." A 1962 report to the Committee on Natural Resources, National Academy of Sciences, National Research Council, Publication 1000-D.

Kaufman, G.M., Y. Balcer, and D. Kruyt. 1975. "A Probabilistic Model of Oil and Gas Discovery." In *Methods of Estimating the Volume of Undiscovered Oil and Gas Reserves, Studies in Geology*, edited by J.D. Hahn. Tulsa, OK: American Assoc. of Geologists.

MacAvoy, P., and R.S. Pindyck. 1975. *The Economics of the Natural Gas Shortage [1960-1980]*. Amsterdam: North-Holland Publishing Co.

Ryan, J.M. 1975. "National Academy of Sciences Report on Energy Resources: Discussion of Limitations of Logistic Projections." *Bulletin of the American Association of Petroleum Geologists* 49(10).

Wattenbarger, R.A., and M.E. Villegas. 1994. "Trends in U.S. Natural Gas Production." Mimeo.

DISTRIBUTIONAL AND
ENVIRONMENTAL
CONSEQUENCES OF TAXES
ON ENERGY:
A PARTIAL EQUILIBRIUM MODEL OF U.S.
HOUSEHOLD ENERGY DEMAND

Hadi Dowlatabadi, Raymond J. Kopp,
and F. Ted Tschang

ABSTRACT

Several recent research efforts have been directed toward an economic
analysis of various U.S. energy tax schemes designed to raise revenue
and mitigate global warming by reducing emissions of carbon dioxide.
These studies focus on the implications of alternative tax schemes for
economic growth and sectoral production, prices, and employment.
While these studies find the effects on economic growth to be quite

Advances in the Economics of Energy and Resources, Volume 9, pages 203-235.

ISBN: 1-55938-922-2

small if the tax revenues are used to reduce labor taxes, they neglect an equally important set of economic and political variables, specifically the distribution of the energy tax burdens across U.S. households and the environmental gains that such taxes may bring forth.

The purpose of this study is to examine the regional consequences of various energy tax schemes, both those designed for fiscal reasons and those "green taxes" related to environmental policies. Our goal is to examine that level of taxes paid by U.S. households under alternative energy tax policies and to document the changing pattern of household emissions as a result of such taxes. To accomplish this goal we have constructed a detailed partial equilibrium model of household energy consumption. The model describes household demand for four types of energy products and differentiates household demand by geographic region. The household model is linked to electricity, petroleum, and natural gas pricing models enabling taxes on coal, crude petroleum, and natural gas to be reflected and in the prices paid by households for the energy products they consume.

I. INTRODUCTION

For both environmental and fiscal reasons, one might expect taxes on energy products to have a substantial following among Washington policymakers and politicians. Conventional Washington wisdom suggests that every one cent increase in the tax on gasoline, for example, raises one billion dollars of revenue, and recent research on large-scale computable general equilibrium (CGE) leads one to believe that even modest broad-based energy taxes can lead to reductions of all the criteria air pollutants and carbon dioxide as well (see Goulder, 1993).[1] However, the recent experience with President Clinton's deficit reduction package and the much publicized and ill-fated Btu tax, suggests otherwise.[2]

While acknowledging the wholesale defeat of the Btu tax, it is hard to believe that taxes on energy will not be reconsidered in the future.[3] The U.S. budget deficit still remains large and the pressure to fund new domestic programs, such as health care, is great, suggesting strong incentives to continuously pursue additional revenue sources. Moreover, the United States faces constant pressure to reduce greenhouse gas emissions.[4]

This all suggests that energy taxes will reappear and likely be adopted in either a piecemeal or perhaps wholesale fashion. If this presumption is correct, it will be important to study and understand the political and economic implications of widespread taxes on energy.

Several recent research efforts have been directed toward an economic analysis of various U.S. energy tax schemes designed to mitigate global warming by reducing emissions of carbon dioxide. Two of the most notable early studies are those produced by the Congressional Budget Office (1990) and by Jorgenson and Wilcoxen (1990). These studies focus on the implications of alternative tax schemes for economic growth and sectoral production, prices and employment.[5]

The newest and perhaps best energy tax study is that conducted by Lawrence Goulder of Stanford (Goulder, 1993). Goulder employs a state-of-the-art computable general equilibrium model of the U.S. economy specifically designed and constructed to examine U.S. tax policy. Goulder adds information to the model that links the usage of various fuels and the level of sectoral production to emissions of a vector of airborne pollutants.[6] Using the model, Goulder examines three tax schemes: a tax similar to the now defunct Btu tax, an increase in personal income tax, and a value added tax (VAT) all generating the same level of revenue. Goulder shows that on the basis of traditional public finance measures of tax efficiency, the energy tax is significantly less efficient than either the increase in personal income tax or the VAT.[7] Goulder notes that the efficiency loss suffered by the energy tax is due to "its relatively narrow industrial base and the fact that it applies to gross output (which includes intermediate inputs) as opposed to net output (which excludes such inputs)" (Goulder, 1993, p. 34).

While the Jorgenson and Wilcoxen, and Goulder studies are quite good, and concern themselves with important economic considerations, and in the case of Goulder, environmental concerns as well,[8] they neglect an equally important set of economic and political variables, specifically the distribution of the energy tax burdens across U.S. households. Analyzing the tax burden is important for several reasons, but certainly the most obvious reason is political. If taxes on energy are to pass Congress, their chances are much improved if House and Senate members believe the burden is spread "thinly" and "evenly" over the voting public. All else unchanged, excessively large tax payments in the form of higher prices for the energy products purchased by households will surely doom new energy tax initiatives and perceived inequities in the distribution of even a small tax on the basis of geography or other relevant demographic characteristics will surely make passage difficult.

In addition to the distribution of the tax burden, it is instructive to learn of the tax revenues generated from the household sector and the associated household contribution to reduced airborne emissions resulting from the tax. If household generated revenues and associated emission reductions are low, it may make more political sense to exempt households from the tax altogether or to target the household energy tax to maximize the emission reductions for any given tax burden.

The purpose of this study is to take a first look at the distributional consequences of various energy tax schemes, both those designed for fiscal reasons and those "green taxes" related to environmental policies. Our goal is to examine the level of taxes paid by U.S. households under alternative energy tax policies and to document the changing pattern of household emissions as a result of such taxes. To accomplish this goal we have constructed a detailed partial equilibrium model of household energy consumption. The model describes household demand for four types of energy products and differentiates household demand by geographic region. The household model is linked to electricity, petroleum, and natural gas pricing models enabling taxes on coal, crude petroleum, and natural gas to be reflected in the prices paid by households for the energy products they consume.

The plan of the paper is as follows. In the next section we discuss the sources of data used in the modeling effort and provide some descriptive information on the price paid, quantity consumed, and total expenditure made by U.S. households for electricity, fuel oil, natural gas, and gasoline in 1990. Section III describes how we measure the burden of energy taxes, while section IV discusses the construction of the household energy demand model. Section V reviews the dowlelopment of the electricity supply model and petroleum and natural gas pricing models, while sections VI and VII present the results of applying the models to various energy tax proposals. Section VIII describes the carbon reducing potential of the taxes and section IX contains concluding remarks.

II. U.S. HOUSEHOLD ENERGY CONSUMPTION

The primary source of information on household consumption of electricity, natural gas, and fuel oil is the Department of Energy, Energy Information Agency (EIA) Residential Energy Consumption Surveys (RECS) conducted in 1990.[9] Gasoline consumption and price data for 1990 were drawn from the 1990 Nationwide Personal Transportation Survey (USDOT, 1992).

The EIA survey aggregates households regionally to the nine U.S. Census divisions. Thus the regional specificity of the model described in this report is also maintained at the census division level. States comprising the census divisions and the number of resident households in each division are displayed in Table 1.

The household energy demand model presented in the next section provides demand equations for four energy types: electricity, natural gas, petroleum products, and gasoline. Petroleum products are an aggregate of fuel oil, kerosene, and LPG. We perform the aggregation by forming a quantity index based on the sum of the Btus of the three fuels and a price index that is found by the sum of all expenditures on the three fuels divided by the Btu quantity index.

One of the purposes of this study is to examine the geographical distribution of the burden of taxes on energy. Most of the distributional story is told by the geographic variation in the quantities of energy consumed and prices paid prior to imposition of any tax. Consider Table 2. Each column displays the regional variation in average household consumption of energy by type and in total. Average household consumption is calculated by simply dividing total household consumption of a particular energy type within the region by the number of households in that region. We can examine the variation in regional consumption by comparing the average household consumption of a region to the simple unweighted average (i.e., unweighted averaging down a column without regard to regional population differences) consumption of the nine census divisions. In 1990 the unweighted average household consumption of all forms of energy measured in millions of Btus (MMBtu) was estimated to be 292. The variation in this consumption defined over census divisions is captured by the standard deviation of consumption and is estimated to be 29 MMBtu. The greatest amount of energy is consumed in the Mountain states (27% above the average), while the lowest consumption is in the Pacific states (10% below the

Table 1. Census Division, States and Number of Households

Census Division	States	Households
New England		4.5
	Vermont	
	New Hampshire	
	Maine	
	Massachusetts	
	Connecticut	
	Rhode Island	
Middle Atlantic		14.7
	New York	
	Pennsylvania	
	New Jersey	
East North Central		16.6
	Wisconsin	
	Michigan	
	Illinois	
	Indiana	
	Ohio	
West North Central		6.5
	North Dakota	
	South Dakota	
	Nebraska	
	Kansas	
	Minnesota	
	Iowa	
	Missouri	
South Atlantic		16.6
	West Virginia	
	Virginia	
	Delaware	
	Maryland	
	Washington DC	
	North Carolina	
	South Carolina	
	Georgia	
	Florida	
East South Central		6.4
	Kentucky	
	Tennessee	
	Mississippi	
	Alabama	

(*continued*)

Table 1.　(Continued)

Census Division	States	Households
West South Central		9.3
	Oklahoma	
	Texas	
	Arkansas	
	Louisiana	
Mountain		4.8
	Montana	
	Idaho	
	Nevada	
	Wyoming	
	Utah	
	Arizona	
	Colorado	
	New Mexico	
Pacific		14.6
	Washington	
	Oregon	
	California	
	Alaska	
	Hawaii	

Table 2.　Average Annual Household Consumption of Energy (MMBtu)

	Electricity	Natural Gas	Petroleum Products	Gasoline	Total
New England	23	78	81	167	349
Mid Atlantic	25	89	73	119	306
East N. Central	28	117	45	151	340
West N. Central	30	99	56	173	358
South Atlantic	41	76	27	147	282
East S. Central	43	72	31	153	299
West S. Central	44	67	30	182	323
Mountain	30	88	55	197	369
Pacific	27	59	24	152	262

average). Thus, average households in the Mountain states consume an estimated 40% more energy than do average households in the Pacific states.

While households in the Mountain states consume more aggregate energy than do Pacific households, the consumption of individual energy types varies considerably. For example, the regional average (unweighted column average) of U.S. household gasoline consumption is estimated to be 143 MMBtu. Households in the Mountain states consume 197 MMBtu of gasoline (38% more than average), while Mid-Atlantic households consume about 119 MMBtu (16% less than the average of the U.S.). Household electricity consumption is highest in the West South Central states and lowest in the Pacific states (44 MMBtu versus 23 MMBtu), but New England consumes vastly greater quantities of petroleum products, primarily used for home heating.

Turn now to Table 3 which displays the prices U.S. households pay for energy products. Consider first the price of electricity in $/MMBtu. The average price is estimated to be approximately $23.40/MMBtu, with a standard deviation of $4.69. The lowest electricity prices are paid in the East South Central states ($19.70/MMBtu, 14% less than average), while the highest prices are paid in the Mid-Atlantic states ($34.82/MMBtu, 49% above the average). Thus, there existed in 1990 a regional disparity of over 75% in electricity prices charged to households.

In contrast to electricity prices, gasoline prices are much more uniform across the United States. The average price paid by U.S. households in 1990 was $9.06/MMBtu and the percent difference between the highest and lowest priced region was 9% (New England was the highest and the West South Central states were the lowest).

Table 4 combines the price and consumption data and displays the levels of household expenditure on energy products. In 1990 it is estimated that the average U.S. household paid $3,104 for energy. The highest per household expenditures were in the New England states ($3,931/year) and the lowest expenditures were in the Pacific states ($2,914/year).

Table 3.   Household Prices for Energy ($/MMBtu)

	Electricity	Natural Gas	Petroleum Products	Gasoline
New England	$32.62	$8.60	$9.03	$10.66
Mid Atlantic	$34.82	$7.71	$8.74	$10.22
East N. Central	$25.79	$5.51	$9.76	$10.40
West N. Central	$24.79	$5.18	$9.18	$9.96
South Atlantic	$24.90	$7.49	$11.07	$10.04
East S. Central	$19.17	$5.29	$10.95	$10.13
West S. Central	$24.24	$5.84	$9.55	$9.78
Mountain	$24.24	$5.18	$11.22	$10.31
Pacific	$26.01	$6.06	$12.08	$10.22

Table 4. Average Annual Household Expenditures on Energy

	Electricity	Natural Gas	Petroleum Products	Gasoline	Total
New England	$753	$668	$728	$1,781	$3,931
Mid Atlantic	$860	$684	$638	$1,221	$3,403
East N. Central	$729	$642	$439	$1,565	$3,375
West N. Central	$742	$512	$518	$1,722	$3,494
South Atlantic	$1,010	$500	$304	$1,478	$3,292
East S. Central	$830	$381	$336	$1,548	$3,094
West S. Central	$1,072	$391	$284	$1,779	$3,525
Mountain	$716	$455	$620	$2,029	$3,820
Pacific	$713	$358	$294	$1,550	$2,914

III. MEASURING THE TAX BURDEN

One of the purposes of this study is to examine the level and distribution of energy tax burdens on U.S. households. An obvious measure of the burden would be the monetized change in household utility engendered by energy tax programs. Changes in monetized utility are the most theoretically appealing measure of tax burden·and would permit one to capture the effect energy taxes have on all products using energy in their production, distribution and sale. However, for a very practical reason we have chosen to focus on a measure that approximates the level of actual taxes households pay rather than the household's change in utility. The reason for this choice is the harsh fact that only economists think like economists, and the continuing debate over energy taxes will be conducted primarily by noneconomists, that is, politicians and special interest groups. The level of their understanding will likely not rise above the simple notion of the taxes households pay. Moreover, our study does not employ a general equilibrium framework. Therefore, the indirect effects which energy taxes have on the prices of other goods in the economy is not to be captured by our model and, therefore, the fact that monetized utility changes could account for these secondary effects is unimportant.[10]

We measure the per household burden of energy taxes by constructing a model of household demand for goods and services of which energy products are a subset. This model gives rise to a set of household demand equations for the energy products. We employ the demand equations to gauge the responsiveness of household energy demand to tax-induced changes in energy prices. We calculate the after-tax quantity of each type of energy consumed by the household, multiply it by the tax-induced change in the respective energy type's price. We then sum across all energy taxes.

The measure of tax burden discussed earlier may be a close approximation to the level of actual energy taxes attributable to the household sector, but in most cases it will not be a true measure of those taxes. It is not a true measure because the change in the price of energy may be greater or less than the tax. In the simple case, imagine a tax placed on electricity at the household meter box of one cent per KWh. If changing household demand for electricity had no effect on the cost of electricity supply, the household burden we describe here would accurately reflect the tax. However, if electricity demand falls in response to the higher tax-induced prices, utilities may require further price increases to maintain their rates of return and therefore prices may rise above the tax level. It would be inappropriate, then, to aggregate all the estimated household burdens and claim this represented the portion of total taxes paid by households, but it is legitimate to state that the aggregate is a reasonable political measure of the tax burden since these price rises would not have occurred had it not been for the tax. Moreover, the level of price rise will be a function of the tax implementation parameters (e.g., the point of tax collection).

Our measure of tax burden will obviously vary with the level of the tax, the tax implementation parameters, and the structure of the energy supply sectors; but perhaps most important, the burden will vary with the household's ability to adjust to changing energy prices. If households make no adjustments in their energy consumption patterns we would expect to see the greatest burdens. While economists rail at the mere mention of zero elasticity of demand, it is a fact that many of the participants in the Btu tax debate relied on models that embodied just that assumption. The greater the adjustment the less the burden, and generally, the longer the period over which households can adjust, the greater will be the adjustment. Thus, a critical modeling decision has to do with the adjustment period assumed to underlie the models' implied demand elasticities.

IV.   HOUSEHOLD MODELS OF ENERGY DEMAND

A.   The Role of Adjustment Time

Rather than choose a single set of household adjustment assumptions, we have chosen to model three adjustment scenarios.

The first, which we term the *naive model,* follows the zero elasticity of demand school and assumes households do not respond in any way to tax-induced changes in energy prices. By all accounts this is wholly unrealistic and we include it solely for the purpose of comparison with previous or future studies that employ the zero elasticity assumption, but may choose other sets of data upon which to base their analysis.

The second scenario has more realism and we term it the *conservation model.* In this view of household behavior, the household maintains a varied stock of long-lived energy-using capital. At one end of the capital asset lifetime spectrum, one finds small inexpensive household appliances (e.g., light bulbs, toasters, hair dryers, etc.). As we proceed to longer lifetimes we find larger more expensive appliances (e.g., TVs, dishwashers, refrigerators, etc.), and then automobiles, and eventually the residential structure itself. In the conservation model the household may roll-over some of the small to medium appliances and replace them with more efficient units, and it may adjust the utilization rates of the larger appliances (e.g., turning down thermostats on heating units, driving less, etc.), but the household does not make large-scale capital investments that would permit it to significantly alter the energy-using composition of household capital. For example, the household would not replace oil-fired home heating with natural gas or electric heat pumps.

The final adjustment scenario is captured by our *long-run model* where all the household's energy-using capital stock may be replaced. We are willing to assume that the long-run model represents adjustment over a 15- to 25-year time period, while the naive model assumes zero time for adjustment and the conservation model represents adjustments over a 5- to 7-year period.

Notation

INDEXES

r indexes region of households residence. $r = 1, ..., 9$, where {$r = 1$: New England; 2: Mid Atlantic; 3: East North Central; 4: West North Central; 5: South Atlantic; 6: East South Central; 7: West South Central; 8: Mountain; 9: Pacific}.

g indexes household consumption good aggregates. $g = 1, ..., 5$, where {$g = 1$: Food, 2: Consumer Goods, 3: Capital Services, 4: Consumer Services, 5: Energy}.

(continued)

Notation (Continued)

INDEXES

e indexes household energy products. $e = 1, ..., 4$, where {$e = 1$: Electricity, 2: natural Gas, 3: Petroleum Products, 4: Gasoline}.

SCALARS

V Indirect utility of household h in region r defined over all household consumption good aggregates.

H Indirect utility of household h in region r defined over all household energy products.

p_g Prices of household consumption good aggregates.

q_g Quantity of household consumption good aggregates.

q_g^* Model predicted optimal quantity of household consumption good aggregates.

p_e Prices of household energy products.

q_e Quantity of household energy products.

qe^* ϵ_{ii}^e Own price elasticity of demand for household energy products.

ϵ_{ij}^e Cross price elasticity of demand for household energy products.

M Household expenditure on consumption good aggregates.

M_e Household expenditure on energy products.

t_e Tax rate on energy (per Btu, or pound of carbon).

T Burden of energy taxes per household.

VECTORS and MATRICES

A 1x18 vector of household demographic attributes. Family size; (1, 2, 3, 4, 5, 6, 7, or more persons); age of household head (15-24, 25-24, 35-44, 45-54, 55-64, 65+); race (white, nonwhite); type of residence (urban-rural)

P_g 1x5 vector of regional prices of household consumption good aggregates.

Q_g 1x5 vector of regional quantities of household consumption good aggregates.

P_e 1x4 vector of regional prices of household energy products.

Q_e 1x4 vector of regional quantities of household energy products.

t 1x4 vector of tax rates on energy.

i conforming row vector of ones.

α 1x5 vector of parameters.

β 5x5 matrix of parameters.

γ 5x18 matrix of parameters.

δ 1x4 vector of parameters.

λ 4x4 matrix of parameters.

τ 4x18 matrix of parameters.

The Naive Model

The naive model assumes,

$$\epsilon_{ii}^{e} = 0, \text{ for all } i = 1,\ldots, 4 \text{ and } \epsilon_{ij}^{e} = 0, i \neq j \text{ for } i, j = 1,\ldots, 4.$$

Under the zero elasticity assumptions, the after-tax quantities of energy products consumed by the representative household in the rth region are,

$$Q_{e}^{\circ} = Q_{e}. \tag{1}$$

The tax burden of households in region re is then calculated as,

$$T = \left[(t + P^{e}) Q^{e*'} - P_{r}^{e} Q^{e'} \right]$$
$$= t Q^{e*'} \tag{2}$$

The Conservation Model

The conservation model assumes,

$$\epsilon_{ii}^{e} < 0, \text{ for all } i = 1,\ldots, 4 \text{ and } \epsilon_{ij}^{e} = 0, i \neq j \text{ for } i, j = 1,\ldots, 4.\,^{[11]}$$

Under the nonzero own-price elasticity and zero cross-price elasticity assumptions, the after-tax quantities of energy products consumed by the representative household in the rth region are,

$$Q^{e*} = \left(\left(i + \Delta P^{e} \middle/ 100 \right) E^{e} \right) \times Q^{e}.\,^{[12]} \tag{3}$$

The household's tax burden is,

$$T = t Q^{e*'}. \tag{4}$$

The Long-run Model

The long-run model we employ draws on a system of hierarchical consumer demand equations. Under the assumption that energy consumption forms a weakly separable subset of the arguments in the household utility function, we define the uppermost system of equations to correspond to the household demands for consumer goods aggregates: (1) food and clothing, (2) other nondurable goods, (3) capital services, (4) consumer services, and (5) energy. In a second level of the hierarchy, household energy consumption is divided into: (i) electricity, (ii) natural gas, (iii) petroleum products, and (iv) gasoline.

While there exist in the literature numerous studies of household energy demand, few are based on explicit characterizations of household utility functions (assuring consistency with neoclassical consumer theory), while even fewer provide estimates of complete energy demand systems where all household energy substitution patterns are considered. The set of studies is narrowed even more when one seeks to find demand estimates that account for demographic differences.

To the best of our knowledge, only one econometric study of household energy demand exists that estimates a complete and theoretically consistent hierarchical system of household demand equations that accounts for demographic differences. Various pieces and versions of this study have appeared in Jorgenson, Lau, and Stoker (1982), Jorgenson and Slesnick (1987), and Jorgenson, Slesnick, and Stoker (1988). In each of these papers, results are based on the estimation of a system of consumer demand equations derived from an indirect translog utility function. The estimation exploits the theorems of exact aggregation due to Lau (1977, 1982) and combines time series and cross-section data to account for demographic differences in energy demand.[13]

The model presentation begins with an indirect utility function, defined over household consumption good aggregates, for household h living in region r.[14]

$$\ln V_h = F(A_h) + \alpha\ \mathbf{ln}(P_g/M_h)' + .5 \ln(P_g/M_h)\ \beta\ \ln(P_g/M_h)' + \mathbf{1N}(P_g/M_h)\lambda A_n' \tag{5}$$

Suppressing the h subscript, the share of household h's aggregate expenditure on good g, living in region r is specified as,

$$S_g = \frac{1}{D} \alpha' + \beta\ \ln(P_g/M)' + \gamma\ A' \tag{6}$$

$$\text{where: } D = -1 + i\beta \ln P'_g$$

Using information on household expenditures, budget shares, and prices for consumption good aggregates, we can define the optimal long-run quantities of consumption good aggregates as,

$$Q^o_g = (MS_g) \div P_g.^{15} \tag{7}$$

We now specify the indirect utility function, defined over household energy products, for household h living in region r as,

$$\ln H = G(A) + \ln M_e + \delta \ln P'_e + 5\ln P_e\lambda \,\mathbf{ln}\boldsymbol{P'_e} + \ln P_e\tau A' \tag{8}$$

and the share of household h's expenditure on energy type e, living in region r as,

$$A_e = -(\delta + \lambda \ln P'_e + \tau A). \tag{9}$$

Using information on household energy expenditures, budget shares, and prices for household energy products, we can define the optimal long-run quantities of household energy products as,

$$Q^*_e = (M_eS_e) \div P_e. \tag{10}$$

Following the two-stage budget allocation model in Jorgenson, Slesnick, and Stoker (1988), we define an index of household h's energy prices in region r as,[16]

$$\ln P_e = -[G(A) + \delta \ln P'_e + .5\ln P_e\gamma \ln P'_e + \ln P_e \,\tau A']. \tag{11}$$

The two-stage budget allocation model begins by feeding a vector of household h's energy prices in region r into the energy price index. The resulting aggregate energy price index is then passed to the household indirect utility function defined over consumption good aggregates. Corresponding expenditure shares are calculated and, using the share of aggregate energy, the level of aggregate energy expenditure is computed.

The same vector of household h's energy prices in region r is passed to the indirect utility function, defined over household energy products and the shares of individual energy products in total household energy expenditure are calculated. Using these shares, the level of aggregate household energy expenditure and the prices of the individual energy products, we calculate the optimal long-run quantities of household energy demand.

The household tax burden is computed in a manner analogous to the naive and conservation models and is given by,

$$T = t Q_e^* \, i'. \tag{12}$$

V. TAX INDUCED CHANGES IN HOUSEHOLD ENERGY PRICES

A. Natural Gas, Petroleum Products, and Gasoline

The household energy demand models presented in the previous section model taxes on energy as if they were imposed at the point of retail sale. In actuality, taxes on the carbon or Btu content of primary fuels are likely to be imposed much further upstream, perhaps at the mine mouth, wellhead, or port of importation. Thus, it is important to be able to model the journey of the tax as it moves downstream to the consumer. However, the task of determining how taxes applied on primary energy affect the prices paid by households for final energy consumption is nontrivial. In particular, we must map taxes on coal, crude petroleum, and natural gas to household prices for electricity, fuel oil, natural gas, and gasoline.

For the purpose of the present analysis, we assume that the taxes on primary energy products are passed on in their entirety to final consumers. Certainly, an alternative assumption would be to admit the oligopolistic and regulated nature of energy markets and develop theoretical and empirical models of pricing behavior for each of these markets; however, such an effort is well beyond the scope of the current study.[17]

In the case of natural gas, we assume that households consume natural gas as a primary energy product and the tax (per thousand cubic feet) is added directly to the price paid by households. Fuel oil and gasoline are refinery products that are manufactured using crude petroleum as a feedstock. The production technology of petroleum refining is decidedly joint, implying that allocating a cost increase for any one input to the marginal costs of production of the multiple outputs is exceedingly difficult, even if one knows the production technology. Given this difficulty, we use a simple rule that states that the added crude oil cost (i.e., the tax) is passed on according to the Btu content of the final energy products. For example, in the case of the 1990 Stark bill which called for a tax of \$3.25/barrel of crude oil by 1995, the tax per million Btu is \$.5603. Given the Btu content of a gallon of gasoline and a gallon of fuel oil, their taxes amount to \$.07 and \$.08 per gallon, respectively. These taxes are then added to actual per gallon prices paid by households to model the price increase due to the carbon tax.

B.　Electricity

Unlike the provision of natural gas and the refining of petroleum products, primary energy represents a small portion of total production cost in the generation and distribution of electricity. Moreover, the industry has been heavily studied giving rise to numerous industry models that might be employed to trace the effect of taxes on primary energy input through to changes in household energy prices.

We model the electricity sector with an engineering cost approach that couples detailed historical plant cost data on the supply side with additional data on the energy-demanding sectors. Using data on individual plants in a particular North American Electric Reliability Council (NERC) region, we calculate the average cost of generation, and the operating costs for each plant, which are the marginal costs needed to rank the plants in their order of dispatch (EIA, 1987b). The demand response to a tax-induced electricity price change is found and used to recalculate the new quantity of electricity that has to be generated. This is then used to recompute the dispatch order.

Since it was not possible to distinguish the electricity supplied by each plant to the residential sector from that supplied to the industrial and other sectors, we have to model the change in demand in each of the three demand sectors (residential, commercial, and industrial). Losses in transmission and distribution are also included in the system. Ultimately, this ensures the balance between supply and demand, which is necessary for the equilibrium determination of prices. The following sections describe how the features of the electricity sector were modeled.

The electricity supply model determines the costs of generating electricity demanded (in Gigawatt-hours or GWh) in each of the nine

NERC regions which differ from census regions in their compositions of states. The electric sector is made up of seven kinds of plants: nuclear, hydroelectric, and fossil-fired steam (coal, oil and gas), and fossil-fueled turbines (oil and gas). The order in which plants are dispatched is based on the relative costs of operating the plants. Different characteristics determine the types of technology that are to be used for meeting different parts of the load (or demand). Hydroelectric plants typically have the lowest operating costs, and are flexible enough to be used for any part of the load. As a result, they are usually fully utilized.[18]

Generating cost and the price of electricity. We use standard utility methods for computing the average cost to a utility of supplying electricity, also known as the revenue requirement (EPRI, 1986). The cost of using a particular plant can be broken down into the following components: (1) capital cost, (2) operations and maintenance (O&M) costs, and (3) fuel costs. We define a simple revenue requirement model as the average cost of supplying electricity.

$$\text{Average Cost}_r = \sum_{j=1}^{n} \frac{(\text{O\&M cost} + \text{fuel cost} + \text{capital cost})_{rj}}{\sum_{j=1}^{n} (\text{energy supplied})_{rj}} \tag{13}$$

where: $j = 1, \ldots, n$ indexes plants.

We determine the initial cost of supplying a region by calculating the revenue requirement of the plants dispatched to meet the actual total generation reported by the EIA for the base year (1986). This simple revenue requirement model must be distinguished from the actual price of electricity. The latter is determined through regulatory rate-making action and must account for the historical and existing financial conditions of the electric utility in question.

Furthermore, the revenue requirement only pertains to the cost of generation as a guideline for the utilities' capital planning decisions. It does not include returns on investment and a number of other costs which are included in the consumer's actual price, such as the cost of distribution and transmission, planned new capacity, and other utility overheads like administrative costs. Much of this additional cost may be considered as a fixed amount per unit since it is not significantly altered by price-induced changes in the amount of power dispatched or the dispatch order. Given this assumption, we calculate the household electricity price by combining the simple revenue requirement with an adder which represents the difference between the revenue requirement and the initial price (based on actual data). The adder then represents a fixed markup per unit of electricity sold that is constant over the entire range of costs of production.[19] Given a rise in the average cost of production due to a tax on primary fuels (Btu or carbon), the percent change in price of electricity passed on to consumers in region *i* is given by:

$$\% \Delta P_{er} = \frac{(AC^t + adder_r) - (AC^o{}_r + adder_r)}{AC^o{}_r + adder_r} \tag{14}$$

where: AC_i = average cost of producing electricity in region *r*, superscript *t* signifies after-tax cost and ^{o} signifies pre-tax cost.

Determining the price equilibrium. When taxes are imposed on primary fuel inputs, the electric utilities' input fuel costs increase, causing the electricity price to increase. We calculate the cost of producing electricity under the new fuel costs with equation 13, and the new consumer price with equation 14. This price change causes a reduction in demand which causes plants to be taken off-line and the average cost of generation to change due to the new plant mix. The energy tax also affects the relative production costs between plants, which changes the dispatch order. Utilities may substitute fuels over a long period of time by modifying the generation equipment, but since the costs of modification are very uncertain, it does not add value to the analysis at this time to make such assumptions.

In order to accurately match total electricity demand with the total supply, the demand response in nonresidential sectors must be included in the model. We model the electricity demand in the commercial and industrial sectors using an elasticity equation similar to equation (3) used in the household model. Short- and long-run elasticity estimates employed for the commercial and industrial sectors are drawn from Bohi and Zimmerman (1984).[20] The demand for energy from other uses (aggregated into a fourth sector) is assumed to be unaffected by price changes. The sum of demands in all four sectors minus imports then becomes the new level of demand that must be met by the generation.

VI. TAX POLICIES: THE BTU TAX

We consider two energy tax policies. The first policy is the Btu tax proposed by the Clinton Administration in January 1993 and passed by the House of Representatives May 27, 1993. The second policy is a tax on the carbon content of primary fuels that would raise approximately the same revenue as the House-passed Btu tax.

The Btu tax examined in this paper was based on a tax rate of 25.7 cents/MMBtu for all fuels and a supplemental tax of 34.2 cents/MMBtu on oil products.[21] Nuclear fuel and hydropower used in electricity generation were taxed on the basis of the average fossil fuel Btu input required to generate equivalent electricity.

It is important to note that if the Btu tax rates had passed into law they would have been passed on to consumers in one form or another as additions to prices for household energy products over the period 1994-1996. However, the data underlying our models of household energy demand represent energy consumption and more importantly, energy prices in 1990. Thus the tax rates cited here are larger fractions of 1990 prices than 1994-1996 prices. Since our energy demand models are sensitive to changes in relative prices, we have deflated the Btu tax rates passed by the House to 1987 and 1990 price levels, conducted the demand analysis and then inflated the result to 1993 dollars.[22]

Each tax policy we investigate abstracts from the actual phase-in embodied in the House energy tax or likely to be embodied in any carbon tax proposal. We assume that the full amount of the tax is levied in the first year of the program.

A. Revenues Generated

Certainly one of the more politically important aspects of a tax policy is the amount of revenue it will generate. Using 1990 energy prices and consumption patterns as a base, Table 5 displays the revenue generated by the Btu tax under each of the three household adjustment assumptions embodied in our models. The table also displays the amount of revenue attributable to each of the nine census regions.

It comes as no surprise that the greatest aggregate revenues are generated under the no-adjustment assumptions maintained by the naive model. The 1990 naive model predicts revenues of almost $12

Table 5. Total Btu Tax Revenues (Millions 1993 $)

	Naive Model	*Conservation Model*	*Long-run Model*
New England	600	594	549
Mid Atlantic	1,583	1,559	1,438
East N. Central	2,114	2,048	1,884
West N. Central	962	942	864
South Atlanatic	1,995	1,936	1,787
East S. Central	811	776	714
West S. Central	1,461	1,418	1,301
Mountain	733	717	649
Pacific	1,712	1,701	1,545
Total	11,972	11,692	10,731

Table 6. Per Household Btu Tax Burden (1993 $)

	Naive Model	*Conservation Model*	*Long-run Model*
New England	166	132	122
Mid Atlantic	137	106	98
East N. Central	154	123	113
West N. Central	169	145	133
South Atlantic	146	117	108
East S.Central	153	121	112
West S. Central	170	152	140
Mountain	179	149	135
Pacific	135	117	107
Column Mean	157	129	119

billion. The 1990 long-run model estimates revenues in the $10.7 billion range.

B.   Household Distribution of Tax Burden

While the absolute magnitude of likely revenues to be generated by a tax on energy is of obvious political importance, the magnitude of the tax burden borne by each household and the distribution of that burden across households, is perhaps of even greater political importance. One of the objectives of this study has been to assemble data and design models that can examine these distributional questions. Table 6 displays the regional per household burden of the Btu tax.

The naive model suggests that the mean household would pay $157 per year in energy taxes. The difference in tax burden between households paying the greatest tax (Mountain region) and those paying the least (Pacific region) is in excess of 30%. The long-run model suggests that energy adjustment serves to decrease the disparity in the distribution of energy tax burden. The percentage difference in the long-run model between the highest tax paying regions and the lowest falls a few percentage points to 26%.

VII.   TAX POLICIES: A CARBON TAX

Until the Clinton Administration's Btu tax proposal came along, the most often discussed broad-based energy tax was a tax on the carbon content of fossil fuels. The motivation behind the carbon tax was the desire to mitigate the emission of carbon dioxide (CO_2), but the revenues generated by the tax were not overlooked by those desiring to finance federal deficit reduction, additional federal spending, or engage in substantive federal tax reform.[23]

Since climate change, the deficit, federal spending, and tax reform are all squarely on the public agenda, it would be unwarranted to argue that taxes on the carbon content of fuels is not a politically viable policy even though no important legislation currently is pending. Therefore, we have conducted an analysis of a carbon tax similar in all respects to that conducted for the Btu tax. The size of the tax on carbon considered in this analysis was set so that it would generate the same revenue from the household sector as the Btu tax.

A.   Revenues Generated

The revenue levels were taken from the predictions of the short-run model and set at approximately \$11,710 million. These revenue targets gave rise to a carbon tax of approximately \$22.20/ton.[24]

While the \$22/ton carbon charge is employed in our analysis because it raises the same level of revenue as the Btu tax, it is interesting to note that Jorgenson and Wilcoxen (1994) solve a large scale computable general equilibrium model for the carbon tax that would stabilize U.S. carbon emission at 1990 levels (1,576 million tons). This tax in the year 2020 is found to be \$22.71/ton.

Table 7 presents the carbon tax revenues predicted by the models. Although the level of the carbon tax was set to mirror the long-run model Btu tax predictions, the naive model carbon tax revenues are

Table 7.   Total Carbon Tax Revenues (Millions 1993 $)

	Naive Model	*Conservation Model*	*Long-run Model*
New England	571	580	536
Mid Atlantic	1,660	1,676	1,536
East N. Central	2,233	2,155	1,968
West N. Central	943	933	854
South Atlantic	2,038	1,989	1,825
East S. Central	859	814	744
West S. Central	1,435	1,403	1,289
Mountain	643	643	583
Pacific	1,493	1,518	1,382
Total	11,876	11,710	10,716

predicted to be very close to the Btu tax revenues. However, this is where the similarity ends. Under a carbon tax, revenues derived from taxes on fuels used to generate electricity are almost 60% *higher* than those generated by the Btu tax, while the taxes on petroleum reflected in gasoline purchases are 30% *lower* under the carbon tax scheme. The same pattern holds for both the conservation and long-run models, but the magnitude of the percentage differences is somewhat mitigated as household adjustment is admitted.

B.   Household Distribution of Tax Burden

Table 8 displays the regional per household burden of the carbon tax. Our model results indicate that a carbon tax generating the same level of aggregate revenue as the Btu tax is more unevenly distributed across U.S. households on the basis of geography. In the case of the

Table 8.   Per Household Carbon Tax Burden (1993 $)

	Naive Model	*Conservation Model*	*Long-run Model*
New England	163	129	119
Mid Atlantic	148	114	104
East N. Central	168	130	119
West N. Central	175	144	131
South Atlantic	152	120	110
East S. Central	165	127	116
West S. Central	172	151	139
Mountain	170	134	122
Pacific	123	105	95
Column Mean	160	128	117

Btu tax, the difference in burden between the highest taxed region and the lowest taxed region was 32% (based on the naive model). In the case of the carbon tax this percentage rises to 42%. If we use the long-run model and perform the same calculation the ratio rises from 42% for the Btu tax to 46% for the carbon tax.

VIII. ENVIRONMENTAL EFFECTS OF TAXES ON ENERGY

This analysis of the Btu tax and a comparable carbon tax reveals the carbon tax to be more unevenly distributed than the Btu tax. Such a result is not surprising, the Btu tax was crafted with an eye toward distributional consequences. However, if the goal of the tax is to reduce emissions of carbon while raising some fixed level of revenue, most economists would agree that a tax directly on the carbon content of fuels would be the most efficient means of accomplishing the goal. In other words, if one compares a Btu tax and a carbon tax yielding the same level of tax revenue, one can expect the tax on carbon to reduce carbon emissions by greater amounts than the Btu tax. In such a case, the effectiveness of the carbon tax in abating carbon emissions would serve to at least partially offset its politically undesirable distributional consequences.

While economists might readily agree among themselves that a tax on carbon is a more effective means of abating carbon emissions than a tax on the Btu content of fuels, it is not possible a priori to state how large a difference in effectiveness one would expect between the two policies. Energy production and consumption in the United States is a complex process characterized by a great deal of geographic heterogeneity. Only an empirical study can quantify the differences.

As part of our analysis of energy tax policy we have modeled the reductions in carbon emissions that would be derived from changes in energy consumption behavior on the part of U.S. households in response to Btu and carbon taxes. Our analysis concentrates on the results from our conservation and long-run models since the naive model assumes no household energy consumption adjustment and, therefore, would give rise to no reductions in carbon emissions.

We begin our presentation of the results on the carbon emission analysis with Tables 9 and 10 that provide estimates of carbon

Table 9. Conservation Model: Aggregate Carbon
Emission Reductions from Carbon Tax (million tons)

	Electricity	Natural Gas	Petroleum Products	Gasoline	Total
New England	0.03	0.00	0.05	0.10	0.19
Mid Atlantic	0.14	0.02	0.11	0.23	0.50
East N. Central	0.21	0.04	0.04	0.35	0.63
West N. Central	0.07	0.01	0.02	0.18	0.28
South Atlantic	0.28	0.01	0.03	0.35	0.67
East S. Central	0.11	0.01	0.01	0.14	0.27
West S. Central	0.05	0.01	0.01	0.27	0.35
Mountain	0.06	0.01	0.00	0.14	0.21
Pacific	0.17	0.01	0.01	0.33	0.51
Total	1.12	0.12	0.28	2.09	3.60
Shares	0.31	0.03	0.08	0.58	

Table 10. Long-run Model: Aggregate Carbon
Emission Reductions from Carbon Tax (million tons)

	Electricity	Natural Gas	Petroleum Products	Gasoline	Total
New England	0.05	0.18	0.48	1.12	1.83
Mid Atlantic	1.26	1.12	1.02	2.71	6.11
East N. Central	2.67	2.00	0.32	4.02	9.02
West N. Central	0.88	0.74	0.14	2.03	3.78
South Atlantic	3.34	0.45	0.24	3.89	7.91
East S. Central	1.40	0.32	0.10	1.62	3.45
West S. Central	1.51	0.64	0.12	3.09	5.37
Mountain	0.51	0.56	0.03	1.76	2.86
Pacific	1.41	0.88	0.06	4.01	6.37
Total	13.03	6.90	2.52	24.25	46.70
Shares	0.28	0.15	0.05	0.52	

emission reductions due to the carbon tax under study. There are
two features of these results we wish to bring to the reader's attention.
First, not surprisingly, there is a significant difference in the predicted
emission reductions between the conservation and long-run models.
Indeed a difference of an order of magnitude. The long-run model
suggests that a carbon tax of $22.20/ton would reduce emissions of
carbon due to households energy consumption by approximately 45
million tons annually.

The second feature of the tables worth some consideration is the
mix of the carbon emissions and how this mix changes as households
adjust. The mix can be seen by examining the row on each table

labeled "Shares" which are the percent of total emission reduction accounted for by each energy type. In the conservation model, reductions in gasoline consumption account for over half of the carbon reductions, while natural gas use is relatively unchanged. However, in the long run, reductions in natural gas usage account for 15% of the emissions and gasoline now accounts for less than half. The share of reductions in emissions due to reduced electricity consumption remains roughly the same.

Finally, we turn our attention to the reduction in carbon emissions that would likely have come about from the Btu tax proposed by the Clinton Administration. Tables 11 and 12 present these results.

Table 11.   Conservation Model: Aggregate Carbon
Emission Reductions from Btu Tax (million tons)

	Electricity	Natural Gas	Petroleum Products	Gasoline	Total
New England	0.03	0.00	0.03	0.12	0.19
Mid Atlantic	0.09	0.01	0.06	0.29	0.46
East N. Central	0.12	0.03	0.02	0.44	0.61
West N. Central	0.04	0.01	0.01	0.22	0.29
South Atlantic	0.16	0.01	0.01	0.44	0.62
East S. Central	0.06	0.00	0.01	0.17	0.25
West S. Central	0.03	0.01	0.01	0.35	0.40
Mountain	0.05	0.01	0.00	0.18	0.23
Pacific	0.14	0.01	0.00	0.41	0.56
Total	0.73	0.10	0.15	2.63	3.60
Shares	0.20	0.03	0.04	0.73	

Table 12.   Long-run Model: Aggregate Carbon
Emission Reductions from Btu Tax (million tons)

	Electricity	Natural Gas	Petroleum Products	Gasoline	Total
New England	0.05	0.16	0.35	1.23	1.78
Mid Atlantic	0.96	0.95	0.72	2.93	5.56
East N. Central	1.89	1.70	0.23	4.37	8.18
West N. Central	0.68	0.64	0.10	2.23	3.64
South Atlantic	2.60	0.40	0.17	4.36	7.53
East S. Central	1.08	0.28	0.08	1.76	3.20
West S. Central	1.27	0.56	0.09	3.45	5.36
Mountain	0.48	0.51	0.02	1.99	3.00
Pacific	1.33	0.81	0.05	4.59	6.78
Total	10.32	6.00	1.81	26.91	45.03
Shares	0.23	0.13	0.04	0.60	

We have only two points to make with regard to the Btu tax and both points can be made by considering the long-run model results. First, we have what we believe to be a fairly surprising result and one of some policy import. In particular, the Btu tax reduces aggregate carbon emission by an amount that most would agree is indistinguishable from the reductions that would be brought about by a revenue comparable carbon tax (45 million tons for the Btu tax and approximately 47 million tons for the carbon tax). Second, the Btu tax gains more carbon reductions from household reductions in gasoline consumption than does the carbon tax; whereas the carbon tax gets more reductions out of electricity consumption than does the Btu tax.

IX.　CONCLUDING REMARKS

This research has been concerned with the energy using behavior of U.S. households as affected by taxes levied on energy products. We have constructed a detailed model of U.S. electric utility sectors and three models of household energy-using behavior that differ on the basis of assumptions regarding the adjustment flexibility of the household. These models are driven by 1990 annual data describing the prices households face for energy products and the related levels of annual energy consumption. These data permit us to conduct a geographically differentiated analysis at the level of the nine U.S. Census regions.

We have employed the models and data to explore four distinct questions which may be asked of any tax on energy that is applied in such a fashion as to cause the prices of energy products to households to rise. The first question asks what will be the magnitude of the tax revenues collected from the household sector? Second, how much tax will be paid annually by representative households in each of the nine U.S. Census regions? Third, how equitably will the tax be distributed across households when equity is defined solely on the basis of the amount of tax burden per representative household in a region?[25] And fourth, how much environmental improvement will be brought forth by the imposition of the tax when environmental improvement is measured solely on the basis of tons of carbon removed from baseline conditions (i.e., nontax state of the world)?

Each of these four questions has been analyzed with respect to two policy relevant energy tax schemes, the Clinton Administration's Btu tax proposal of 1993 and a hypothetical carbon tax of \$22.20/ton that would produce approximately the same level of revenue as the Btu tax. Jorgenson and Wilcoxen (1994) believe the \$22/ton tax would be sufficient to stabilize U.S. emissions at 1990 levels.

Our results can be easily summarized. First, the Administration's analysis of the House-passed Btu tax suggested that upon full phase-in (FY 1998), aggregate revenues would be approximately \$22 billion. Our analysis using our long-run model suggested the revenues derived from the household sector would total between \$9 billion and \$10 billion.[26] Thus, in answer to our first question, we find that the household sector is a major revenue source. Since our carbon tax analysis produces similar results we believe it is safe to say that it would be unreasonable to consider a revenue motivated energy tax policy of any form that exempted households.

Second, again using our long-run model, we estimate that the average household will pay between \$110 and \$120 per year in energy taxes under the proposed Btu tax or the \$22/ton carbon tax. Relative to other taxes, for example social security, these are not large taxes.

Third, the Btu tax as proposed by the Clinton Administration and passed by the House is spread across U.S. households in a remarkably even fashion if the only parameter is geography.[27] The same cannot be said for the revenue comparable carbon tax.

Finally, we have calculated and presented estimates of the carbon that would be removed from emissions due to household changes in energy consumption brought about by a Btu tax or a carbon tax. Using our conservation model that assumes no changes in energy using capital and very little adjustments to energy mix due to conservation, we find trivial changes in carbon emissions. However, the fully adjusting long-run model suggests fairly large carbon reductions.

Perhaps the most interesting of all of our results is the fact that a revenue comparable carbon tax produces about the same carbon reductions as the Btu tax. One would have expected the targeted carbon tax to be more effective at reducing emissions. While we have not calculated the social dead weight loss associated with the Btu tax and the revenue comparable carbon tax, we feel it is not too outlandish to suggest that as a climate control policy or a revenue raising device a carbon tax is inferior to the Btu tax proposed by the Clinton Administration, due to its uneven distributional consequences.

When considering our carbon emission results, it is important for the reader to be cognizant of the substantial implications of our approach to electricity supply modeling compared to say that of Jorgenson and Wilcoxen (1990, 1994). Our model is very disaggregate and engineering based, whereas the Jorgenson and Wilcoxen model is aggregate and relies on parameters econometrically estimated from aggregate time series data. The structural differences in these models give rise to a very different modeled response to energy taxes. Whereas small carbon taxes in the $20-30/ton range are sufficient, in the Jorgenson and Wilcoxen model, to induce substantial movement by the electric utility sector away from coal, our model suggests these tax levels are too low to induce the massive new investments needed to bring about the reduction in coal usage. Consequently, our model suggests more conservative reductions in carbon emissions than a model constructed along the Jorgenson and Wilcoxen lines.

NOTES

1. Criteria air pollutants are those for which National Ambient Air Quality Standards exist. They include: carbon monoxide, sulfur dioxide, nitrogen oxide, lead, ozone, and particulates.

2. The Btu tax was really not a straight tax on the Btu content of fuels, but rather was a politically palatable tax (at least that was the thinking) that was derivative of a straight Btu tax. The tax had two rates, a base rate of 25.7 cents/million Btu and an oil supplement of 34.2 cents/million Btu. In terms of physical units this amounted to $5.57 per short ton of coal (varies somewhat on the Btu content of the coal), $3.47 per barrel of oil, and $0.26 per million cubic feet of natural gas. Nuclear fuel use in electricity generation was taxed on the Btu content of the nuclear fuel, and hydropower used in electricity generation was taxed on the basis of the average fossil fuel Btu input required to generate equivalent electricity. Nonfuel uses of fossil fuel, exported fossil fuels, and nonconventional fuels (solar, geothermal, biomass, wind, and other) were excluded. Finally, the tax was to be phased in by thirds, with the first third in place by July 1, 1994, the next third July 1, 1995, and fully phased in by July 1, 1996.

3. Even the fairly intense debate over the Btu tax led to a tax on gasoline, albeit a fairly small tax of approximately 4 cents/gallon.

4. In response to such pressure, both foreign and domestic, the Clinton Administration announced its Climate Change Action Plan on October 19, 1993

(Clinton and Gore, 1993). The plan calls on the United States to "return greenhouse gas emissions to 1990 levels by the year 2000" and proposes to do so through a system characterized by voluntary actions, that is, actions not stimulated by command and control regulation or significant economic incentives. From an economist's viewpoint, such an approach seems to be of uncertain efficacy. Finally, the Clinton-Gore plan does not *stabilize* emissions at 1990 levels as many of the critics of U.S. policy had hoped for. If stabilization is deemed a worthy goal in the future, it is difficult to see how true stabilization can be attained without the imposition of some form of direct regulation or the imposition of taxes on the carbon content of fuels.

5.   Jorgenson and Wilcoxen report that a tax of $15.00/ton of carbon would lead to a 0.5% fall in real GNP (p. 40). This tax would be sufficient to stabilize CO_2 emissions at 1990 levels by the year 2020. We note that other studies have found more pronounced effects on macroeconomic variables. See the study by the National Association of Manufactures (1990).

6.   The emission factors employed in the Goulder model are derived from work conducted by the Environmental Law Institute for the U.S. Environmental Protection Agency.

7.   By "traditional efficiency" Goulder means "...the aggregate net benefit or cost to the economy, as obtained by adding up the dollar value of the welfare change to each person" (p. 1).

8.   The Goulder study shows that the non-energy taxes provide trivial reductions in airborne pollutants while the energy tax provides reductions an order of magnitude or larger.

9.   The survey was designed by the Energy Information Administration (EIA) of the U.S. Department of Energy to provide information on how households in the United States and District of Columbia use energy; the RECS collects data on energy use within the home. The 1990 RECS was the eighth in a series; previous surveys were conducted in 1978, 1979, 1980, 1981, 1982, 1984, and 1987.

10.   We note that we have ignored these secondary effects not because we believe them to be unimportant, but because we have chosen to focus on detailed aspects of household energy consumption and regional supply, aspects which have yet to be incorporated into CGE models of the United States. We do however acknowledge and applaud the advances made by Jorgenson and Wilcoxen with respect to demographic disaggregation of the household sector in their model.

11.   Demand Elasticities for the Conservation Model

	Electricity	*Natural Gas*	*Petroleum°*	*Gasoline*
Electricity	-0.089	0.000	0.000	0.000
Natural Gas	0.000	-0.032	0.000	0.000
Petroleum	0.000	0.000	-0.187	0.000
Gasoline	0.000	0.000	0.000	-0.160

Note: *Petroleum includes: fuel oil, kerosene, and LPG.
Source: Blattenberger, Taylor, and Rennhack (1983), U.S. Department of Energy (1981).

12.   The symbol "✕" denotes element-by-element multiplication.

13.   The model described here, based on a complete system of consumer demand equations, is an extremely long-run model of household energy demand. The model assumes that all patterns of energy use have been optimally adjusted to prevailing prices. This implies that both housing and automobile stocks have been optimally adjusted. It is difficult to place an accurate estimate of the adjustment period associated with this model, but it surely is longer than 15 years and may more reasonably be in the 20-25-year period.

14.   The following set of parameter restrictions have been imposed on the indirect utility function.

$$i\alpha' = -1, i\beta = 0 \mathrm{m} i\beta' = 0, i\gamma' = 0$$

15.   The symbol "$\times$" denotes element-by-element division.

16.   If the household's energy price index is normalized to unity when the individual energy price components are unity, the function $G[A]$ is zero and the price index reduces to:

$$-\ln P_e = [\delta\ 1\mathrm{m}p_e' + 5\ln P_e\lambda\ln P_{\overrightarrow{e}} + \ln P_e\tau A'].$$

17.   Unfortunately, it is not possible to determine a priori whether such sophisticated models would lead to consumer prices higher or lower than those embodied in our assumption of full tax pass through. Moreover, there are several competing models from which one must choose, with no particular model necessarily superior to the others. The benefit of using a simple full pass through is that the implication of the assumption is transparent and the sensitivity of the results to the amount passed along is easily determined.

18.   Hydropower is usually used to the maximum ability of the water source for creating energy. The critical parameter is the "run of the river," which measures the proportion of river flow that the plant is dependent on.

19.   The average cost of generation in a region will vary with demand due to the dispatching order of the generating plants in the region. The dispatching order of a plant depends on the plant's efficiency which in turn is a function of engineering design features and economic variables. In this study, the dispatch order of a plant depends upon: type of technology, capacity (Megawatts), generation (GWh), and heat rate (Btu/KWh).

20.   The short- and long-run commercial elasticities are -0.28 and -1.00 respectively, while the short- and long-run industrial elasticities are -0.18 and -.60.

21.   Nonfuel uses of fossil fuel, exported fossil fuels, and nonconventional fuels (solar, geothermal, biomass, wind, and other) were excluded from the tax.

22.   The deflater used is the "fixed weighted price index for domestic product, final sales to domestic purchasers," as published in the *Survey of Current Business*, July 1992 and August 1993. The effective Btu tax rates in $/MMBtu are: natural gas -0.23, fuel oil/kerosene -0.54, gasoline -0.54, LPG -0.23, coal -0.23, hydroelectric -0.23, and nuclear -0.23.

23.   Such tax reform would include using the revenues generated by a carbon tax to offset reductions in distorting taxes on labor and capital income.

24.   The effective carbon tax rates in $/MMBtu are: natural gas -0.32, fuel oil/kerosene -0.48, gasoline -0.48, LPG -0.32, coal -0.60, hydroelectric -0.00, and nuclear -0.00. These rates are equivalent to $22.2/ton of carbon.

25.   One can, of course, define many other reasonable measures of equity. For example, if one adopts the "polluter pays principle," one may wish to compare the distribution of the tax burden divided by the Btu or carbon content of all the energy consumed by a household.

26.   Readers are reminded that for the most part energy producers and distributors (i.e., the petroleum industry and natural gas and electric utilities) are passing the energy taxes along to all customer classes.

27.   In April of 1993 the Office of Tax Policy at the Treasury Department released its predictions of the geographic distribution of the Btu tax. It is unknown to these authors how the Treasury estimates were made, but they do bear a close resemblance to some of ours if you assume that Treasury Department estimates are on a household basis rather than on a per capita basis as they state on the table. Their estimates are presented without further comment here.

Census Region	Tax Increase (Per Capita)	Census Region	Tax Increase (Per Capita)
New England	$124	West North Central	$110
Middle Atlantic	$115	West South Central	$106
South Atlantic	$113	Mountain	$104
East North Central	$110	Pacific	$108
East South Central	$102		

REFERENCES

Berndt, E.R., and D.O. Wood. 1979. "Engineering and Econometric Interpretations of Energy-Capital Complementarity." *American Economic Review* 69 (3): 342-54.

Blattenberger, G.R., L.D. Taylor, and R.K. Rennhack. 1983. "Natural Gas Availability and the Residential Demand for Energy." *The Energy Journal* 4 (1): 23-45.

Bohi, D.R., and M. Zimmerman. 1984. "An Update on Econometric Studies of Energy Demand Behavior." *Annual Review of Energy* 9 (Annual Reviews, Inc.): 105-154.

Clinton, President W.J., and Vice-President A. Gore, Jr. 1993. "The Climate Change Action Plan." The White House Office of the Press Secretary, Tuesday, October 19.

Congressional Budget Office. 1990. "Carbon Charges as a Response to Global Warming: The Effects of Taxing Fossil Fuels." U.S. Congress, August.

Dowlatabadi, H., and W. Harrington. 1990. "Uncertainty and the Cost of Acid Rain Control." *Contemporary Policy Issues* 8, July.

Dowlatabadi, H., and M. Toman. 1989. "Changes in Electricity Markets and Implications for Generation Technologies." Energy and Natural Resources Division Discussion Paper ENR89-01, Resources for the Future, Washington, DC.

Energy Information Agency. 1981. "Price Elasticities of Demand for Motor Gasoline and Other Petroleum Products." U.S. Department of Energy, DOE/EIA-0291.

Goulder, L.H. 1993. "The Choice Between Energy and Other Taxes: Traditional Concerns and Environmental Considerations." Department of Economics, Stanford University, August.

Jorgenson, D.W., L.J. Lau, and T.M. Stoker. 1982. "The Transcendental Logarithmic Model of Aggregate Consumer Behavior." Pp. 97-238 in *Advances in Econometrics* (volume 1), edited by Baseman.

Jorgenson, D.W., and D.T. Slesnick. 1987. "Aggregate Consumer and Household Equivalence Scales." *Journal of Business and Economic Statistics* 5 (2): 219-32.

Jorgenson, D.W., D.T. Slesnick, and T.M. Stoker. 1988. "Two-Stage Budgeting and Exact Aggregation." *Journal of Business and Economic Statistics* 6 (3): 313-326.

Jorgenson, D.W., and P.J. Wilcoxen. 1990. "The Cost of Controlling U.S. Carbon Dioxide Emissions." Paper presented at the Workshop on Economic/Energy/Environmental Modeling for Climate Policy Analysis, October 22-23, Washington, DC. Sponsored by the University of Tokyo and the Massachusetts Institute of Technology.

Jorgenson, D.W., and P.J. Wilcoxen. 1994. "The Economic Effects of a Carbon Tax." Paper presented at the 1994 Annual Meeting of the American Economic Association, Boston, Mass., January 3-5.

Lau, L.J. 1977. "Existence Conditions for Aggregate Demand Functions." Technical Report 248, Stanford Institute for Mathematical Studies in the Social Sciences.

Lau, L.J. 1982. "A Note of the Fundamental Theorem of Exact Aggregation." *Economic Letters* 9: 119-26.

National Association of Manufactures. 1990. "An Analysis of the Stark Carbon Content Fuels Tax," Taxation and Fiscal Policy Department, NAM, Washington, DC.

U.S. Department of Transportation/Federal Highway Administration (FHWA). 1992. Summary of Travel Trends: 1990 Nationwide Personal Transportation Survey, Report No. FHWA-PL-92-027, FHWA, Washington, DC., March.

COMMENTARY

M. Douglas Berg

With growing public concern over the environmental damage caused by the burning of fossil fuels, an energy tax appears to be every politician's dream. Proponents of an energy tax can claim to be fighting pollution and reducing the federal deficit at the same time. But regardless of how politically attractive such a tax may seem, three questions naturally arise.

1. How much money will the government collect from the energy tax?
2. What is the regional variation in the average household burden of the tax?
3. How much will airborne emissions be reduced?

These are the questions that Dowlatabadi, Kopp, and Tschang focus upon when comparing the two energy tax schemes most recently discussed in the political arena, Clinton's 1993 proposal of a Btu tax and a carbon tax designed to yield the same amount of revenue.

Advances in the Economics of Energy and Resources, Volume 9, pages 237-241.
Copyright © 1995 by JAI Press Inc.
All rights of reproduction in any form reserved.
ISBN: 1-55938-922-2

They go about answering these questions by first determining for each tax the after-tax market price and quantity for each energy product. Because of the complexity of following the tax all the way from the point of imposition to the household level, the authors assume "…that the taxes on primary energy products are passed on in their entirety to final consumers." Natural gas is considered to be a primary fuel to the household, hence the after-tax price is simply the pre-tax price plus the tax. A barrel of crude oil can be refined into a number of products, each containing a different number of Btu's. Therefore, the tax on a barrel of oil is apportioned out to the refined products on the basis of each product's Btu's.

The after-tax price of electricity is modeled using an engineering cost approach. Using a large set of data on the power plants across the country, and a set of decision rules for determining when a particular power plant is put into action, they compute the average cost of supplying electricity by region before and after the tax. The percentage change in average cost is then applied to the pre-tax price of electricity to yield the after-tax price.

The authors estimate the quantity response to the tax induced change in price under three models. The *naive* model assumes that the own-price demand elasticity is zero. Therefore, the quantity demanded before and after the tax is the same. The *conservation* model allows for some change in the quantity demanded, but does not allow the capital stock to be adjusted in response to a price change. Using a set of elasticities estimated outside of their study, the authors use the percent change in price times the elasticity number to represent the percent change in quantity demanded due to the tax. One plus this number times the pre-tax quantity demanded results in the after-tax quantity demanded.

The *long-run* model allows the household to fully adjust to a change in price. The time frame suggested by the authors is 15 to 20 years. The first step in determining the after-tax quantity demanded of any particular energy product, is to determine the optimal after-tax quantity of energy products in aggregate relative to other household consumption goods. This is done by first computing an after-tax aggregate price index for energy, which is then fed into the share equations of a translog indirect utility function. (The parameters for these share equations are taken from papers by Jorgenson, et al.) The result is the optimal percentage of the average household in region *r*'s total expenditures that should be spent on energy products in total.

The second step is to compute the proportion of optimal aggregate energy expenditures that should be devoted to any one energy product. This can be done by placing the after-tax vector of individual energy product prices into the share equations of a translog utility function defined over household energy products. The output will be the percentage of total energy expenditures devoted to each energy product. Given the average household's total expenditures and multiplying it by the optimal aggregate budget share computed above results in the optimal dollar amount spent on energy products in total. Multiplying this by the budget share percentages computed in the second step results in the optimal dollar amounts spent on each energy product. Finally, it is a simple step to divide the optimal dollar amount for each energy product by its after-tax price to yield the after-tax quantity demanded.

For each tax scheme, this entire process is performed for 1987 and 1990. The Btu tax rate is 25.7 cents/MBtu. The carbon tax rate was chosen so as to generate the same amount of tax revenue from the household sector as the Btu tax. This rate turns out to be $22.20/ ton of carbon.

In answer to the first question, regarding how much revenue each tax will generate, refer to Table 1. As expected the carbon tax generates approximately the same amount of revenue as the Btu tax. The average across all three models for 1987 is $9.8 billion and $11.5 billion for 1990 (measured in 1993 dollars). Notice that the long-run estimate of tax revenues is lower than the conservation estimate, which in turn is lower than the naive estimate. This is to be expected given the adjustment assumptions of each model.

Table 1. 1987 and 1900 Estimated Tax
Revenues in Millions of 1993 Dollars Under
Each of the Three Models for Each Tax

Model	1987 Total Revenue	1990 Total Revenue
	Btu Tax	
Naive	10,168	11,972
Conservation	10,079	11,692
Long-Run	9,240	10,731
	Carbon Tax	
Naive	10,253	11,876
Conservation	10,060	11,710
Long-Run	9,229	10,716

Concerning the political feasibility of any proposed energy tax, the answer to the second question will help determine the likelihood of enactment. If the tax burden varies greatly between regions the likelihood of enactment will be low. Referring to Table 2, the maximum difference between regional household tax burdens, $52, takes place under the carbon tax naive model for 1990. According to the *Economic Report of the President, 1992* (p. 387), the federal government collected $466.9 billion in individual income taxes for 1990. For the same year, the *Statistical Abstract of the United States* (Table 60), reports the total number of households as being 91,947,000. This implies that the average federal income tax burden per household is $5,078 in 1990. In this light, the $52 regional variation in the household energy tax burden appears to be very small, slightly greater than 1% of the 1990 average household income tax burden. It is a useful contribution simply to show that both tax schemes have equivalent burdens across regions.

The final question to be addressed by the authors is the reduction in airborne emissions. They report the reduction in "carbon emissions" without specifying whether by "carbon" they mean CO_2, CO, or both combined. No mention is made of how the reduction in carbon emissions is calculated. It is my guess that they multiply the reduction in quantity demanded for each energy product by some pollutants-to-quantity-of-fuel ratios. Table 3 summarizes their estimates of reductions in carbon emissions. As is expected, the long-run model shows greater reductions in emissions than the conservation model. The interesting thing about their results is that both the Btu and carbon tax reduce carbon emissions by about the

Table 2.   The Difference Between the
Highest Regional Household Tax Burden
and the Lowest, in 1993 Dollars

Model	1987	1990
	Btu Tax	
Naive	$20	$44
Conservation	21	46
Long-Run	19	42
	Carbon Tax	
Naive	$39	$52
Conservation	32	46
Long-Run	30	44

Table 3. Reductions in Carbon Emission
Measured in Millions of Tons Per Year

Model	*1987*	*1990*
	Btu Tax	
Conservation	3.13	3.60
Long-Run	39.51	45.03
	Carbon Tax	
Conservation	3.08	3.60
Long-Run	39.59	46.70

same amount, 45.03 and 46.7 million tons respectively. According to the *Statistical Abstract of the United States, 1992*, national carbon monoxide emissions (CO) in 1990 amounted to 60.1 million metric tons. It should be noted that CO emissions have fallen from a peak of 101.4 million metric tons in 1970 to the 1990 level just mentioned, without the imposition of an energy tax.

Overall, I would say that the authors accomplished their goal of developing a framework to answer the three central policy issues of an energy tax. Their estimates of tax revenue under the three different models are consistent with economic theory in that tax revenue is lower the more time is allowed for adjustment to higher tax-induced energy prices. The variation in average household energy tax burden between regions is relatively small in comparison to the average household's federal income tax burden. And finally, the reduction in carbon emissions predicted by the long-run model are significant when compared to 1990 levels of carbon monoxide emissions.